A
Primer
for Poets
&
Readers
of Poetry

ALSO BY GREGORY ORR

Poetry

River Inside the River
Burning the Empty Nests
The Red House
We Must Make a Kingdom of It
New and Selected Poems
City of Salt
Orpheus & Eurydice
The Caged Owl: New and Selected Poems
Concerning the Book That Is the Body of the Beloved
How Beautiful the Beloved

Prose

Stanley Kunitz: An Introduction to Poetry
Richer Entanglements: Essays and Notes on Poetry and Poems
Poets Teaching Poets: Self and the World
Poetry as Survival
The Blessing

A Primer *for* Poets & Readers *of* Poetry

GREGORY ORR

W. W. NORTON & COMPANY
Independent Publishers Since 1923
New York • London

For information about permission to reproduce
selections from this book, write to Permissions,
W. W. Norton & Company, Inc.,
500 Fifth Avenue, New York, NY 10110

For information about special discounts for bulk purchases,
please contact W. W. Norton Special Sales at
speacialsales@wwnorton.com or 800-233-4830

Manufacturing by Quad Graphics Fairfield
Book design by JAM Design
Production manager: Lauren Abbate

ISBN: 978-0-393-25392-4 (pbk.)

W. W. Norton & Company, Inc.
500 Fifth Avenue, New York, N.Y. 10110
www.wwnorton.com

W. W. Norton & Company Ltd.
15 Carlisle Street, London W1D 3BS

1 2 3 4 5 6 7 8 9 0

For Trisha

Contents

PART FOUR: WHY POEMS? WHY POETS?

Preface

(To a poetic student and friend.) I only seek to put you in rapport. Your own brain, heart, evolution, must not only understand the matter, but largely supply it.

WALT WHITMAN, "After Trying a Certain Book"

I've spent my life reading and writing poetry and teaching both the reading and the writing of it. In putting together this book, I asked myself what I would have liked to know when I was a young poet. What would have been useful or interesting to me back then? What could have helped me grow as a poet by deepening my excitement about, appreciation of, and understanding of this curious and compelling art?

This small book represents one poet's informal exploration of language and self in relation to the impulse to write lyric poetry. I think of it as a series of brief provocations presented in the hope that they will lead the young poet or reader toward an active response of his or her own. If it encourages you to write poems, or if it clarifies your personal engagement with and excitement about poetry, then it will have succeeded. Inevitably, this book bears the stamp of my own interests and preoccupations—probably even where I imagine myself to be least personal or biased. I'm not trying to convert anyone to my ideas or preoccupations, but only to share them and to articulate what I find to be wonderful and urgent about poetry. I think it's preferable for young poets or readers to have a set of ideas and observations to orient them at the outset, rather than muddling their way into something as complex (or simple) as poetry. If any of my ideas strike you as wrong or not true to your experience, that's fine. You, the reader, are invited to make use of anything that seems worthwhile and to discard the rest. But to do either—to assimilate or reject—is to become what Ralph Waldo Emerson calls "an active soul," and that is essential if you wish to engage poetry.

Poetry resists logical progressions and insists on clusters of relationships. I've done my best to organize this book under brief topics and made some attempt to present them in a sensible order. That said, readers should feel free to investigate any topics that interest them in whatever order they choose. I've also periodically suggested certain activities a reader might do to directly experience some notion in the text; for lack of a better word, I've called them exercises. If, in responding to any of these exercises, you write something that so engages you that you work on it to the point of considering it a poem of your own, then that's all to the good. But it isn't essential that the exercises lead to full-blown poems. Rather, they should be approached in the spirit of experiment and fun.

■ ■ ■

When starting out in poetry, it's often the case (as it was for me) that the urge to write poems is stronger than the urge to read them. That said, sooner or later you have to read lots of poems in order to develop as a poet. The more poems you read, the more you realize the various and amazing things that poets can do with language. But I don't intend this book to be an anthology, and I don't reproduce many complete poems in it. Throughout, I suggest a number of poems by title and author; if you're curious and have access to the Internet (today's global library), you'll probably be able to find them and read them to see if they are useful or interesting to you. Likewise, in the early stages of your growth as a writer or reader of poetry, teachers and peers will happily guide you to poems that they find exciting and worthwhile. Quite possibly, you are using this primer in a class alongside an anthology chosen by your teacher, who will enthusiastically present the poems she or he most admires. That's as it should be. It's how most of us entered the world of poetry as young writers—guided by the enthusiasms and insights of our first teachers. But ultimately, each poet must find his or her own way to grow authentically—at least partly through reading poems. Perhaps one poem or poet that you love will lead you to another—you'll become aware of influences and shared preoccupations of style or content—and soon you'll be finding on your own those poems through which you can develop a clearer sense of your own identity as poet and person. I hope this book encourages that very important and brave purpose.

■ ■ ■

This primer is, as all texts must be, a reflection of the attitudes and biases of its author. In it, you will find very little discussion of traditional forms. For example, I say nothing much about sonnets, though some of my favorite poems are sonnets; nor villanelles, though I've written almost a dozen myself. I admire both forms, but I think their study should come later in a poet's growth, and only if those particular forms attract you. Of course, if you're studying with a teacher who has the desire and ability to teach how to write those forms, that's all to the good. If I neglect the traditional forms, I say even less about so-called experimental poetries. My reasons for neglecting experimental poetries are more deeply rooted: in my experience, most poets are eager to connect words to both the world around them and the worlds inside them, and to do so in terms of understandable themes and experiences. Certain experimental poetries are based on severing the bond between Word and World; while this can be exhilarating for a while, I feel it is a flirtation with alienation and isolation that ultimately undermines the social purpose of language, which is to connect us to the world of our experience and to each other.

While I'm listing my sins of neglect and omission, I should add that I haven't a lot to say about meter and metrical scansion of poems. Although traditional meters are a profoundly honorable form of ordering language in poetry, I find the topic to be more intimidating than welcoming to young poets and readers. What's more, I think an early preoccupation with meter can distract from what I consider to be the central project: the encouragement of intelligent and engaged self-expression. If you feel otherwise, I urge you to continue your studies in these directions, either on your own or under the guidance of a more experienced poet-teacher.

Were I to continue this list of the shortcomings or omissions of my primer, I could hardly expect you to have enough curiosity to give it a chance, so I'll stop now and wish you well on this most exciting of adventures: the expressive joy of writing poems.

Part One

DISORDER AND ORDER

formance. What unites lyric poetry and popular song isn't the quality of language use, but its expressive purpose.

LYRIC POETRY: EVERYWHERE AND ALWAYS

Lyric poetry is the voice of the individual making sense of his or her experience. When I say that lyric is the most basic form of poetry, I mean two things—"everywhere and always." "Everywhere" refers to the fact that lyric poetry is present in every culture on the planet. No matter where you go, if people are there, then lyric and song are also there. If my blanket claim of "everywhere" is global, then my claim of "always" is historical: lyric poetry and song have been present throughout history in every culture whose writing has been recorded and preserved. There's also little reason to doubt that it was present in cultures without written languages.

Let me reiterate briefly: the personal lyric exists universally—everywhere and always. Poems about love, or loneliness, or fear, or wonder. Poems about what someone did, or what happened to him, or what she dreams of doing. Sometimes lyric poems don't use the pronoun *I*, but they are always expressive of an individual viewpoint—what some imagined person is saying or feeling or doing in the world.

Lyric poetry is present in all times and places because it helps us live by expressing our experience and at the same time moving that experience a bit away from us—to the world of words, where it can be shaped or dramatized into meaning. When writing a poem, we turn our world into words and arrange them into patterns of pleasure or urgency or coherence. This second world created out of words is intensified and structured for expressive gratification. When reading a poem, we enter this second world—one that the poet's imagination has created to express his or her vision of life and, indirectly, to connect with us.

Humans need lyric poetry. Most of us know that, based on our own experiences of adolescence, when emotions and events threat-

CHAPTER ONE

Poetry Is Both Simple and Complex

In many ways, lyric poetry is the simplest and most obvious thing in the cultural world. You'll notice that I say "lyric poetry." I don't have much to say about epic poetry, or even extended narrative poetry. Lyric poetry is the most basic and omnipresent form of poetry. Not only that, but ever since the romantic period lyric has been the dominant form of poetry in the West. Once you realize that lyric poetry includes popular song, it's obvious that it is at the center of human emotional life as it seeks expression in words. Who among us could imagine growing up without some form of popular music—songs whose lyrics express the inner life of the self and its responses to the world and to other people? In America, this could be rock 'n' roll, hip-hop, blues, country, folk, rap, or emo. Why should it matter what kind of music we personally respond to? It all has the same purpose: to dramatize human experience and to emphasize its subjective dimension. Although the lyrics of popular song are poetry—an opinion I find powerfully validated by the recent award of the Nobel Prize in Literature to Bob Dylan—language in song is seldom as well organized and carefully constructed as the language of poems written for the page. After all, so much of the energy and emotion of song is carried by melody, instrumentation, and vocal per-

ened to overwhelm us even as time propelled us relentlessly toward biological and cultural adulthood. And many of us still turn to lyric in times of crisis. Even before adolescence, many young people feel the urge to write a poem when a beloved pet dies or death takes someone they know. Not to mention that other great crisis of human experience: romantic love—the urgencies and delicious tribulations of it, the longing to love and to be loved. Who in the throes of first love hasn't written a poem or wished that he or she could? Maybe, plagued by shyness or confusion, we sought out someone else's poem to speak for us.

I argue that writing a lyric poem serves two basic functions. One is that it feels good to express what is in us. Who hasn't at some point experienced the sense of being a separate person isolated from others and yet bursting with emotion? Lyric poets have always claimed that expressing that emotion in words can heal, bringing a transformative sense of release and relief. William Wordsworth put it this way:

> To me alone there came a thought of grief:
> A timely utterance gave that thought relief,
> And I again am strong: . . .
> from "Ode: Intimations of Immortality from
> Recollections of Early Childhood" (1807)

Closely related to this expressive function, yet even more important, is the fact that the writing of lyric poems helps to restabilize a self that has been destabilized by experience (inner or outer experience, or both). Lyric helps a poet restabilize by turning a personal experience into words and then applying the ordering principles that poetry and individual imagination abound with. When the poet translates her distress or confusion into words and then orders those words, she achieves what Robert Frost identified as a main goal for poetry: "a momentary stay against confusion." To put it more positively, the poet actively restabilizes herself through expressive writing. She turns her rich and bewildering world into words with the awareness that lyric poetry's enormous array of ordering principles will both express her situation and stabilize it.

■ ■ ■

It often seems that writing a lyric poem should be easy and gratifying. We all use language, after all. We know that poetry can be composed aloud or written down. Speaking is a natural human activity; most everyone does it. Granted, writing words is a more complicated process, but most of us do that too. Either way, to write poetry might seem to be a simple thing—just "speak out what's in you." It would seem that all we have to do is use words and a pen or laptop to write out what's percolating inside us or to evoke a pleasant or unpleasant memory.

And that's partly true. Some of the most moving poems and songs use very simple language and seem to speak directly to us. But there's a paradox here: poetry is both a "simple" use of language and a very complicated one. The reason poetry is so useful for emotional and spiritual expression—and for human survival—is that it is also a rich and complex use of language for creating order. Both the obvious and the subtle orderings of poetry serve to hold words together—to forge them into solid but dynamic structures that contain and channel the chaotic inner and outer experience that we humans seek to express.

A DOUBLE AWARENESS: THE PRESENCE OF DISORDER, THE NEED FOR ORDER

Before saying more about the paradox of the simplicity and complexity of lyric poetry, I want to talk about the simplicity and complexity of being a person in the world, since that is at the heart of the impulse to engage with poetry. If we give it a moment's thought, we realize that being a person in the world brings two awarenesses that can deeply impact us.

First, there is a great deal of disorder in experience. Please understand that I use the word *disorder* as a conceptual term; it isn't a moral category. Disorder is neither good nor bad, though it can be either, or even both at the same time. Disorder can take many forms and show many qualities—it can be exhilarating or terrifying, depending on the situation. It can be outside us in the world—think of war, weather, a loved person or creature, traumatic violence, or being lost in a city or a forest. Disorder can be inside our bodies—think of pain or illness. It can be in our minds—think of the fluctuations in emotion that we experience on an almost daily basis, the bad memories or nostalgic longings that disturb us, or the giddy intoxications we sometimes seek. Disorder can also occur when we think of the future and become anxiously aware of the uncertainty of what next week or next year will bring. The examples I've just given can be weighted toward happiness as well as negativity—the disorder of romantic love is often highly prized, and daydreams can be the mind's pleasurable playfulness with the unknown future. Outdoor adventure or sports can be the body's dynamic encounter with the unpredictable physical world. Whether disorder is experienced as exhilarating or life threatening, it is real. In various forms and degrees, it is undeniably present in our daily lives.

Second, along with the reality of disorder in experience is the equally powerful human need for a sense of order. We value it in social and political situations (we want peace; we want civility and goodwill from neighbors and strangers). But we also crave order in our own lives: we enjoy our private habits immensely, those little rituals that establish reassuring patterns—whether it's how we brush our teeth or how we arrange our possessions and our rooms. Consider even the cosmic order of nature's cycles: the predictable rising of the sun and moon, the stable rotation of the stars in the night sky, the recurring circle of the seasons. All these natural patterns have given humans an enduring sense of reassurance from prehistoric times until now.

THE VANISHED PAST, THE UNKNOWABLE NEXT MOMENT, AND RADIO FREE BRAIN

One of the odd and disturbing facts that goes with being a body exist-
ing in time is that everything that happens to us vanishes as soon as it
occurs. Where is yesterday and all it contained—its events and char-
acters? It's gone; it's completely vanished. Yes, the tree outside our
window is still there, just where it was yesterday, and we take genu-
ine if unconscious reassurance from that. But what about last week or
our childhood—aren't they both gone completely in physical terms?
Is there any place where last week or our childhood still exists in the
world? No, they're gone, and that's a fact. I call this form of disorder the
Vanished Past. The medieval French poet François Villon gave an elo-
quent and haunting phrase for this vanishing in the refrain of a lament:
"où sont les neiges d'antan?"—"Where are the snows of yesteryear?"

The fact that everything that has happened to us has vanished—
everything we've done or seen or thought or felt—can be a sad and
disturbing realization; it can seem a high price to pay for living inside
time. And I should mention another sad realization: not everything
vanishes with the same certainty. Those who have had traumatic expe-
riences know that some of the worst things they've endured live on
inside them and can return in nightmares and flashbacks with terrify-
ing vividness. It seems one of life's injustices that these violent disor-
ders persist or surge up in our minds with more intensity than many
pleasant memories that we would love to re-experience vividly.

But it isn't just that everything that has already happened disap-
pears as we move through time. The future is also unpredictable.
What will happen to you tomorrow, or even later today? Do you really
know, beyond the human basics of moving, eating, and sleeping? Isn't
the future mostly unseeable? Yes, the sun will rise (which is funda-
mentally reassuring), and weather of one sort or another will happen.
We can even pretend that our days are so predictable as to be boring.
But really, who knows what will happen next, whom we might meet,

what we might see? So much of the future is what I call the Unknowable Next Moment. Whether this fact about the unpredictable future fills us with excitement or apprehension depends on our personality and our circumstances, but it's a simple existential dimension of life.

Think, too, about what's inside our minds, inside that circle of self. Isn't there a voice constantly chattering in there? It's a voice; it's speaking words (at least mine does, and I assume yours does also). I call it Radio Free Brain—a 24/7 station. If you wake up at four o'clock in the morning, the voice is still broadcasting; if you paused after reading the last sentence, it probably had something to say before you began reading again. But this inner voice doesn't come from a steady, single station. Instead, it's like a radio permanently set on "scan"—shifting from one channel to the next with hardly a pause for station identification. And we, who are listening, have very little control over it. Pause sometime during your day, and listen to that voice for a mere sixty seconds—in just that brief time, notice what odd and unpredictable things it says. A running commentary on your life, yes, but also the voice seems to be all over the place: saying "my back hurts" or "I'm hungry" or "I'm cold" and "wonder what I'll do for dinner" and "that guy reminds me of someone from my high school" and "I'm feeling blue" and so on. And there isn't just the jazzy static of Radio Free Brain; there's also the fundamental flux of our subjective states and those larger swings of mood from exhilaration to depression that don't seem under our control, much less predictable.

Disorder outside us (past and future); disorder inside us (shifting moods and anxious fantasies, the scattered chatter of the voice). In the ordinary, mildly chaotic world of daily life, we somehow manage to balance between disorder and order. We usually keep ourselves steady enough and moving forward more or less purposefully and responsibly through our day. But when something destabilizes us, it might well qualify as a crisis of self. And it is precisely to help us respond to such crises—be they positive or negative, minor or major—that culture invented lyric poetry.

HOW POETRY HELPS US, HOW WE HELP OURSELVES THROUGH POETRY

Poetry is compelling in a crisis not just because it is concise and imme-
diate, but also because it is superbly designed to handle both aspects
of experience: the reality of disorder and the self's need for some kind
of order.

We might wish our lives to be stable and calm, but they aren't
for the most part. (And wouldn't they be boring if they were too safe,
too calm?) It's in the nature of experience to destabilize us—whether
through a crisis of trouble (grief, illness, trauma, divorce, suffering,
violent accident) or a crisis of something positive (romantic love,
adventure, joy, wonder). Nor does the crisis have to be in the pres-
ent moment: consider the recollection (re-emergence?) of past trauma,
the longings of homesickness or nostalgia, the memories of a loved
one who is gone forever. Many people know how these feelings have
the power to disturb and destabilize.

Culture offers a number of large ordering schemes to help deal
with experiences of disorder. In particular, religions and philosophies
offer ordering explanations and beliefs that seek to make sense of our
confusing experience and help us through it. But to my thinking, lyric
poetry has several major advantages over all other orderings. For one
thing, it is adapted to our specific issues and experiences. It emerges
from or addresses our lives individually and specifically. When we
write a poem (or song), we write the story of *our* crisis (joyous or grief-
filled)—we turn *our* individual world into words, and then we order
those words into an expressive structure. That structure, that poem,
is turbulently alive with the disorder that plagues or exalts us, but it
also manifests the ordering power of poetry—the ability to compress
experience into a small and lively space of language. When I write a
poem and turn my world into words, I order those words and thereby
order my world. It's a world I can shape, one in which I dramatize my
disorder but also create a patterned structure to contain it. I displace

or "translate" my instability into words, and in that second world of the poem I restabilize. I may suffer or be confused in the real world of my life, but in the world of the poem I am able to dramatize my confusion and take control of it—turn it into an expressive but stable thing: a lyric poem.

Doesn't everyone, at some time, write a poem or at least want to write one? The expressive impulse can grip us when we're in grief or when we're in joy. Maybe we don't actually write a poem because we don't know how to or don't feel adequate to express what we're experiencing; but we may find solace or release in someone else's poem, as if that person had said it for us. Or maybe we wait a while—maybe we'll live a bit with our confusion before we can order it. But poetry is there, waiting for us, offering its resources when we're ready to dramatize our experience and shape it into something fixed and stable, yet pulsing with life.

■ ■ ■

More often than not, the experience of disorder seems to be confusing or upsetting—think of poems of despair or grief or suffering. But oddly and importantly, there is also a poetry in which disorder is a positive, desirable quality. I'm not just thinking of romantic love's confusions as a form of pleasurable uncertainty and adventure. There are other times when our daily lives seem too orderly and we begin to consider a little disorder as something we could welcome. There's the simple but serious feeling of boredom when our daily lives are too dull to bear and the disorder of kicking loose exerts a powerful attraction. And then there's the sinister "order" of political oppression that can make disorder as liberty seem alluring and positive. This sense of the too-much order of political and economic oppression led the pre-romantic poet William Blake to speak of "mind-forged manacles"—restrictive laws that he felt oppressed both himself and his fellow citizens:

> I wander through each chartered street,
> Near where the chartered Thames does flow,

And mark in every face I meet,
Marks of weakness, marks of woe.

In every cry of every man,
In every infant's cry of fear,
In every voice, in every ban,
The mind-forged manacles I hear:

How the chimney-sweeper's cry
Every blackening church appalls,
And the hapless soldier's sigh
Runs in blood down palace-walls.

from "London" (1794)

For Blake, kings and priests were co-oppressors—from their centers of power in palace and church, they both restricted and oppressed other humans and diminished their lives.

In another poem, Blake describes a "Garden of Love" that used to welcome lovers with its flowers and opportunities for intimacy, but now is full of tombstones and "priests in black gowns making their rounds / and binding with briars my joys and desires." In a more contemporary world, Allen Ginsberg's "Howl" is a Blakean visionary cry of anguish and rebellion against the oppressive conformity of mid-twentieth-century American life.

Whether disorder has a positive or a negative charge depends on the particular poet and the circumstances of the particular poem. That being said, it's true that probably in 85 percent of poems disorder is experienced as threat or negativity, and the poem's ordering is felt as an affirmation.

What is crucial about lyric poetry is that it can dramatize the presence of both disorder and order. What this might mean and how it manifests in particular poems we'll consider in a moment, but first it might be useful to explore one aspect of our minds that has a huge influence on poetry.

MEMORY, EXPERIENCE, AND THE SELF

> Great is the power of memory, a thing, O my God, to be in awe of,
> a profound and immeasurable multiplicity; and this thing is my
> mind; this thing am I.
>
> Augustine of Hippo, *Confessions* (fourth century CE)

It's time to open the door to a rich disorder and variety that's as close to home as we can get: the world of memory. I've mentioned that as each of us moves through our day or our life, our experiences vanish almost as soon as they happen. That's true in a physical sense—yesterday's landscape, thoughts, and sensations are utterly gone from the world today, and we don't give much thought to what's gone if we're actively engaged in the present moment. But of course, much of what we experience and all of our past is stored in our minds as memory images, and there it persists within us—"a profound and immeasurable multiplicity," to use Augustine's phrase.

A brief consideration of memory will go a long way toward revealing some of the mysteries and urgencies of lyric and how they relate to our lives. As the quote from Augustine indicates, our sense of self, our unique and individual identity, is profoundly tied up with our personal memories—"I am this person who has these particular memories." Anyone who doubts that claim should listen to the poignant testimony of amnesiacs about the depression that accompanies their condition, caused in large part by their sense that they have no identity because they have no personal memories. Along the same lines, we often speak of certain memories as "formative"; with that one word, we acknowledge the crucial role of memory in creating our sense of having a unique identity as an individual—"I am the person shaped and formed by these powerful memories." Even though we forget much of what we see and experience, in another sense memory can seem almost infinite—a gigantic inventory of what we've seen, tasted, smelled, touched, and otherwise done, stored in our brain cells and waiting for opportunities to become a meaningful part of our lives, or, equally common, waiting to pop into our consciousness in a seemingly random way.

It's easy to see that memory has this huge and peculiar role in our lives, but it's another thing to experience its odd qualities firsthand. To my mind, one of the most remarkable instances of an effort to do that—to foreground the rich strangeness of personal memory—is a poem entitled "I Remember" by the American poet Joe Brainard (1941–1994). The poem orders itself as a long list (and when I say long, I'm not kidding—one published version of Brainard's poem is 266 pages long!). A list is one of the most curious of language orderings, because it is arbitrary and yet focused. And lists are seemingly easy to make. Your grocery list consists of a jotting down of things you plan to buy the next time you go to the supermarket (you make it to help your memory). The order of the items in a grocery list is random (disorder), but the list itself has a unity and an internally coherent logic. For example, the list consists of things you want and expect to find in your local market—you don't add "flamingos" unless you intend to be deliberately whimsical (and you certainly don't expect to find them there, even in the gourmet section). Unlike a shopping list, Brainard's list has no such restrictions as to content—anything he remembers can be on it. To counteract and structure the freewheeling nature of his project, Brainard makes use of one obvious "ordering" pattern: each line of his poem begins with the phrase "I remember." Another principle he seems to use is that he keeps each memory short—never more than a few sentences; often, just a single, simple sentence.

I should also note that Brainard's memories are specific to his moment in history and his place in his culture—he's a white, American, gay male born and raised in Tulsa, Oklahoma, in the middle of the twentieth century. Many of the things he remembers—bola ties, iceboxes—belong to his time, not to yours, and yet they are precise and particular and various. Here's a small sample from early in his poem:

I remember the first time I got a letter that said "After Five Days
Return To" on the envelope, and I thought that after I had kept
the letter for five days I was supposed to return it to the sender.

I remember the kick I used to get going through my parents' drawers
looking for rubbers. (Peacock).

I remember when polio was the worst thing in the world.

I remember pink dress shirts. And bola ties.

I remember when a kid told me that those sour cloverlike leaves we
used to eat (with little yellow flowers) tasted so sour because dogs
peed on them. I remember that didn't stop me from eating them.

I remember the first drawing I remember doing. It was of a bride
with a very long train.

I remember my first cigarette. It was a Kent. Up on a hill. In Tulsa,
Oklahoma. With Ron Padgett.

I remember my first erections. I thought I had some terrible disease
or something.

I remember the only time I ever saw my mother cry. I was eating
apricot pie.

I remember how much I cried seeing *South Pacific* (the movie)
three times.

I remember how good a glass of water can taste after a dish of
ice cream.

I remember when I got a five-year pin for not missing a single
morning of Sunday School for five years. (Methodist)

I remember when I went to a "come as your favorite person" party as
Marilyn Monroe.

I remember one of the first things I remember. An ice box. (As
opposed to a refrigerator)

I remember white margarine in a plastic bag. And a little package of
orange powder. You put the orange powder in the bag with the
margarine and you squeezed it all around until the margarine
became yellow.

I remember how much I used to stutter.

I remember how much, in high school, I wanted to be handsome and
   popular.

I remember when, in high school, if you wore green and yellow on
   Thursday it meant you were queer.

I remember when, in high school, I used to stuff a sock in my
   underwear.

I remember when I decided to become a minister. I don't remember
   when I decided not to be.

I remember the first time I saw television. Lucille Ball was taking
   ballet lessons.

I remember the day John Kennedy was shot.

I remember for my fifth birthday all I wanted was an off-one-
   shoulder black satin evening gown. I got it. And I wore it to my
   birthday party.

I remember a dream I had recently where John Ashbery said that my
   Mondrian period paintings were even better than Mondrian.

I remember a dream I have had often of being able to fly. (Without an
   airplane)

I remember many dreams of finding gold and jewels.

I remember a little boy I used to take care of after school while his
   mother worked. I remember how much fun it was to punish him
   for being bad.

I remember a dream I used to have a lot of a beautiful red and yellow
   and black snake in bright green grass.

I remember St. Louis when I was very young. I remember the tattoo
   shop next to the bus station and the two big lions in front of the
   Museum of Art.

I remember an American history teacher who was always
   threatening to jump out of the window if we didn't quiet down.
   (Second floor)

                                     from *I Remember* (1975; 1995)

Brainard's poem goes on like this for hundreds of pages—it is both
boring and exhilarating to read, an odd and unpredictable combina-

tion of the significant and the trivial. (Perhaps our lives are the same.) I wonder if anyone has read it cover to cover at one go. But I think he's on to something very exciting for poets: the depth and mystery and radiant ordinariness of our lives among things and people. And also the fact that we can, through the power of language, bring those memories out of our consciousness and onto a page.

■ ■ ■

"I REMEMBER" EXERCISE

For this first exercise, I propose that you try imitating Brainard's poem and write ten pages of "I remembers" from your own life. When you do this, one thing is essential: *know that the list you are making is not to be shown to anyone else.* Only you will (or should) see your list. That freedom, that privacy, that permission you give yourself is essential to the full experience of this exercise. Think of your list as a private dialogue between yourself and your past. Equally important is that you not sit in judgment on your list. It's crucial that you approach this exercise by giving yourself permission to write down whatever memories come to mind.

You are welcome to try to guide the flow of your list, although my years of experience talking with students who have done such lists indicates that there's only just so much control we can exert over the way our memories present themselves. Writing ten pages of "I remember" may be easy for you or difficult; it varies from person to person. Nor must you do it all in one sitting—many of my students have preferred to take periodic breaks when memories got too intense or confusing. You can write it by hand or type it out on a computer—whatever works best for you. But do attempt it, or you won't be able to test the accuracy of my assertions about memory against your personal experience.

If you were my students (instead of my readers), after doing this exercise we would all sit together in a classroom. I would ask you to hold up the printout of your "I remember" list so that you could make physical contact with it and thus reconnect to the experience of writing it. Then I would say, "So what was it like to do this? I don't want to know any specific memories—those are entirely your business—but is there anything you'd like to share? Was it fun? Scary? Sad? All of the above? Did it focus on a particular time in your life, or a particular place? Did you get caught in any 'whirlpools'? If so, what was that like?" And so on—most people who have done this are eager to talk about the experience, because it stirs you up a bit (or quite a bit sometimes). Many people are eager to share some of their memories out loud (and why not, as long as they get to choose what they share?). But as a general principle, know that the *actual content* of the list will remain completely confidential, because to think that someone else might see it (even a close friend or relative) is to create an inhibition and self-consciousness that can short-circuit the richness of the process.

■ ■ ■

SOME ASPECTS OF MEMORY

One of the first things you'll probably notice about your list is that it consists entirely of concrete, sensory images. You cannot remember "beauty" or "love" or "sadness" or any other abstraction. You can, of course, remember the first time you felt that something was beautiful or the first time you felt "loneliness," but the memory itself is always concrete and specific—always "who, what, where, when."

The concrete, sensory nature of memory may well be at the heart of William Carlos Williams's often-quoted line: "no ideas but in things." Certainly, it is central to the impulse to precision and specificity that is common to many poetries—the sense that poetry is made vivid by what William Blake called "the bright particulars."

In making your list, you also will have become more aware of what you already knew: that memory is a huge storehouse of images that indicate who you are and what you've seen and done (and tasted and touched and smelled). At certain points in the process, you may have realized that this ten-page list could be extended indefinitely—that there are hundreds of thousands of images stored in your memory. Once you begin listing memories, the very process stimulates recollection of even more. Many of the memory images seem rather trivial; after all, not everything stored in an attic or basement is interesting.

However, as you let yourself down into the rapidly flowing stream of memory, you probably encountered more than a few that were rich in emotional association—that made you suddenly feel happy or sad or anxious or full of shame. Some of those emotions might have surprised you; you wouldn't necessarily have predicted them. Sometimes people making "I remember" lists feel as if they're caught briefly in a vortex of emotionally charged memory images—as if being sucked into a wounded place in their lives that has a kind of whirlpool power over them. This is obsessive memory, and it can be scary. Disturbing though they are, obsessive memories are the raw material of many lyric poems—a deep pain or sorrow that awaits transformation and redemption through the act of writing a poem.

I would add that a list can just as easily flow into a swirl of positive associations—where one vivid and pleasant memory leads to another.

When I make an "I remember" list, it's often difficult to stop at a single thing. Before I know it, one memory leads to another, and I have to struggle to prevent my list from flowing into paragraph-long (or longer) anecdotes. Having done more than a few such "I remember" lists, I'm always impressed by how Brainard knew when to stop. Part of the achievement of Brainard's poem (I know this sounds odd) is in his *restraint*.

Before we consider the ordering principle of the list, I want to make one more point about your "I Remember." When we value our memories enough to write them down on a page, we are also validating our own experience. This simple act can be an important first step in believing that our experiences and our lives might have value— which is an attitude that underlies and nourishes the very existence of lyric poetry.

LIST AS STRUCTURE

As you made your list, there was probably a certain amount of pattern to the memories: for example, remembering one movie title may have led to another one (this is called associative memory). Because each of us has seen plenty of movies and remembers plenty of movie titles, you could easily have filled ten pages with nothing but movie titles. But the odds are that you didn't do that, because we humans take pleasure in pattern only when it is accompanied by variety. Or, put simply: we get bored easily. We like connections; but once things become too predictable, we quickly lose interest. This tension between the pleasure of pattern and the need for variety becomes important when writing poems.

A list structure might seem arbitrary and even whimsical, and it probably took a bit of nerve (and exhibitionism) on Brainard's part to declare his book-length list a poem. But a list can also be a meaningful structure for a poem. For example, the German poet Günter Eich wrote a poem called "Inventory" at the end of World War II. In a sense, Eich's poem is a simple list of the things he possesses at that moment. But that moment of the poem has to do with his situation in the world: he is a young German soldier who has spent a year in a prisoner of war camp near the end of World War II. Knowing this biographical and historical context is essential to understanding what the poem dramatizes:

Inventory

This is my cap,
this is my overcoat,
here is my shave kit
in its linen pouch.

Some field rations:
my dish, my tumbler,

here in the tin-plate
I've scratched my name.

Scratched it here with this
precious nail
I keep concealed
from coveting eyes.

In the bread bag I have
a pair of wool socks
and a few things that I
discuss with no one,

and these form a pillow
for my head at night.
Some cardboard lies
between me and the ground.

The pencil's the thing
I love the most:
By day it writes verses
I make up at night.

This is my notebook,
this my rain gear,
this is my towel,
this is my twine.

Günter Eich (1946), translated by Joshua Mehigan

This "inventory" is a list of all he possesses in the desolation and deprivation of his imprisonment. The poem itself isn't necessarily about war or trauma, but about having almost nothing and living in confinement and destitution—a deprivation so complete that a single nail is precious. It's the voice of a solitary individual reduced to almost nothing, isolated and untrusting (he keeps the nail hidden from his fellow prisoners, who would want it and steal it). The poem implies that this is a complete list, *all* that the speaker (Eich) possesses in the world.

It's important to note two things. First, on a cultural level, this poem became famous in a postwar Germany where everything had been destroyed—both the physical world and the social community—by years of Nazi rule and warfare and Allied bombardment. Eich's laconic and unemotional list of all he had left in the world also spoke eloquently for many other Germans, both soldiers and civilians, who emerged from the war with nothing and with their world ruined. Second, two (similar) objects in this list are given extra space—their own stanzas—and are connected to the poet's emotions (the other objects, no matter how important, are simply named). The first emotionally charged object is the nail. One of the reasons it is "precious" is that it has enabled him to scratch his name into his food plate (think: nail as writing tool). That scratched name is not just important for claiming possession, but also for asserting his personal existence ("my name"—i.e., I, Günter, exist). The second object that is connected to special value is a pencil, which he "loves most." It is the thing that enables him to write poems, to sustain his emotional and spiritual life. If you ever wonder whether poetry is "important," think of this desolate list, which is also, in a paradoxical way, a celebration of life and the individual's desire to live and to retain dignity and some control over life. Eich's list is proof that he is "still in charge" even though he is obviously powerless in the prison camp—he still has a name, a pencil and his creativity, and the power to list the material objects that he owns and that sustain his existence, both physical and emotional. Beyond that, his poem has enabled him to communicate with people in the wider world and thereby restore some semblance of meaning as connection between himself and others.

There are other ways to turn the arbitrary structure of a list into the meaningful ordering that we often seek in poems. In "The Day Lady Died," the poet Frank O'Hara seems to arrange his poem as a simple chronology of the things he did on a certain day as he walked around New York City. That day was July 17, 1959, and it was a pretty ordinary day and a pretty ordinary list of activities, considering O'Hara's sophisticated bookishness and social life. This list culminates in the moment when he notices a picture of the great jazz singer and songwriter Billie Holliday (whose nickname was Lady Day) on the front page of a newspaper and realizes that she has just died. The photograph immediately causes him to remember what becomes the final event on his list: a memory of hearing her sing years ago in a small club, a moment so cherished and special that the poet and everyone else in the club "stopped breathing" in awe:

The Day Lady Died

It is 12:20 in New York a Friday
three days after Bastille day, yes
it is 1959 and I go get a shoeshine
because I will get off the 4:19 in Easthampton
at 7:15 and then go straight to dinner
and I don't know the people who will feed me

I walk up the muggy street beginning to sun
and have a hamburger and a malted and buy
an ugly NEW WORLD WRITING to see what the poets
in Ghana are doing these days
                         I go on to the bank
and Miss Stillwagon (first name Linda I once heard)
doesn't even look up my balance for once in her life
and in the GOLDEN GRIFFIN I get a little Verlaine
for Patsy with drawings by Bonnard although I do
think of Hesiod, trans. Richmond Lattimore or
Brendan Behan's new play or Le Balcon or Les Nègres
of Genet, but I don't, I stick with Verlaine
after practically going to sleep with quandariness

and for Mike I just stroll into the PARK LANE
Liquor Store and ask for a bottle of Strega and
then I go back where I came from to 6th Avenue
and the tobacconist in the Ziegfeld Theatre and
casually ask for a carton of Gauloises and a carton
of Picayunes, and a NEW YORK POST with her face on it

and I am sweating a lot by now and thinking of
leaning on the john door in the 5 SPOT
while she whispered a song along the keyboard
to Mal Waldron and everyone and I stopped breathing

Frank O'Hara (1964)

O'Hara's poem is a list, but a list with a difference. By the poem's
end, he has suddenly been transported out of his ordinary day and
into the past—into a vivid memory of a moment so filled with wonder
that everyone "stopped breathing." When we realize that this is an
elegy for the singer, who has herself "stopped breathing," we know
we're in a magical place that only poetry can dramatize, a place where
the mysteries of death and intensified life are braided together as a
single strand.

List structures can also generate poems that are profoundly
grounded and affirmative. For example, the traditional Navajo song
known as "Night Chant" is an incantatory celebration of (and prayer
for) positive experiences that centers itself in the wonder of encounter-
ing the awesome beauty of the world and locating oneself in relation
to that beauty and that world:

House made of dawn,
House made of evening light,
House made of the dark cloud
. . . .
Dark cloud is at the house's door,
The trail of it is dark clouds,

The zigzag lightning stands high upon it

. . . .

Happily may I walk.

Happily, with abundant showers, may I walk.

Happily, with abundant plants, may I walk.

Happily, on the trail of pollen, may I walk.

Happily may I walk.

May it be beautiful before me.

May it be beautiful behind me.

May it be beautiful below me.

May it be beautiful above me.

May it be beautiful all around me.

In beauty is it finished.

DISORDER AND THE POET'S PEN

There's a passage in a play by Shakespeare that gets directly to the heart of poetry's positive ordering power, and it does so, oddly, by comparing the poet to two other figures who are overwhelmed by their minds' contents, though each in a different way. Like much of Shakespeare, these lines are dense and somewhat dated—they aren't easy to understand, but they're worth working at a bit, because they get at something important to us as poets:

Lovers and madmen have such seething brains,
Such shaping fantasies, that apprehend
More than cool reason ever comprehends.
The lunatic, the lover, and the poet
Are of imagination all compact:
One sees more devils than vast hell can hold,
That is, the madman; the lover, all as frantic,
Sees Helen's beauty in a brow of Egypt;
The poet's eye, in a fine frenzy rolling,

Doth glance from heaven to earth, from earth to heaven;
And, as imagination bodies forth
The forms of things unknown, the poet's pen
Turns them to shapes, and gives to airy nothing
A local habitation and a name.

from *A Midsummer Night's Dream*, 5.1

The speaker of these lines begins by claiming that two representative figures—the impassioned lover and the lunatic—have such intense and powerful imaginations that they create their own realities, realities that are not reachable by "cool" reason or logic. He then adds a third figure to his list—the poet—and claims that all three have a consciousness entirely made up of dynamic imagining. Having lumped the three figures together, he then proceeds to distinguish them from one another in terms of how their imaginations work. The lover, it turns out, is so besotted with his beloved that his idealizing imagination overwhelms reality. Shakespeare's lines imply that the bedazzled lover perceives his beloved as a pale-browed beauty (an English ideal in Shakespeare's time, oddly assumed to correspond to the legendary Greek beauty, Helen of Troy), whereas her actual complexion has a Gypsy (Egyptian) darkness. In short, an infatuated lover projects his own cultural ideal of beauty onto his beloved's actual appearance and sees what he wants to see.

If the lover overwhelms reality with his idealizing passion, then the madman is himself overwhelmed by the negative image-making power of his mind, a power he can't control at all: he "sees more devils than vast hell can hold"—that is, more than there could be in hell, or anywhere, really. These monsters exist only in his imagination, but this disturbed imagination is terrifyingly infinite and means him harm.

The madman's gaze could be said to be frozen in terror at the sight of the devils pouring up out of hell before his eyes. Likewise, the infatuated lover can be imagined to be mesmerized by his version of the beloved's face. Of the three figures, only the poet has a freedom of eye movement that symbolizes a deeper freedom of imagination. Glancing freely back and forth, the poet negotiates a balance between the ideal (heaven) and the real (earth) and then has the right tool (a pen for writing words) to shape what he or she imagines and "bodies forth" into the "forms of things unknown" (i.e., previously unknown, newly created by the poet). The end result? Something new has entered the world: a poem, a vital entity that has been given "[a] local habitation and a name" by the poet with pen.

The Three Realms

Shakespeare's image for how a poet works with pen and imagination is quite flattering to poets—he seems certain that poets can handle levels of chaos and disorder that could easily disable other types of people (as they do the lover and the madman). But I have one quibble with it: he only mentions two realms in relation to the poet's glance and grasp—heaven and earth. I'm concerned that these two geographies can be reduced too quickly to the human experience of the ideal (an image our minds can create) and the real (what our senses reveal to us of the world). It's as if the ideal and the real were the only options and the poet's task were to combine the two in whatever proportions seem truest to him or her and to "body them forth" as words in a poem. But I'm pretty sure there's a third realm that Shakespeare neglects to mention in relation to the poet: hell. After all, where did those devils come from that overwhelmed the madman's self? Of course, when I say "hell," I'm not speaking about some awful world we encounter when we're dead. As Shakespeare's lines point out, hell and its devils are potentially as present in our daily lives as are the realms of heaven and earth. Maybe I should say, "as constantly present in our nightly lives." Aren't all of us in our dream-life occasionally haunted by demons or strange powers that seem to come from just such a third realm?

Since the time of the romantics, certain Western lyric poets have specialized in glancing from earth to hell and back before they bodied forth in poems. One of the prime examples from the nineteenth century is the great French poet Charles Baudelaire, who noted in a prose poem: "Life swarms with innocent monsters." In his view, a poet might well "leap into the abyss—heaven or hell, who cares, as long as we arrive at the Unknown." But less likely poets, such as Emily Dickinson, also sent their bold and unafraid glances toward the demonic and terrifying. Nor should we neglect the Sylvia Plath of "Daddy" and "Lady Lazarus." In the first poem, she's persecuted by a demon dead-daddy and his living counterpart (the "vampire who said he was you"—her husband). In "Lady Lazarus," she herself takes on the demonic power and becomes something made by a devil-alchemist ("Herr Lucifer") but now filled with (avenging) power of her own as she resurrects herself from the pile of ashes she's been reduced to:

> I rise with my red hair
> And I eat men like air.

CHAPTER TWO

Letting In the Disorder

say that Shakespeare's poet has the tools (pen, language) and the positive imaginative power (that ability to "give form to airy nothings") to order disorder. But what do I mean by *disorder*, and what does it have to do with us in the twenty-first century? I'm using the term *disorder* to cover huge areas of human experience, most of which have existed for millennia. For starters, disorder can refer to events that disturb or excite us, and that become the subject matter of poems. Experiences of love and loss are major instances of disorder—falling in love, having your heart broken, losing someone you love or some place or creature you love. Love for some person or some thing can be a delirious disorder that a poet might wish to organize and dramatize in a poem of celebration. Leaving something or someone behind forever, either by chance or by choice, and feeling grief, regret, or backward longing—that's another disorder that poets often dramatize. So are experiences of illness, suffering, and trauma. And the brief or persistent experiences of intense emotion—rage, joy, despair, fear—are other forms of disorder that lyric poets body forth in poems.

In daily life, we often push down as much as we can of disorder or disturbance—ignore it or repress it in order to keep our forward momentum and to stay focused on the world before our eyes and our tasks in that world. It's possible to say that with poetry we pause and step aside to make a place for that disorder, whatever it is (feeling or event)—invite it into our poem and try our best to express and order it there. It may be that you took note of the examples of disorder I gave in the previous paragraph and applied them to your own life; but if you didn't, they might seem a bit abstract and generalized. So before I say more about how poets incorporate disorder into the thing we call a poem, let me bring the issue closer to the personal specifics that matter to you as a poet and a unique individual. When you did the "I Remember" exercise, you probably encountered a number of instances of disorder—memories that excited or saddened or disturbed you. That's what I mean by disorder: not anything abstract and theoretical, but your own actual experiences—the who, what, when, and where of it. These personal experiences of disorder are what lyric poetry is superbly designed to engage and make sense of.

There's more to be said on this topic—in fact, I think it's one of the key aspects of lyric poetry—so let's return to Shakespeare and work forward toward our own time as we consider what insights several other great writers have provided into the issue of disorder and order in creativity. In the passage from *A Midsummer's Night's Dream*, Shakespeare gives a cool and complimentary picture of poetic creativity in action—the poet is clearly in charge, and we watch as he handles what neither lover nor madman can. But in the Shakespeare scene, we're watching the poet from outside. It's as if we were seeing a movie of the poet sitting at her or his desk and rolling eyes up and then down, then back up again—heaven to earth, earth to heaven. Then the poet splits the difference between the two places and, using a pen and language, bodies forth a kind of compromise: something never seen before, a form of things (previously) unknown. It's a nice scene, and it's gratifying to poets (Look how we do it! Look how we take control with our pen or laptop and body forth!). But is it that simple? I mean, a poet observed from a distance writing a poem might resemble this cosmic, slightly cartoonish eyeball-roller, but what does it feel like to the poet in the act of creating? We see the glancing, but what is the poet actually experiencing?

THE CREATIVE PROCESS: TWO GODS PRESIDING

Let's shift forward several centuries for a different story about the creative process that might give a more vivid sense of what it feels like to the poet as he or she creates. The nineteenth-century German philosopher Friedrich Wilhelm Nietzsche had a lot to say about creativity. Let's begin with a quote of his from *Thus Spake Zarathustra* that picks up some of the wildness of disorder that Shakespeare attributed to imagination. Nietzsche has this to say about poets and creativity in general: "Who has no chaos inside him will never give birth to a dancing star." Let's assume that a poem could be imaged as a "dancing star" (personally, I like that image for its dazzle and energy and grace and strangeness). Okay, a poem is a dancing star—end product of the poet's creativity. But notice Nietzsche says "chaos inside him"—his aphorism claims the end product (dancing star or poem) can only emerge from a chaotic subjective place inside the poet.

So Nietzsche says we need chaos in us, but what do we do with it? How does that relate to creativity? To making poems? In *The Birth of Tragedy from the Spirit of Music*, he has another, more extended image for creativity—it's a two-part process, he tells us, by saying that there are two gods who preside over the creative act: Dionysus and Apollo. These two ancient Greek gods both bring their particular energies and attributes to the same process—but only one god at a time is in charge. First comes Dionysus: god of chaos, wine, wild flute music, intoxication, ecstasy, excess, even madness. He starts the process. Only after he has asserted his presence as wild disorder can the second god appear to finish the process, to complete the art. And so Apollo enters: god of beauty, proportion, rationality, harmony, the music of a harp—where different notes are harmonized as chords. First the god of chaos and confusion; then the god of order and clarity. Neither can do the job (i.e., make the poem) alone. Dionysus represents the aspect of imagination that is wild and out of control; Apollo represents the "shaping of imagination"—that which asserts control and molds the shapeless chaos into a coherent form.

This story of the two gods is fairly easy to translate to our contemporary world and to our interest in poetry. First Dionysus, then Apollo: at the outset, the poet has to let disorder in, give permission to let chaos happen—she must permit herself to write down on the page what might seem jumbled and crazy or out of control (Dionysus), trusting that eventually Apollo will come along with a new ordering beyond what the poet's self could have predicted or forced into being. Thus, first we must give ourselves over to the confusion of our early drafts. But I don't just mean confusion about plot or anything structural; I mean a deeper confusion of letting ourselves feel disorder, allowing ourselves to put anything and everything down on the page in the hopes of letting some significant disorder enter our process of creation. We must suspend judgment about what comes out of us, letting words flow onto the page regardless of whether they're coherent or dignified or logical or what we intended to say. When Dionysus is present, we are not in charge; we are whirled around. This first stage is necessarily messy and even embarrassing, and it can also be scary. How can we be sure that Apollo will even show up for the next phase? What if we give ourselves over to the chaos of Dionysus and his serene partner doesn't arrive in time to roll up his sleeves and set things in order? It's a risk that poets take in order to write significant poems.

Nietzsche's point (my point, really) is that disorder precedes order in poetry. You need to let in enough disorder before you try to order. It means giving yourself permission. You did this to a great extent during the "I Remember" exercise—you let your memory swirl around in a kind of Dionysiac dance. (Or let's say, more accurately, that both gods presided at the same time: your memory jumped and raced around for seven pages like a young, untrained dog, but Apollo was holding the leash the whole time with his ordering principle of "I remember" and his ordering advice to not go on too long, to try to keep each memory limited to a single phrase or sentence.)

Suppose this story of Dionysus and Apollo, chaos evolving into harmony, has some truth in it. We're still looking at the process from a slight distance. Why not hear firsthand testimony from a person who initially is quite convinced he's taken that initial risk, has given himself over completely to Dionysus—surrendered control of things in order to arrive at some intense and significant state of being. This testimony is in the form of an intriguing poem by the twentieth-century poet and novelist D. H. Lawrence entitled "Song of a Man Who Has Come Through." The speaker seems to feel that he has opened himself to disorder—"I yield myself and am borrowed" is the way he puts it—in order to get to some special place: to "come at the wonder," to "find the Hesperides" (a magical garden on a mythical island). He opens himself to disorder, and all goes well until he suffers a rude shock near poem's end. Here's the poem:

Song of a Man Who Has Come Through

Not I, not I, but the wind that blows through me!   1
A fine wind is blowing the new direction of Time.
If only I let it bear me, carry me, if only it carry me!
If only I am sensitive, subtle, oh, delicate, a winged gift!
If only, most lovely of all, I yield myself and am borrowed   5
By the fine, fine wind that takes its course though the chaos of
     the world
Like a fine, an exquisite chisel, a wedge-blade inserted;
If only I am keen and hard like the sheer tip of a wedge
Driven by invisible blows,
The rock will split, we shall come at the wonder, we shall find
     the Hesperides.   10

Oh, for the wonder that bubbles into my soul,
I would be a good fountain, a good well-head,
Would blur no whisper, spoil no expression.

What is the knocking?
What is the knocking at the door in the night?   15
It is somebody wants to do us harm.

No, no, it is the three strange angels.
Admit them, admit them.

                                        D. H. Lawrence (1917)

All the way up through line 13 of the poem, the speaker seems
quite confident that he has let himself be open to the vital disor-
der of the world—that he himself has become a shifting and flexi-
ble being—he floats, seemingly like a weightless seed; he becomes
the tip of a chisel splitting a rock that pours out "wonder" like a
fountain; he even imagines that he has become the fountain that
speaks wonder. And then . . . ? And then he hears something that
frightens him deeply: a "knocking at the door in the night." (Who,
reading this poem, would have ever known it was taking place at
night or that the poem was set inside the speaker's house?) It is a
weird knocking—one that doesn't simply surprise and unnerve the
speaker, but that generates paranoid fantasies of malicious disor-
der seeking him out ("somebody wants to do us harm"). And next
an even stranger thing happens: some other voice speaks. (Who
even knew some "other" was present in this poem?) This other
voice speaks with great calm and authority, correcting the original
speaker and calling a halt to his panic with clear instructions as to
what to do:

No, no, it is the three strange angels.
Admit them, admit them.

They are angels, the voice tells the poem's original speaker (and us), but they are "strange angels." Chances are, these nocturnal visitors are bringing in more disorder or some message from a different dimension (the English word *angel* comes from the Greek word for "messenger"). It seems the original speaker is being reassured by this authoritative voice, but also urged toward a further action—a further, risky faith in the mysterious. It's not hard to imagine that opening a door in the middle of the night can be dangerous. Even as a metaphor, we sense that the issue might be: Am I letting in too much disorder? Am I risking madness or destructive chaos?

My own, milder version of Lawrence's admonition ("Admit them, admit them") is this mantra: *give yourself permission.* Open yourself to a bit of chaos at the beginning of the writing process. Don't judge the words you put down on the page in a first draft. Just let the flow happen, and don't worry about where it's going. I don't just mean, as in the opening lines of Lawrence's poem, letting yourself float on the language or hammer against something that resists like a rock; instead, think about opening yourself as one opens a door in the night: there is something alive out there, some entity or theme that wants to enter your room—the room of your mind, the room of the page. Don't be afraid to put words down, no matter what they are—it's essential to admit a few strange and unpredictable angels.

THE THRESHOLD IN POETRY

In the ceaseless interplay of disorder and order in our daily lives, it is possible (and crucial) to imagine that there are certain situations in which that ceaseless interplay can be held briefly in a steady state. One such suspended moment is the poem, which freeze-frames the interplay as language so that we can contemplate it, feel it, and concentrate on it. Robert Frost characterized poetry as "a momentary stay against confusion," and his phrase expresses the power of poetry to lift

moments of clarified drama up out of the ceaseless and discombobu-
lating flow of experience. Imagining the poem's moment as a thresh-
old between disorder and order can reveal a lot about poetry and also
about ourselves.

When the speaker in Lawrence's poem hears that knock on his door
in the night, he wants to retreat from it, maybe even cower behind a
couch. Instead, he is instructed to go to the door and open it—to stand
on the threshold and welcome (or at least admit) the strange angels.
The threshold is a crucial place in poetry because it symbolizes poet-
ry's power to present both disorder and order.

What is a threshold? What do I mean by this term? In the simple,
dictionary sense, a threshold is the place of transition that a door
makes in a house. Imagine, for a moment, standing on the threshold
of a house: the door is open, and we're facing out into the street and the
wider world. Behind us, at our backs, we have the sense of the geomet-
rical order and stability of the room we're facing away from. Behind
us, we know the room's furniture is staying put, that its walls and
floor and ceiling are solid and unmovable, completely stable. In front
of us is the street—cars going by, clouds moving through the sky, tree
branches waving in an unpredictable but strong way as they respond
to the wind. Perhaps our dog runs a zig-zag on the lawn, following the
inspirations that her nose announces. There is nothing threatening in
what's before us, but it is alive and in motion and essentially unpredict-
able in its events (e.g., we can't know what cars or trucks will go by, or
whether the dog will discover and chase a squirrel). We are standing
on the simplest and most basic of thresholds, a place where we expe-
rience both order (behind us) and disorder (before us). We are at the
place where they meet.

A threshold is the place where two different states meet. I'm using
the term *threshold* to stand for that place in poetry where disorder and
order meet. It is the place where urgent and significant poems are writ-
ten. Each one of us has his or her own personal threshold. In order to
write well, a poet must locate and write from this threshold.

The Personal Threshold and Poetry

> The edge is what I have.
> Theodore Roethke

Each of us has his or her own personal threshold: the place where order passes over into disorder. It's a matter of how much order we need to feel safe and yet how much disorder we need to feel vitally alive.

In poetry, the threshold is that place in the poet where disorder and order meet. It could be a place of subject matter—a theme. Or it could be a formal disorder that the poet is encountering—experimental poets sometimes scramble ordinary syntax (the word order in a sentence that establishes meaning) or disrupt logic in order to create an encounter with linguistic or imaginative disorder.

Poets tend to go to their thresholds to create their best poems. Why? The first reason would be that thresholds are places where energy exchange is happening, where something real is at stake for the poet. In his essay "The Figure a Poem Makes," Robert Frost puts it this way: "No tears in the writer, no tears in the reader. No surprise for the writer, no surprise for the reader." The poet must go to his or her threshold and authentically experience the disorder (in this case, the disorder of emotion: tears and surprise) in order to move the reader. The poet is not and cannot be a puppet-master using language gifts to manipulate the reader while remaining personally detached—that is the realm of advertising and political rhetoric, not poetry. The threshold that poets must approach is a place where the ordering powers of imagination are responsive to the stimulus of disorder. When, in the same essay, Frost defines poetry as "a momentary stay against confusion," he is acknowledging the significance of thresholds as a place where disorder and order meet and are held in dynamic tension by the power of the poet's imagination. (Nietzsche might say that after Dionysus arrives with tears and surprise, Apollo shows up to shape it all into a "momentary stay," or the brief stability that the poem embodies.) In Frost's statement, confusion of all kinds (from anguish and despair to wonder and joy) is understood to be the ordinary, human mental condition, and poetry (a poem) helps to clarify or dramatize that confusion in such a way as to stabilize the self. Elsewhere in the same passage, Frost points out that culture also supplies "large" stays against confusion—religions and certain other systematic ideologies claim the power to order and make sense of the world—but that poetry doesn't make such grand claims. It's a "momentary" stay, a momentary clarification or victory for the self—and one that invites a similar experience in the reader.

Each individual reader has his or her own threshold. Like the poet's, it is formed by two forces: one innate, the other experiential. The genetic part has to do with our inborn temperament or personality and includes attitudes and qualities that are biologically inherited. A lot of who we are seems to be established from birth and doesn't budge much—if you don't believe scientists, you can ask your parents (if they're available). They're probably pretty aware of how set and solid certain aspects of your personality were right from birth. The experiential part concerns the way environment affected or altered your basic temperament; this part has to do with experiences and events that happened to you, especially during the formative years of childhood and adolescence. The threshold is a different place for every poet and reader.

The Personal Threshold in Writer and Reader

When we read a poem that takes us to our threshold, we know it. When a poem takes us way beyond our threshold—into a chaos we can't make sense of or feel stimulated by—we know it. When a poem doesn't even approach our threshold, instead seeming to squat safely in the middle of a sealed room, we know that too—we feel a bit stifled, a sense of claustrophobia. Each poem has a threshold, and we read in hopes of finding poems that will take us to our own threshold or show us a new and persuasive one.

Because your own personal threshold is formed by your temperament and personality (the innate element) and also by your experiences during childhood and adolescence, the two factors together determine what proportion of disorder and order you find stimulating or enlivening. The threshold is not a moral category—it has nothing to do with good or bad, right or wrong. But it's something just as important—it's an existential category. In other words, your threshold has a lot to do with who you are: how much disorder you need to feel alive or real, how much order you need to feel that (as the poet Robert Duncan put it) "certain bounds hold against chaos."

■ ■ ■

Innate temperament and early experiences (childhood and adolescence)—these seem to me the major factors in determining where your threshold is: how much disorder you can tolerate and enjoy; how much order you need to feel safe. But it's not *predictable* from these two factors. The impact of early experiences is especially complex. For example, having had a chaotic or dysfunctional childhood doesn't necessarily mean you can handle *lots* of disorder, more than someone from a less turbulent background. It could go either way. Your chaotic background could make you more sensitive and even "allergic to" disorder, less tolerant of it. You might feel: "I had so much disorder and violence in my childhood that I need lots and lots of order now to make up for it, to calm me." Or the opposite: "I have a high tolerance for (even a need for) disorder, because I had a lot of it early on and now I crave a certain level of it in order to feel that something is real." There's no predicting, but the issue isn't about prediction. The issue is this: What do *you* feel about it? How would *you* locate yourself on a spectrum of disorder to order?

Disorder ←——————————————→ Order

Where you fall on such a spectrum may vary from topic to topic, but still I think we all have a general sense of our own needs and inclinations in this regard.

■ ■ ■

A threshold can concern subject matter, content, theme. I know people who absolutely will not read a poem about a sexual assault. I also know people who will willingly read and even seek out poems on that subject. As a teacher, I wouldn't conclude anything about those two facts. But the reader who is attracted or repulsed by such a subject would certainly be experiencing something to do with his or her threshold. Likewise, a personal threshold can concern formal qualities of poetry. I know students who are intrigued by and attracted to poems that rhyme, and others who dislike rhyme so much that they cannot enjoy any poem whose rhyme scheme is apparent. Again, a personal threshold is at work in these responses. Rhyme isn't good or bad; nor is any subject matter in poetry good or bad, appropriate or inappropriate, in our present-day American culture. We cherish the diversity of our experiences and try to honor and enjoy the variety of it. But a threshold is a real thing for each of us, and it comes powerfully to the fore in our reading and in our writing.

■ ■ ■

Poems that matter to us take us to our threshold: either in subject matter or in style, or both. We grow as poets, as readers, as people by extending our thresholds. Poems invite us to their thresholds; poets do also. One way we grow as poets, as readers, as people is by extending our thresholds, and reading lots of poems helps us to do that.

■ ■ ■

Often, arguments about taste, about whether or not a particular poem is "great," are simply the result of differences in readers' thresholds.

To say that we find a poem "boring" is another way of saying that it doesn't bring us close to any threshold in us. To say that a poem seems to us "meaningless chaos" is just another way of saying that it throws us way out past our threshold. No one "wins" these arguments about taste, because they are really just disguised ways of discussing our own thresholds.

■ ■ ■

When reading a poem we don't consciously think about its threshold, but we do have an intuitive feel for the play of disorder and order in the poem. We assess the threshold with a part of our minds, but still there's not much point in rushing to judge a poem's worth on the basis of its threshold—to say (as if speaking with objectivity and authority): "not enough significant disorder here" or "this is way too chaotic and jumbled." It's more important to become aware of how someone's poem relates to our threshold than it is to judge the poem. A poet's job is to go to his or her threshold, not to *your* threshold. Of course, if it doesn't go to your threshold, you'll have a less positive response to it. But we're all of us different—different things have happened to us, matter to us, have hurt or thrilled us. Our job as poets is to engage those things in a way that feels real to us and let the reader respond as best he or she can. Frost's "No tears in the writer, no tears in the reader" is a good principle to remember when we write.

■ ■ ■

Above all, threshold is an awareness about yourself—a sense of how you feel in relation to certain topics and/or, in poetry, to certain ways of using language; an awareness of how the intuited relative proportion of disorder and order makes you feel. It's important to adapt the term to *your* needs and experiences—to use it when and where it's helpful to you as poet or reader. But I argue that the threshold is a real thing—with roots deep in the human psyche.

THE CULTURAL THRESHOLD

In addition to the personal threshold that each person, poet, and reader has, there is a cultural threshold. It is different in different cultures and also can change *within* a given culture, depending on where that culture is in its historical development. It has to do with the society-wide agreement about how much disorder and order should be present in an act of imagination.

In America, the cultural threshold has been rising steadily over time: we're able to tolerate increasing levels of disorder in our cultural products. Consider what seemed to be a terrifying horror movie fifty years ago (*The Blob*, which was just a gelatinous sofa that oozed around slowly like an amoeba made of jelly) and what can be shown and eagerly viewed on movie screens now in the horror genre—dismemberment and gore galore. Consider the threshold for violence shown on television or in movies, or the acceptable level of verbal violence in those media. To note this cultural threshold shift is not to judge it, either morally or aesthetically, but simply to note it as a part of the environment in which a poet's individual threshold is situated. As a poet (or reader), we may feel as if we're in harmony with the cultural threshold of our moment, or we may feel out of tune with it—either way out ahead of it, or lingering behind as if we were nostalgic for a gentler mix of disorder and order. This cultural threshold is one more factor in our creative lives, and it can lead to a sense of buoyancy or tension.

What matters most is your own exploration of your personal threshold—that place where important poems are written. When you write a poem from your threshold, you can feel it. You know it in your bones.

THRESHOLDS OVER TIME

A poet's threshold can shift over time. Young William Wordsworth was a poet of radical disorder—in both subject matter and style—*for his time* (the late 1700s, say). We may read Wordsworth now and find him very dull (as many of my students do), but in his youth he was considered so radical and chaotic that his poems were deemed not poetry at all, but the ravings of a fool or a dangerous subversive. Yet as Wordsworth grew older, he got tired of being so far out at the edge. He'd written so many poems that were (in his youth) experimental and risk-taking in terms of subject matter and style that he began, in his early thirties, to lose his taste for disorder. He wanted to come in out of the chaos and write from a more ordered, culturally acceptable place—a place where he could feel less exhausted by his freedom. Consider these lines from what I'm tempted to call his surrender poem, "Ode to Duty":

> I supplicate for thy (Duty's) control;
> But in the quietness of thought:
> Me this unchartered freedom tires;
> I feel the weight of chance desires:
> My hopes no more must change their name,
> I long for a repose that ever is the same.

It wasn't long after this ode that Wordsworth began writing one sonnet after another and celebrating the narrow confines of its formal restrictions, which he now experienced as the safety of a convent cell:

> Nuns fret not at their convent's narrow room;
> And hermits are contented with their cells . . .

For Wordsworth, the intense formal ordering of the sonnet form was a welcome refuge.

Wordsworth wasn't the first person (or poet) to become more con-servative as he grew older—to draw back from his threshold, or to feel his threshold shift beneath him. You are young poets starting out, so you don't need to think much about this issue; but as an old poet I think a lot about how to keep my poems vital by trying to find new thresholds. I like to think of how T. S. Eliot worked hard to move in an opposite direction from Wordsworth as he grew older, pressing out against the unknown by writing a new kind of poem in his fifties and announcing in one such poem that "Old men ought to be explorers."

■ ■ ■

THRESHOLD EXERCISE: THRESHOLD AND YOU

During the course of the "I Remember" exercise in Chapter 1, you may have felt yourself drifting on a flood or stream of associative memories and then found yourself caught in the occasional whirlpool that swirled around a painful or traumatic memory scene. You may have felt caught in its downward spiral and sensed an urgent need to break free. I've had students say that they had to stop completely, clear their heads, and start over again in order to feel safe and secure, or free of sadness or danger.

For this exercise, I want you to go back to your ten pages of "I remember" statements and circle those memories that had strong emotion associated with them: for example, fear or shame or pleasur-able excitement. When a memory arrives attached to strong feelings, positive or negative, it's a signal that you're in a threshold situation. You don't have to be able to name the emotion or understand exactly what it is. In fact, one purpose of writing poems is to come to a better understanding of what feeling or feelings are involved in our experi-ence. Poets have been known to say: "How do I know what I feel until I see what I write?"

Now comes the harder part of this exercise. While your "I remem-ber" list is in front of you, try to recall some memories that you decided *not* to write down during the original exercise. Memories that were too intense—too disturbing or embarrassing or painful or exciting or shameful. Memories that carne up and you shunned, blinked your eyes to dismiss; or if you did write them down, you crossed them out (even though you weren't going to share your list with anyone—you crossed them out as a way of reasserting control over them through silence or suppression). I don't have any moral or artistic point to make here. I'm not saying that these are the memories you should write about. I don't believe that. My only point is this: you definitely experienced a significant threshold there.

■ ■ ■

READERS APPROACHING THRESHOLDS

Both poet and reader risk the instability of thresholds in poems. The poet risked it first, when she or he wrote the urgent poem in which something real was at stake—in which he or she approached a threshold where disorder and order meet. The poem exists, so we know *by way of that simple fact* that the poet succeeded in the effort to successfully order material encountered at the threshold. But now the *reader* is experiencing the poem, entering into the dynamic of disorder and order that is the poem unfolding. The reader, in order to be moved by the poem, must also experience the thrill and risk of the threshold. If we as readers are not moved, then we have not reached a threshold in ourselves or been affected by the poet's threshold.

But how does this transaction between poet and reader take place? How does the poet's threshold become the reader's threshold? It takes place when the reader is able to identify with the speaker of the poem. If there's no identification, then there's no ability to be moved by the poem, no matter how great it is said to be. To give an ordinary example of how important identification is to pleasure, think of a time when you watched a movie and couldn't identify, even slightly, with any of the characters. If you were in a movie theater, you probably spent a long and boring (or irritating) ninety minutes in the dark as you endured something you couldn't have cared about in the least. Detachment and alienation are the enemies of enjoyable participation in any art form. But when this identification is successful, in poetry it is the glue that binds us to the poem and to its pleasures and discoveries. I call this essential transaction between poem/poet and reader the lyric invitation.

CHAPTER THREE

The Lyric Invitation

When we write a poem, most of us want other people to read it. We hope they will read it with excitement and interest. However, we have written a lyric poem—a poem that dramatizes our own emotional, experiential, or imaginative lives (or a combination of them all). Why should any readers be interested in our poem?

TRANSCENDING THE SELF TO CONNECT WITH OTHERS

We might begin considering this by asking how it is that human individuals transcend their separate selves, each person's isolation in a separate body and mind, in order to "connect" with other people. Or we could approach it this way: *Do* we transcend our separateness and isolation? *Can* we? It was a question that haunted the eighteenth-century Scottish humanist and moral philosopher Adam Smith. On the very first page of his first book, *The Theory of Moral Sentiments* (1759), Smith boldly sketches a stark situation in which a person is being tortured as other individuals (including us, his readers) look on:

Though our brother is upon the rack, as long as we ourselves are at our ease, our senses will never inform us of what he suffers. They never did, and never can, carry us beyond our own person, and it is by the imagination only that we can form any conception of what are his sensations. . . . *By the imagination* we place ourselves in his situation, we conceive ourselves enduring all the same torments, *we enter as it were into his body, and become in some measure the same person with him.* (emphasis added)

In this remarkable passage, Smith challenges us to admit a disturbing truth about our senses, which we use to orient ourselves physically and morally in the world—if we're honest, we must admit that we do not (cannot) feel through our own bodily senses the suffering that another body endures, even if that other body is only two feet away from us. Another person's physical agony, no matter how intense it is or how close they are to us, cannot actually be communicated to us by our own bodily senses. That's a disturbing thought; a deeply disturbing fact. Yet Smith goes on to name that human power we all possess through which we can transcend our senses: imagination. In his book, Smith calls this imagination-based act of connecting with another person "sympathy" and "sympathetic identification." Today we name it "empathy," a word not invented until the twentieth century.

Let me give a few more instances of this power of imagination that Smith places at the heart of moral being. A hundred years after Smith formulated his notion, Walt Whitman adopted it as one of the key principles of his poetry. In his Preface to *Leaves of Grass* (1855), Whitman claims that two "pillars" support poetic consciousness: pride and sympathy. He insists that the best poets move flexibly between these two principles: "pride," which is a centering in the self's physical being in a celebratory way; and "sympathy," which uses the imagination to enter into the being of another person, to *assume* the identity of another person. Here is how Whitman introduces this dual project of pride and sympathy in the opening lines of his central lyric sequence, "Song of Myself":

I celebrate myself and sing myself
And what I assume you shall assume
For every atom belonging to me as good belongs to you.

Throughout "Song of Myself" Whitman continues to make "assump-tions"—his punning reference both to his ideas about the world and to his assumptions (his taking over) of other people's identities, since he finds other people as "divine" and wonderful as himself and delights in becoming them. Whitman claims that the poet (or anyone with imagi-nation) can become anything: another person, a rock, a whale, a cloud, a flower—anything that truly interests him or her. Indeed, he goes so far as to claim that sympathetic identification is the *only* thing that connects people to other things and other people: "A man is only inter-ested in anything when he identifies himself with it." Whitman makes extreme (supernatural?) claims for his own powers of identification:

I do not ask the wounded person how he feels, I myself become the
    wounded person,
My hurts turn livid upon me as I lean on a cane and observe.
                                        from "Song of Myself," section 33

Notice how intense his interest is in the wounded person. Whitman's lines claim that the other person's wounds actually appear on his own body—and yet he is also, paradoxically, a detached observer who can casually "lean on a cane."*

Whitman is equally clear about the morbid isolation that awaits anyone who is incapable of feeling empathy for another person: "And whoever walks a furlong without sympathy walks to his own funeral drest in his shroud" ("Song of Myself," section 48). How's that for a

---

* Google "Francis of Assisi stigmata" for a similarly intense story of bodily trans-formation triggered by identification. In Francis's case, the identification was with Jesus Christ, on whose life Francis had modeled his own. Late in his life, wounds appeared spontaneously on Francis's body where the crucifixion nails had pierced Christ's body.

grim image of isolation? Without sympathy (or empathy), you are the walking dead, and your only destination is your own funeral. Nor should you expect to find many people there at that bleak locale when you finally arrive.

But what does sympathetic identification have to do with the *reader* of lyric poetry? Everything. It's at the heart of the lyric invitation. When a lyric poem engages us, we don't just find ourselves interested in listening to its voice; we experience the poem fully by giving up our sense of self and "becoming" the poem's speaker, becoming the *I* of the poem—seeing, hearing, feeling, and thinking what that *I* sees, hears, feels, and thinks. It's a temporary loss of our own sense of self, but an essential one; to my mind, it's part of what Samuel Taylor Coleridge calls the reader's "willing suspension of disbelief." This voluntary suspension of our own self and assumption of the poet's self is what I think of as accepting the lyric invitation.

As readers, we are held to the poems we deeply enjoy not just by curiosity but also by our acceptance of this invitation to identify with the poet. Seventy years after Whitman's preface, William Carlos Williams negotiated this lyric invitation directly with the reader at the beginning of his book *Spring and All* (1923), and his phrasing teases out the peculiar intimacy that can occur among poet, poem, and reader:

> In the imagination, we are from henceforth (so long as you read) locked in a fraternal embrace, the classic caress of author and reader. We are one. Whenever I say "I" I mean also "you." And so, together, as one, we shall begin.

T. S. Eliot, a contemporary of Williams, isn't quite as insistent that the reader merge and fuse with him right away. He begins his poem "The Love Song of J. Alfred Prufrock" with a more genial suggestion:

> Let us go then, you and I,
> When the evening is spread out against the sky . . .

Eliot invites us to be his companion on an evening stroll through a city, a walk during which he will tell us private and important things about himself—his longings, anxieties, and despairs.

I have chosen to call this possibility that begins our reading of poems an invitation for a simple reason—like all invitations we receive, we can either accept it or decline it. And it's easily and frequently rejected—we do so all the time by not finishing a poem that we've started to read. Or by not even going past its opening lines—by choosing not to "assume" what it assumes. We give the poem a brief chance to enthrall us and pull us in—"so long as you read," notes Williams.

SOME MOTIVES FOR ACCEPTING LYRIC INVITATIONS

The lyric invitation is one of the boldest and most mysterious of thresholds. Why would a reader cross this threshold, identify with the poem, yield to this curiously intimate union in imagination? I certainly don't want to lose sight of Adam Smith's original insight—that such identifications are essential as we seek to orient ourselves toward right and wrong in a moral universe. But poetry isn't only about morality; it's also about pleasure and about being an individual self in the world. The romantic poet John Keats loved the ability to lose himself in other identities—he called the poet a chameleon, that remarkable lizard that takes on the colors of whatever surrounds it. To lose, briefly, the burden of self and become some other thing or person, to take on some other color—it's not always a moral issue, and Keats says so candidly: "What shocks the virtuous philosopher, delights the chameleon poet."

In a passage from Ralph Waldo Emerson's *Journals*, the word *delight* comes up again in relation to the act of reading and how we participate in a poem we love—how both the poet and the reader journey out into disorder:

> The maker of a sentence . . . launches out into the infinite and
> builds a road into Chaos and old Night, and is followed by those
> who hear him with something of wild, creative delight.
>
> from *Journals* (December 19, 1834)

It thrills us to be the poet making those roads into chaos, but it also
thrills us to follow a poet as she or he makes such bold sentences and
embarks on such a journey. Pleasure, then, is central, a kind of basic
ecstasy induced by language and imagination when we accept a poem's
lyric invitation. But that's not the only reward we get when giving
ourselves over to the poem. I'll briefly list just a few others that many
readers will recognize from their own experience:

The Discovery That We Are Not Alone

Just imagine: someone else has felt or endured what we have experi-
enced! What a profound moment it is when we hear someone speak
about something that connects with us in a deep way—not just that
he or she seems to speak to us or for us, but that those words seem
actually to "speak us," to articulate some profound aspect of our own
being. When that happens, poetry fulfills itself as "the voice of the
solitary that makes others less alone" (from Stanley Kunitz's poem
"Revolving Meditation"). When this happens, our isolation (and the
quiet despair that often accompanies it) vanishes, and we know again
that we are part of the human community.

The Thrill and Challenge of Intensified Being

Often, we move through life as if half-awake, half in a dream—like
sleepwalkers closed up in a husk of numbness. Lyric poetry offers to
intensify our sense of being alive. In fact, two of the greatest American
lyric poets, Walt Whitman and Emily Dickinson, challenge us to enter
their poems, experience the intensity they offer, and bring that inten-

sity back with us into our own lives. Here's Whitman's way of putting it (and putting us on the spot):

> Long enough have you dream'd contemptible dreams,
> Now I wash the gum from your eyes,
> You must habit yourself to the dazzle of the light and of every
>   moment of your life.

> Long have you timidly waded holding a plank by the shore,
> Now I will you to be a bold swimmer,
> To jump off in the midst of the sea, rise again, nod to me, shout, and
>   laughingly dash with your hair.

from "Song of Myself," section 46

Throughout his amazing poem, Whitman wants us to not be afraid to risk ourselves in the world—to join him on the Open Road—to explore and to feel and to enlarge our lives. Emily Dickinson, of course, is a far more interior lyric poet than Whitman; her risks have to do with subjectivity and the extremes of emotion—joy, despair, madness, love. How do such emotions manifest in her poems; how does she extend her lyric invitation? "Dare you see a Soul *at the White Heat*," she challenges in the opening line of poem 365. She's not picking a fight with us; she's revealing the fierce intensity of her own being and showing us that it is bearable, even beautiful—like the fire in a blacksmith's forge that is pushed past the ordinary red color of fire to the ferocious intensity of no-color and "unannointed Blaze." She insists that such intensity won't destroy us any more than it has destroyed her, but perhaps it will reveal a new and fierce energy that will enrich our lives (which is one thing lyric poetry surely does). Dickinson's poems (as her image of the forge and the shaping power of the blacksmith's sledge reveal) claim that anguish and suffering can be endured and shaped into something beyond the fire, but that something is only arrived at by going through the fire.

The Possibility of Transformation

Our identification with the speaker in a lyric poem doesn't just offer connection and intensification; it also speaks to our longing for transformation—to be more than or different from what we are in our ordinary lives. When we give up our sense of self and open to the poem that wants to change us, it's an amazing experience. Our identification with the speaker just might lead us toward his or her values and view of the world. When Wordsworth wrote about the beauties of nature, it wasn't just to show us something he enjoyed. In many of his poems, he wanted to change us—to lure us away from the workaday world:

> The world is too much with us; late and soon,
> Getting and spending we lay waste our powers—
> Little we see in Nature that is ours.
>
> from *Poems, in Two Volumes* (1807)

Wordsworth wrote those lines two hundred years ago, but he seems to be speaking directly to many of us who feel trapped in the anxious drudgery of laboring and consuming, of "getting and spending" that depletes and deadens us. Whitman, too, would change us with his poems—would have us love our bodies as well as our souls (aren't they the same thing?, he asks); would have us give up the shame and guilt that cripples so many of us: "Undrape! You are not guilty to me, nor stale, nor discarded." He insists that all humans are equal and lovable; that men and women are equal; that all ethnicities and all aspirations are honorable and should be honored. Nor should we fear death:

> The smallest sprout [of grass] shows there is really no death,
> And if ever there was it led forward life, and does not wait at the end
>   to arrest it,
> And ceas'd the moment life appear'd.

All goes onward and outward, nothing collapses . . .

from "Song of Myself"

Whitman's poetry wants nothing less than to change us utterly toward his mystical and ecstatic vision of democracy and wonder. It's a tall order for any poem, but how many of us have been enthralled by his work and believed it passionately as we gave ourselves over to it, if only for its length and the glorious afterglow that sometimes follows the reading of any poem we love? Not all poets or poems offer to change us; nor do we necessarily want them to. But when they do, they can only do so when we accept their invitation and give over our hearts and minds and imaginations to their promise of a different view of the world and our place in it.

Part Two

POWERS OF ORDERING

CHAPTER FOUR

Imagination at the Threshold

At the outset of this primer, I proposed that an awareness of disorder and randomness and a need for order are two central human attributes. I further claimed that for us as poets the basic strategy is to turn our disorder (be it joy or despair) into words, at which point poetry steps forward with ordering principles to aid us in dramatizing this interaction of disorder and order. I intentionally ended Part One with the notion of the threshold between disorder and order and with the notion that the lyric invitation invites us as readers to identify with the poet and to follow his or her journey into the unknown that hovers at the threshold. But we are first of all poets or would-be poets. Suppose that, as poets, we have approached a personal threshold that is both exciting and perilous—how do we know we can handle the disorder we encounter there?

THE ORDER-MAKING POWER OF THE INDIVIDUAL IMAGINATION

Many of us, approaching our thresholds, fear that we will be incapable of finding the ordering response to the disorder and confusion we have let loose with our "permission." How do we know that if we decide to become Ralph Waldo Emerson's "maker of a sentence" who heads out "into Chaos and old Night," we won't get lost out there? After all, I encouraged you to revisit the more disturbing aspects of Chapter 1's "I Remember" exercise—those memories that most clearly radiated the chaotic power of primal emotions for you.

It might be useful at this point to circle back to the Shakespeare passage we considered on pages 37–38 and look at it in terms of the concept of thresholds. With the infatuated lover and the madman, Shakespeare presented two types who are, in a sense, undergoing the peculiar power of their thresholds. The lover is too far back from his threshold: he doesn't see the beloved in her variety and particularity, but as a cultural stereotype of beauty. It seems as if he is so far back inside his mind that he views his lover through a window shaped like the silhouette of Helen of Troy—an idealized cut-out that obscures the real shape of the beloved as a unique living body. By contrast, the madman is too far out past his threshold: he's surrounded by chaos, by the demons that assail him from all sides. Only the poet stands confidently on his threshold, giving himself to neither ideal nor real, but to a third thing—bodied forth as language emanating from his imagination.

It's fine for Shakespeare to talk boldly of the poet's pen, but how do we know that we ourselves have the poet's power to do that— to take in both unity and variety and form a third thing, a poem? There's a simple exercise that demonstrates that each of us possesses an inherent ordering imagination of some authority, a power capable of creating the coherence we all seek in poems. I call it the random poem exercise.

My Students' Random Poem Exercise

This is the second exercise I do with my poetry-writing students. I'm using as my example a class that consisted of eleven students. In our first meeting, I asked each student to do the following: "Write down

on a sheet of paper a single line from a poem, either from a poem of
your own or from someone else's. Note: not a sentence, just a single
line (most lines of poems don't form complete sentences)." Chances are
the students wrote down a line from one of their own poems. I asked
them to pass in those lines (without their names attached). That gave
us eleven lines. But I needed more than eleven for the exercise, so I
asked them each to write down another line and then pass it to me. I
now had twenty-two anonymous and unconnected lines. Just for fun,
I shuffled them and then read the lines back to the students while they
wrote them down. The result was what I declared to be the rough
draft of a collaborative poem: twenty-two lines in a random order—a
benign form of chaos. My student-poets were placed on a threshold
where disorder seemed to have successfully overwhelmed order, but
the process had only just begun; that is, they had given permission to
let disorder happen, but now it was time to respond to it, to meet it at
the threshold. Of course, the threshold represented by these lines had
been created artificially, and it represented more of a linguistic chaos
than an emotional chaos (which is usually the threshold that disturbs
us most); but what we were working toward here is evidence of inher-
ent order-making power in the individual imagination.

Here are the twenty-two lines as they appeared in that class:

> hirsute penguins
> the only thing that breathes is me
> where the parachute sky
> in an overly patriotic sweater
> like skirts of bruises   5
> sea, struggling to be free yet unable to be
> throw your wrench into scaffolding skies
> there is no reward
> and so cold
> they scream "roll away the stone"   10
> but a concrete night
> a slow sigh

storm clouds, sky, bursting into sea
a wave of porcelain faith
now, dance with me   15
what station is the static on
see it in red letters
across my body, a universe
stood bursting with
sleep visited like a resentful friend   20
in gray folds of
and one of them left me moaning

Now the fun begins. My instructions to my students for the assignment were as follows:

> You are to arrange or rearrange these lines into the most interesting piece of language you can. There are a few *absolute rules*: You cannot change any words in the lines or break up a line into two fragments and insert another line or word between them. Nor can you add anything (anything!) to the lines (or take anything away from them).
>
> However, you do have the following options: You may change the *tenses of any verb* into whichever tense you wish (past to present, present to past or future, etc.). You may also change *any pronouns* you wish (*he* to *she* or *they* or *it* or *we*, etc.). You may also *punctuate* lines in any way you wish (i.e., break up a phrase or sentence into two phrases or sentences using punctuation you provide). *But you may not make any other changes in the given lines.* In addition, you may make a long line into a shorter line by adding line breaks (or make two short lines into a longer one by joining them together), but you may not rearrange any words within the line or drop any words from the lines. You may also supply your own title to the poem.
>
> A subsidiary instruction: try to use as many lines as you can, and feel free to try making several different poems from these lines.

At first, this assignment may seem very difficult, but actually people tend to get engaged by it after a bit and begin to see interesting possibilities.

■ ■ ■

One of the first, curious things to notice is that chance seems to have created moments of coherence and continuity in some of these lines: "a slow sigh(,) / storm clouds, sky, bursting into sea (,) / a wave of porcelain faith" (lines 12–14). These three lines seem to accumulate a tonally coherent picture that mingles personal emotion with external details of landscape or seascape. This passage also brings together what is almost a pun (*sea* and *wave*), although the lines came from three different poets. There's another almost-pun with lines 10 and 11—"they scream 'roll away the stone' / but a concrete night"—where *stone* and *concrete* end up near each other by mere chance. Again and again, there are little snippets of story or sentence continuity: "see it in red letters / across my body, a universe"; "sleep visited like a resentful friend / in gray folds of." So one thing the "first draft" reveals is that even in a set of random lines certain coherences happen, certain lines form briefly plausible continuities.

Here are some of the results from this assignment.

REM

Sleep visits like a resentful friend
Where the parachute sky
Stands bursting with a wave
Of porcelain faith.

But—a concrete night
In gray folds of a slow sigh.
See it in red letters?
The only thing that breathes is me.
There is no reward.

They scream, "roll away the stone,"
"throw your wrench into scaffolding skies."
What station is this static on?

                                                    Rory Finnegan

Notice that the student-supplied title "REM" is scientific shorthand for
"rapid eye movement"—the sleep stage in which most of our dreaming
occurs. It orients us as readers toward the basic story situation ("sleep
visits") and also gives the poet permission to have a fairly high level of
disorder or confusion in her poem, since she's claiming it takes place
in the world of dreams.

Fresh Evening Scars

In gray folds of storm clouds, sky bursting into sea,
sleep visited like a resentful friend.
A wave of porcelain faith, a slow sigh
now dance with me.
Across my body, a universe
see it in red letters,
like skirts of bruises

There is no reward but a concrete night
where the parachute sky in an overly patriotic sweater
stood bursting with sea, struggling to be free yet unable to be.
The only thing that breathes is me.

                                                    Ian Garnett

Relapsing into Dreams of an Exquisite Corpse

Now, dance with me,
hirsute penguins—
what station was the static on
but a concrete night

where the parachute sky
in an overly patriotic sweater
threw its wrench into scaffolding skies,
in gray folds of
storm clouds—sky bursting into sea
like skirts of bruises?
they scream "roll away your stone,"
see it in red letters
across my body, a universe
stood bursting with
sea, struggling to be free yet unable to be—
sleep visited like a resentful friend
and one of them left me moaning
a slow sigh,
a wave of porcelain faith,
and so cold,
the only thing that breathes is me
in an overly patriotic sweater.
there is no reward.

Addie Eliades

The title of this poem that ambitiously includes all twenty-two lines also makes clever use of its title. "Exquisite Corpse" was a word game the French surrealists invented early in the twentieth century. By referencing this game in its title, Addie's poem gives itself permission to be "surrealistic" in its movements and imagery—which is a clever way of justifying more chaos in the poem.

Peter's Song

What station is the static on?
It screams, "roll away the stone!"
but a concrete night stands bursting with
sleep, visiting like a resentful friend.

There is no reward—
a slow sigh,
a wave of porcelain faith,
seeing it in red letters.

Now dance with it.
The only thing that breathes is you,
in gray folds of storm clouds:
sky, bursting into sea.

Kelly Zanotti

■ ■ ■

There are many things worth noting about the responses to this assignment, but perhaps the most important is that each student's rearrangement was in the direction of greater coherence. Note that I never requested that the arrangement aspire to coherence or communication—only that it be "interesting." And yet every student worked (against real odds) to communicate some cohesive mood or scene, or at least to move toward coherence, or (in the case of the surrealist and REM poems) to justify a high level of disorder. Each and every example represents proof that we possess an active ordering power—something in us that not only actively seeks coherence but has the power to produce it.

■ ■ ■

RANDOM LINES EXERCISE

Why not experience that power yourself, firsthand? Here is a set of sixteen lines presented in the order I received them from another group of students. Take them and try to make an interesting piece of writing out of them. A final bit of advice: most of my students testify that this exercise seems impossible at the outset, but becomes alive with possi-

sixteen lines. It would be interesting to see if you could come up with a poem that uses all the lines, but keep in mind the main criterion: "most interesting."

2. You can arrange and rearrange the lines in any order you wish. You can make certain specific changes within the lines you've been given (but only these changes):

You may change the *tenses of any verb* into whichever tense you wish (past to present, etc.).

You may change *any pronouns* you wish (*he* to *she* or *they* or *it* or *we*, etc.).

You may punctuate lines in any way you wish (i.e., break up a sentence into two sentences with a period, or change a statement into a question).

You may make a long line into a shorter line by adding line breaks (or make two short lines into a longer one by joining them together), but you may NOT rearrange any words within the line or drop any words from the lines.

You may also supply your own TITLE to the poem.

(Note: If you are in a classroom situation, of course the idea would be to generate right now *your own set of random lines*, so that this exercise can happen in a more spontaneous and real way.)

VALIDATING SHAKESPEARE'S CLAIM

When you made the random lines into a nine-line poem by rearranging them and altering only verb tenses, pronouns, and punctuation, the lines you worked with didn't matter to you; they weren't expressions of your own concerns and experience. They probably didn't place you at an emotional threshold (though the randomness may have created a certain level of frustration in you, and that itself is a form of threshold). You may even have felt that the lines you were given didn't permit you to "be yourself" or speak from your own individual perspective. But I suspect that in a way your detachment gave you a kind of freedom—

bilities as you persevere. If you give yourself an arbitrary time limit fo
this—say half an hour—it will help to concentrate your ordering imagi
nation. Here are the lines:

> *your hands bloomed around my heart*
> *the patch of space behind the sun*
> *a soft tongue breaks the bone*
> *and the heat*
> *a small child*
> *wonder why the water returns to earth*
> *brushing their teeth with crystals*
> *the underbelly of a sandcastle*
> *the roads we choose*
> *the city rising up in lights to meet us*
> *but of the epitaph: HERE LIES A WOMAN*
> *we swing*
> *crushed and purple under*
> *some tirade*
> *the kitchen in smoke, sear . . .*
> *they walked there, they*

I'll repeat the rules (in a slightly different format from the ones I described earlier). Your task is to make the most interesting poem you can by rearranging the lines above and using as many of the lines as possible to make this poem. One main rule: YOU CANNOT CHANGE ANY WORDS IN THE LINES or break up a line into two fragments and insert another line between them. NOR CAN YOU ADD ANYTHING to the lines. You will work with the lines as they appear, adhering to the following rules:

1. The resulting poem must use at least nine of the lines (as many more as you wish). You can repeat a line if you wish (as a refrain or incantation), but the poem must have at least nine of the original

you weren't anxious about whether the resulting poem communicated something urgent to you or about you personally.

But even granting that these lines didn't express your personal viewpoint, I still insist that you just demonstrated firsthand that Shakespeare was right: your mind does have a "shaping" power to "body forth." You rearranged random phrases into coherence. You not only created a unity of language, but you also probably created an imagined speaker and an imagined situation or dramatic context that helped make sense of your "poem." That's quite an impressive demonstration that your personal imagination is strong enough to come up with significant and credible coherence, even when it starts from randomness or disorder. And consider that you were told to include at least nine lines; had you been told to use only six or seven, your poem would probably have shown even greater unity and coherence.

The chances are very good that in ordering the chaos of these lines, you sought some ordering principle and quite possibly struggled to make them into what I would consider a lyric-inflected story or a lyric poem with a "ghost" of a narrative situation behind it that helped to hold it together. Perhaps it's time to consider narrative and lyric inclinations in poems.

■ ■ ■

CHAPTER FIVE

Lyric and Narrative

Two Fundamental Ordering Impulses

Are there particular kinds of orderings that poetry tends to favor? For the purposes of this book, I'll propose two essential forms of coherence in poetry—lyric and narrative—and assert that each aspires to a distinct kind of unity. The easiest way to talk about them is by way of metaphor. The narrative poem is like a journey. It wanders across a landscape, propelled by verbs (action words) and unified by the need to have a beginning, middle, and end that relate to one another. The narrative poem is searching for something and won't be happy (complete, unified) until it has found it. By contrast, the lyric poem has a different shape. It *constellates* around a single center—usually an emotional center such as a single dominant feeling, though it could also be a dominant image, action, or situation. If the shape of a narrative is the line of a journey meandering down the page, then the shape of a lyric is that of a snow-flake or crystal—an intense, almost geometric concentration around a center. The lyric poem doesn't take the shape of a searching journey because it already "knows" what it knows and feels, and its main struggle is to adequately express that knowledge. The poet Robert Browning caught this already-knowing quality when he said of the lyric poet:

"he digs where he stands." The lyric poet digs into his or her emotion, that single, centered thing.

However different their strategies and aims, lyric and narrative are not opposite kinds of poems. They actually exist on a spectrum with (pure) lyric on one end and (pure) narrative on the other:

Lyric ⟵————————————⟶ Narrative

I've put the adjective *pure* in parentheses because there is no such beast—every lyric has some element of narrative in it, even if only an implied dramatic context for its words. Likewise, every narrative has some element of lyric in it, if only a metaphor placed at some crucial point or a heightening of its rhythmic texture to give it lift as it approaches its narrative climax.

You can spend an extremely interesting afternoon by taking a number of your poems and locating them along this spectrum. (Is this sonnet more lyric than narrative? And how does it compare with this other poem of mine in terms of lyric and narrative elements—which is dominant?) But before trying that, it might make sense to consider the two kinds of poems further.

CARVING THE LYRIC, MODELING THE NARRATIVE

These two types of poems have different temperaments and different ways of coming into being. Lyrics and narratives are the products of different sensibilities, or of the same sensibility operating in two distinct ways. These differences can be understood by analogy with the making of sculpture.

There are two basic ways of creating a piece of sculpture: *carving and modeling*. The carving method involves taking a good-size piece of stone or wood and cutting away toward a desired or intuited shape *within* the original block. The finished piece of art emerges only after the extra material has been stripped away—it's a shape that was "hidden" inside the original block. By contrast, the modeling method calls for the sculptor to construct a skeletal structure out of wood or metal rods or wire that essentially defines the underlying shape of the piece, much as our human skeleton defines the shape of our bodies. This structure is called an armature. After constructing the armature, the sculptor proceeds by slapping lumps of clay or wax onto the armature to further flesh out the shape. This modeling technique is one of *accretion*—the sculptor adds material to make the piece, and the finished piece ends up being larger than what the sculptor began with.

What do these two techniques have to do with poetry? They correspond to the lyric and narrative modes. The lyric poem is created like the carved sculpture—the poet intuits a hidden, compelling shape within the language of the first draft. The lyric secret is to carve away, to eliminate the excess as you work your way toward the lyric's vital center. The motto of the lyric poet is somewhat paradoxical: "less is more." Since the lyric poem seeks a center that is emotionally charged, its highest ambition is toward *intensity*.

The narrative, in contrast, has a different ambition—it wants to tell a story. It wants to add material, to keep things and characters moving, to find out what's over the next hill, what the next sentence might discover. The narrative is a kind of journey, and it needs to add action to action, event to event, line to line. Narrative poems get longer as they're rewritten, because the narrative poet discovers his or her meanings by asking: "What happens next? And then what happens?" The repeated "What next?" pushes the poem's protagonists further as each new line of action tries to answer the question, only to hear it repeated again and again as the poem builds and explores. One of the wittier definitions of narrative thinking came from the contemporary poet Frank O'Hara, who spoke of his work as his "I do this I do that" poems. O'Hara's remark sounds almost glib, but he's articulating the secret of how a narrative gets made. The narrative poet's motto is the sensible "more is more."

Needless to say, neither the narrative nor the lyric is "right"—they are simply primary directions in which a poet might take a poem. But they are also *inclinations* that a poet has, and as such they can be more deeply rooted in the poet's psyche.

Robert Frost is a prime modern instance of a narrative temperament. I don't mean to imply that his poems lack lyric moments; but the lyric was seldom his aim, and lyric unity was not what he usually sought. William Carlos Williams is my candidate for someone whose primary temperament is lyric.

It's probably time to give an example of a narrative poem and how it moves. Walt Whitman's "Song of Myself" is a long poem made up of different kinds of poems, but sections 35 and 36 provide an excellent example of how narratives are structured. "Would you hear of an old-time sea-fight?" Whitman asks in the opening line. His "tale" of a naval battle in the days of sailing ships goes on for forty-eight lines—lines packed with detail, told in sequence from the story's beginning:

> Our foe was no skulk in his ship I tell you, (said he,)
> His was the surly English pluck . . .

We're drawn into the story by our own curiosity ("Would you hear . . . ?"). We're offered an eyewitness account of an intense and authentic experience—Whitman in the poem claims he's telling it "as my grandmother's father the sailor told it to me." Written in 1855, the narrative reminds us that before movies, narrative poems brought unusual and exotic experiences vividly before the eyes of the reader or listener. The two sections are an excellent example of how narrative organizes experience as a series of sequential events: this happened, next this happened, and then this . . . our two ships approached each other, drew alongside, then fired their cannon point-blank, then roped themselves together, and we began hand-to-hand fighting that went on all day and into the dark of night.

Section 35

Would you hear of an old-time sea-fight?
Would you learn who won by the light of the moon and stars?
List to the yarn, as my grandmother's father the sailor told it to me.
Our foe was no skulk in his ship I tell you, (said he,)
His was the surly English pluck, and there is no tougher or truer, and
     never was, and never will be;
Along the lowered eve he came horribly raking us.
We closed with him, the yards entangled, the cannon touched,
My captain lashed fast with his own hands.
We had received some eighteen pound shots under the water,
On our lower-gun-deck two large pieces had burst at the first fire,
     killing all around and blowing up overhead.
Fighting at sun-down, fighting at dark,
Ten o'clock at night, the full moon well up, our leaks on the gain, and
     five feet of water reported,
The master-at-arms loosing the prisoners confined in the after-hold
     to give them a chance for themselves.
The transit to and from the magazine is now stopt by the sentinels,
They see so many strange faces they do not know whom to trust.
Our frigate takes fire,
The other asks if we demand quarter?
If our colors are struck and the fighting done?
Now I laugh content, for I hear the voice of my little captain,
We have not struck, he composedly cries, *we have just begun our part of*
     the fighting.
Only three guns are in use,
One is directed by the captain himself against the enemy's main-mast,
Two well served with grape and canister silence his musketry and
     clear his decks.
The tops alone second the fire of this little battery, especially the
     main-top,
They hold out bravely during the whole of the action.

Not a moment's cease,

The leaks gain fast on the pumps, the fire eats toward the
powder-magazine.

One of the pumps has been shot away, it is generally thought we are
sinking.

Serene stands the little captain,

He is not hurried, his voice is neither high nor low,

His eyes give more light to us than our battle-lanterns.

Toward twelve there in the beams of the moon they surrender to us.

Section 36

Stretched and still lies the midnight,

Two great hulls motionless on the breast of the darkness,

Our vessel riddled and slowly sinking, preparations to pass to the one
we have conquered,

The captain on the quarter-deck coldly giving his orders through a
countenance white as a sheet,

Near by the corpse of the child that served in the cabin,

The dead face of an old salt with long white hair and carefully curled
whiskers,

The flames spite of all that can be done flickering aloft and below,

The husky voices of the two or three officers yet fit for duty,

Formless stacks of bodies and bodies by themselves, dabs of flesh
upon the masts and spars,

Cut of cordage, dangle of rigging, slight shock of the soothe of waves,

Black and impassive guns, litter of powder-parcels, strong scent,

A few large stars overhead, silent and mournful shining,

Delicate sniffs of sea-breeze, smells of sedgy grass and fields by the
shore, death-messages given in charge to survivors,

The hiss of the surgeon's knife, the gnawing teeth of his saw,

Wheeze, cluck, swash of falling blood, short wild scream, and long,
dull, tapering groan,

These so, these irretrievable.

Narratives of battles and heroes doing brave and violent deeds have been the raw material of epics since the days of Homer's *Iliad*, that long poem focused on the struggle of the Greeks against the Trojans. Whitman's story certainly has its heroes (the captain, the sailors), but it ends on a somber post-battle scene: the surgeon sawing off the limbs of injured sailors, the groans of the dying, the sense of loss of life—of the "irretrievable."

For our immediate purposes, though, we are interested in the *structure* of narrative, not its content. What's important here is that the story follows the journey of the battle from beginning to end; the story isn't over until the battle is over. The story, like the battle, is full of twists and turns and reversals—it seems the American ship is doomed, and the British captain asks if the Americans are finally ready to surrender; the American captain replies defiantly, even though his ship is sinking; and indeed the Americans fight on and eventually win although the decks are covered with "[f]ormless stacks of bodies" and the grim debris of battle. A story isn't over until it arrives at its (natural) end-point. If Whitman had stopped his tale halfway through, we readers would have been upset and felt cheated, felt he hadn't lived up to the promise that his "yarn" implied.

If we were placing Whitman's battle scene poem on a lyric–narrative spectrum, I'd be inclined to put it far over toward the narrative pole:

Lyric ←——————————————————— X ——→ Narrative

Lyric poetry doesn't make any such promise—a lyric poem isn't starting out on a journey or a series of linked events. Instead, a lyric focuses on a single dominant emotion that constellates the poem's language around a center. The lyric isn't "going anywhere," because the lyric poet "digs where he stands." In contrast, if a narrative "isn't going anywhere," then it's in danger of failing—failing to keep its promise to satisfy readers' curiosity by relating a series of interesting events that will arrive somewhere. And where the story will arrive can't be told from the opening. That's one reason a narrative resembles a journey: you may have some idea where you're headed, but you won't really know for sure until you get there (and that's part of the fun).

What might a profoundly lyric poem look like in contrast to a narrative such as Whitman's sea-fight? Here is the seventeenth-century English poet Edmund Waller's lyric "On a Girdle." The girdle he celebrates is an embroidered sash or belt that a woman wears around her waist, not the foundation garment of recent fame.

On a Girdle

That which her slender waist confined
Shall now my joyful temples bind;
No monarch but would give his crown
His arms might do what this has done.

It was my heaven's extremest sphere,
The pale which held that lovely deer;
My joy, my grief, my hope, my love
Did all within this circle move.

A narrow compass! and yet there
Dwelt all that's good, and all that's fair.
Give me but what this ribbon bound,
Take all the rest the sun goes round.

Edmund Waller (1664)

Before we look at this poem's lyric qualities, recall that I mentioned that lyric poems often have the "ghost" of a narrative in them. In Waller's poem, that ghost-narrative completes itself as a single act that the poet proposes to do in the opening lines: take his beloved's sash and tie it around his head as a trophy or emblem of his devotion:

That which her slender waist confined
Shall now my joyful temples bind . . .

That's it—that's the single action in the poem. (And even that has the feel of something the poet intends to do rather than has already done.)

If I were to follow my intuition as to where on the lyric–narrative spectrum Waller's poem belonged, I'd be pretty certain it is very lyric:

Lyric ←——————X———————————————→ Narrative

Waller's poem achieves lyric unity in two ways. One is through the single emotion that motivates and animates the poem: praise of the beloved. The poet is at pains to tell us how enraptured he is at the thought of his beloved: he'd rather have her in his arms than the whole world in his possession. Notice that Waller sticks with the single emotion and carries it all the way through the poem. Lyrics tend to do that—locate a single, central emotion and take it to the limit.

The second unifying aspect of Waller's poem is technical—the recurring use of circle images and metaphors. Almost everything is a circle, starting (and ending) with the sash that encircles his girl's waist. In stanza 1 he puts the sash around his head, and that reminds him of the circle of a king's crown and arms around a woman's waist; in stanza 2 he thinks of heavenly spheres and the circle of fence (a "pale") that might confine a deer; in stanza 3 he thinks of his beloved's waist again and (final line) the giant orbit of the sun around the earth. (He's using the old, earth-centered cosmic scheme in this final line.)

I chose Waller's poem to contrast with Whitman's narrative because the very technique that unifies Waller's lyric—a series of metaphors—would work *against* narrative coherence. Why? How? Simply this: metaphors slow a poem down by sending the reader's imagination zooming off to the new connections that the figures of speech introduce. The more metaphors in a poem, the slower the going. The reader has to stop and think (and savor) the comparisons—as you, no doubt, had to when you read Waller's poem. But narrative poems thrive on momentum; they need to keep moving. A good narrative poet knows to beware of metaphors and use them sparingly. Metaphors are a lyric poet's friend, but they can disrupt narrative unity, which is based on unfolding action—on lots of nouns and strong and precise verbs.

A lyric poem can go wrong in many ways, but the most common occurs when the first draft doesn't sufficiently surround its emotional or imagistic center. This is one more reason a poet needs to give himself or herself permission to put down as much as possible in the first draft, without knowing whether it belongs or where it might lead. A lyric poem is almost always certain to become shorter as the poet "carves away" what isn't essential, what doesn't constellate around the poem's central mood or situation.

Likewise, when a narrative poem goes wrong, it can get completely lost and wander aimlessly—one action or event doesn't feel connected to what preceded it or to what follows.

If a poem you're working on is giving you trouble, try to locate it on the lyric–narrative spectrum. If the poem seems to aspire more to narrative, then keep it moving with verbs and actions, and ask yourself where this story best begins, how it develops, how it resolves. If the poem wants a lyric presence and intensity, then ask where its emotional or imagistic center is, and see if you can strengthen it by stripping away extra material that doesn't add to that focus.

STORY: NARRATIVE UNDER LYRIC PRESSURE

Straightforward narrative poetry isn't much in fashion now. For certain historical and cultural reasons, it's hard to imagine genuine narrative poetry ever being central again. Most poetry readers and writers have shifted toward lyric, especially in America, a culture that's fascinated by individuality and subjectivity. What's more, movies and novels cater more effectively to our deep craving for narrative pleasures. But even if narrative poetry isn't what most of us write, the narrative impulse is still powerfully present in all of us as a fundamental way of organizing experience into meaning. It *can't* go away—storytelling may even be an innate way our brains work to make sense of the world; after all, one of the basic premises of experience made into story is that cause and effect are real and important ways of understanding the world.

Stories often clarify the cause-and-effect relation of actions or events. For example, someone might say: "My parents divorced and I became unhappy." One event (my parents divorced) precedes the other (I became unhappy), and the connection between the two is important for the speaker's understanding and search for meaning and order in the world. So I still think it's useful to think about poems on a lyric–narrative spectrum, but to recognize that the narrative impulse in contemporary poetry is heavily influenced by our commitment to lyric emotion.

At this point, it's time to talk about how the narrative impulse manifests in what I'll call story-making. Story is so basic to the human experience that it's sometimes difficult to think clearly about it; but unless we do, we can't understand one of the basic orderings of lyric poetry.

Some Characteristics of Story

You'll notice I've shifted the term from *narrative* to *story*. From here on, I'll be using the term *story* to indicate narrative impulse altered by lyric pressure.

For all we know, the ability to order experience into story may be hard-wired into the human brain. Here is the anthropologist Clifford Geertz on the subject: "Human beings make sense of the world by telling stories about it—by using the narrative mode for constructing reality. . . . Our immediate experience, what happened yesterday or the day before, is framed in the same storied way. Even more striking, we represent our lives (to ourselves as well as to others) in the form of narrative." It's quite possible that stories are the fundamental meaning-making structures that we humans, all of us, use.

A good story is almost magical in its hold on us. I personally find Samuel Taylor Coleridge's "Rime of the Ancient Mariner" a bit long-winded and full of awkward archaisms, but I love the way its opening honors the almost magical power that story can exercise over an audience. The poem begins with the Mariner trying to physically detain the Wedding-Guest, who's late for the festivities. The Guest easily breaks free of the Mariner's "skinny hand," but he has less luck breaking the spell of story that the old man exerts with his "glittering eye" and his words:

> He holds him with his glittering eye—
> The Wedding-Guest stood still,
> And listens like a three years' child:
> The Mariner hath his will.
>
> The Wedding-Guest sat on a stone:
> He cannot choose but hear;
> And thus spake on that ancient man,
> The bright-eyed Mariner.

When story begins, we yield to the joy of curiosity and story's enthralling power that takes us back to childhood: we "cannot choose but hear."

Story involves narrative action, but it also organizes itself around conflict and tension. Notice how Thomas Wyatt's sixteenth-century love lament "They Flee From Me" opens with these lines:

> They flee from me that sometime did me seek
> With naked foot, stalking in my chamber.
> I have seen them gentle, tame, and meek,
> That now are wild and do not remember
> That sometime they put themself in danger
> To take bread at my hand; and now they range,
> Busily seeking with a continual change.

Here is pure story tension: two pronouns—*they* and *me*—and a verb (*flee*) between the pronouns; a verb that establishes the nature of the relation between these two centers of energy. In the second stanza, Wyatt goes on to shift the *they* to a particular person and thereby reveals the extraordinary focusing power of story imagination:

> Thanked be fortune it hath been otherwise
> Twenty times better; but once in special,
> In thin array after a pleasant guise,
> When her loose gown from her shoulders did fall,
> And she me caught in her arms long and small;
> Therewithall sweetly did me kiss
> And softly said, "dear heart, how like you this?"

Conflict is essential to story. Without conflict, there is no dramatic tension. Place the pronouns *I* and *you* in the first line of a poem, and already you have the bare bones of story tension: two pronouns standing for two separate beings, two separate centers of energy. All you need to do is place a verb between *I* and *you*, and the tension takes on the trajectory of emotion that motivates action: *I hate you, I love you, I envy you, I long for you, I fear you.* . . . The story has begun. Already your poem is alive with tension and calls out for more language that will unfold as action seeking to resolve this conflict.

What's essential to story is that there be at least two centers of energy, two poles of awareness around which the conflict can organize itself. When Stanley Kunitz counsels young poets to "polarize their contradictions," he is proposing that this essential conflict can be *internal*, that it can take place inside the speaker, who feels two ways about something. The ancient Roman lyric poet Catullus, in a two-line "love" poem to his mistress Lesbia, gives a wonderful example of how a passionate person can feel internally conflicted:

> I hate and I love. Perhaps you wonder why I do?
> I don't know, but I feel it and it tortures me.

In poems like this, the source of conflict is a "divided self" as it were, rather than two separate people. The Irish poet William Butler Yeats was after the same point when he remarked: "We make out of the quarrel with others, rhetoric; but of the quarrel with ourselves, poetry."

In lyric story, events constellate around a single conflict that evokes a focused emotional situation. For example, in "Those Winter Sundays," Robert Hayden dramatizes such a tension between a father and son. But Hayden's poem also goes on to dramatize the inner conflict of the son-as-speaker:

Those Winter Sundays

Sundays too my father got up early
and put his clothes on in the blueblack cold,
then with cracked hands that ached
from labor in the weekday weather made
banked fires blaze. No one ever thanked him.   5

I'd wake and hear the cold splintering, breaking.
When the rooms were warm, he'd call,
and slowly I would rise and dress,
fearing the chronic angers of that house,

speaking indifferently to him,   10
who had driven out the cold
and polished my good shoes as well.
What did I know, what did I know
of love's austere and lonely offices?

Robert Hayden (1966)

The details of story in poetry (and in memory) often reveal an attitude toward an event or figure. In Hayden's poem, the "good shoes" the father has polished are not only the special shoes the speaker will wear to church, but also an indicator of the father's attitude toward the son: he does kind things for the son specifically (the fire-building and house-heating benefited everyone) despite being treated "indifferently" by his son.

But story in lyric isn't just a way of structuring experience through the organizing of words; it's also a means of sustaining a self. The Danish writer Isak Dinesen seems to have it right when she says: "Any sorrow can be borne if it can be made into a story, or if a story can be told about it." We might think about Dinesen's notion when reading Hayden's poem, which is haunted by the past and the too-lateness of regret. By poem's end, the speaker seems to have recognized the father's love and devotion. The incantatory repetition of "What did I know, what did I know . . . ?" tells us that *now* he understands his father's behavior—now that it's too late to express his gratitude. *Now* he recognizes the love hidden in the father's actions—not just the waking early to heat the house, but the polished shoes given as a kind of offering by the father, much as the priest performs the religious rituals of "lonely offices" in a church. The poet seems to have recognized the father's love too late in terms of the real-world passing of time. And yet one could argue that in writing this poem Hayden has given a belated testimony to the sustaining power of the father's devotion and has partly repaid his complicated debt.

If I were placing Hayden's poem on the lyric–narrative spectrum in order to become more aware of the relative strength and presence of lyric and narrative elements in his poem, I'd probably place it somewhere near the center, but a little bit toward the narrative pole (there's a clear narrative action all the way through line 12, I'd say to myself), but then I'd have to admit that the last two lines are a lyric outcry—and for that matter, the poem has stressed emotions underlying its actions also ("fearing the chronic angers . . ."). I'd give it a little consideration, then go with a gut feeling that places it a bit on the narrative side of the spectrum:

Lyric ←——————————✕——————→ Narrative

One of the things I learn from placing the poem on the lyric–narrative spectrum is how wonderfully lyric and narrative are held in tension in Hayden's poem. But wait a minute, there's that adjective in line 2: *blueblack*—it's an unusual word (invented?), and it's doing a lot of sound work in the poem—the *oo* sound of *blue* connects backward to the *too* (a word that shows the father worked constantly, ceaselessly), and the *ack* of *black* is going forward to rhyme with *cracked* in the next line. And the *b* of *blueblack* is going to alliterate with *banked* and *blaze* a few lines later. And then there's the word itself: *blueblack*. I wonder if it's an invented color, but my listening ear almost flips it to *blackblue*, which makes some part of my mind think *black and blue*, a term often used to describe the bruises of someone who has been beaten. It's subtle, very subtle—I'm not sure what to make of it; but this odd word *is* part of a poem that speaks of "chronic angers" and "fearing." And so we see both the limits and the uses of the lyric–narrative spectrum: it's a way of organizing our responses to a poem and locating places in the poem that convey a feel of lyric concerns or a nudge toward narrative emphasis.

■ ■ ■

In the twentieth century, the psychological century, Sigmund Freud proposed specific archetypal stories such as the father–son rivalry underlying what he called the Oedipus complex and the mother–daughter rivalry underlying what he termed the Electra complex. More broadly, Freud drew attention to the family triad (father, mother, child) as a rich source of urgent stories. Sometimes poets have organized these stories as two-person conflicts, as in Sylvia Plath's "Daddy" or Adrienne Rich's "Snapshots of a Daughter-in-Law" or Dean Young's "Shamanism 101." At other times they've been dramatized with triadic richness, as in Louis Simpson's "My Father in the Night Commanding 'No'" or Stanley Kunitz's "The Portrait" or Theodore Roethke's "My Papa's Waltz."

Here's Roethke's poem:

My Papa's Waltz

The whiskey on your breath
Could make a small boy dizzy,
But I hung on like death:
Such waltzing was not easy.

We romped until the pans   5
Slid from the kitchen shelf;
My mother's countenance
Could not unfrown itself.

The hand that held my wrist
Was battered on one knuckle;   10
At every step you missed
My right ear scraped a buckle.

You beat time on my head
With a palm caked hard by dirt,
Then waltzed me off to bed   15
Still clinging to your shirt.

Theodore Roethke (1942)

It's a poem dramatizing a child caught up by the father's boisterous exuberance and the possible destructiveness of his drunken romp. Although the disorder doesn't seem major in terms of the physical world (pans falling from the kitchen shelf), we do know that the mother is alienated and unhappy, which is a significant form of emotional disorder. Is the child delighted or terrified, or both? Who knows for sure? Evidence based on image details from the poem can point in either direction. What we can say is that there is an unfolding interplay of disorder and order in the poem: the stately order of a waltz, but also the wildness of the father's drunken state; the order of rhyme and the idea of beating time, but the disorder of ". . . beat time on my head / With a palm caked hard. . . ."; the order of the physical intimacy of son and father, but the alienation of the mother, who is powerless to change her disapproval ("countenance / Could not unfrown itself"). Looking at this poem can also be a kind of litmus test for a reader's personal threshold. Readers who have endured and emerged from the dysfunctional dynamics of a family with an alcoholic parent are far more likely to experience the child's situation as jeopardy rather than simple excitement.

I don't want to overemphasize the lyric–narrative spectrum technique or make you think that every poem should be considered in that light. However, it can be a useful tool. Myself, I'd put "My Papa's Waltz" just a bit more toward the narrative pole than Hayden's "Those Winter Sundays." In fact, in the light of the way action dominates Roethke's poem, I'm also tempted to reassign Hayden's poem a bit further toward lyric. It's a game that calls for flexibility, for listening and becoming aware of how each poem achieves its effects. If I were looking for a specific lyric element to point to in Roethke's poem, I'd say the simile in line 3 ("But I hung on like death"), which occurs pretty early on, as contrasted with the way the lyric outburst happens so powerfully in the last two lines of Hayden's poem. Almost all of Roethke's poem is action and description—important, decisive elements of narrative—and yet there's the intensity of focus on that brief, emotionally charged moment and the way the child's emotional state is poised between jeopardy and joy ("romped"), between thrill and disgust ("whiskey on your breath"). In terms of the lyric–narrative spectrum, we can appreciate how every word carries crucial information (a sign of lyric concentration?); and the poem itself practically vibrates with the tension of lyric and narrative pleasures (with, as I mentioned previously, an undertone of anxiety for readers to whom this scene triggers darker memories from childhood about how "innocent" scenes can conceal frightening implications).

■ ■ ■

STORY EXERCISE: MAKING UP A STORY

If the "I Remember" exercise in Chapter 1 is a simple way to sample the rich disorder of our sensory memories, then there's an equally simple way to experience the structuring power of story. First, find a quiet place where you won't be distracted. Now, choose a figure who is known to you—father, aunt, mother, best friend, grandparent, sister, brother, favorite pet. It should be a figure who has a significant relation to you, for better or worse. Close your eyes and visualize that person or creature. Then imagine that figure in a context: What is the location? What time of day is it? What is the person or creature doing? If there is no physical context or activity, then imagine that figure in some place performing some act—make up or remember some context that seems to you appropriate to this figure.

After doing that, you've pretty much arrived at the title for your exercise in story creation: "My Uncle Weeding His Backyard Garden" or "My Aunt Sitting in the Kitchen" or "My Sister Driving Downtown." You have a figure in the "real world"—the sensory world of experience, or memory, or imagination. Now add yourself to the situation, and you have the two pronouns that are the two poles of tension in story. If you don't see how to add yourself to the story, try using this as your opening line:

> I watch as my aunt stirs sugar
> Into her tea . . .

or:

> I watch as my sister steers
> Onto the Expressway . . .

Now that you have the tension of two pronouns (an observing *I* and an observed figure), ask yourself what happens next. Whatever happens next (in your imagination of the scene) is the next line of the poem: "She sets the spoon down and lifts the cracked cup to her lips." You've begun your story and can continue extending it by simply adding one line to another, by asking "What happens next?" and then writing that down. Extend the poem line by line by repeatedly asking that key question.

The only "rule" you might want to apply is this: whatever happens next (the next line) must be more interesting or at least as interesting as the line before it. If the actions or revelations of your poem become less interesting as the poem goes along, the reader will get bored and stop reading. Build the poem line by line. And remember, you (as the *I* of the poem) can also act or respond to or interact with the other figure. If the story you're making up gets less interesting or you run out of memories or can't imagine anything interesting, then just stop. But try to stop at a satisfying place, a place with some kind of dramatic closure or located in a situation that completes this portrait and the figure's relation to you. How long should your poem be? It's hard to say—Roethke covered a lot of territory in sixteen lines; Hayden in fourteen. I'd try for at least that many and consider that each line might represent a strengthening of your story imagination.

If the assignment doesn't "work" for you, pick another figure, another action—and try again.

The reason I urge a context—your uncle in his garden, for example—is to narrow the focus so that you don't try to tell too much in a single poem. If you try to write *directly* about any significant figure or relationship in your life, you could probably tell hundreds of stories or anecdotes, each of which might dramatize some aspect of a complex relationship experienced over time. But when you try to tell everything about a significant relationship, then chances are things will get mingled and turn into mishmash, and the richness will quickly become confusion. By narrowing the focus to a single action and a single moment, you can keenly highlight one aspect of a relationship.

What's more, the action and setting you chose for your figure are usually themselves symbolic of an emotional aspect of your relationship to the figure. Roethke's choice of the drunken dance or Hayden's choice of the wintry house warmed only by a stove or fireplace—both are scenes that reveal or imply meaning through sensory details. Ezra Pound tells us in his 1918 essay "A Retrospect" that "the proper and perfect symbol is the natural object." In other words, the aunt sipping tea or the uncle in the garden are likely to be symbolic actions and placements—symbolic of how the self (the speaker) feels about the figure. Actions and setting reveal the figure's significance for the poet.

■ ■ ■

MORE ABOUT LYRIC AND THE GHOST-NARRATIVE

Western wind, when will thou blow.
The small rain down can rain.
Christ! If my love were in my arms
And I in my bed again!
　　Anonymous, fifteenth century

"Western Wind" is an anonymous poem written down almost five hundred years ago, but it is probably much older. It's a very short poem—only four lines long, and in two of them the speaker is talking to (cursing?) the wind and rain, which does not exactly constitute a narrative plot. But those few lines, those twenty-six words, sketch a dramatic situation and focus the speaker's emotion—and the poem's meaning. The speaker is enduring windy, rainy weather, a circumstance that would be cause enough for misery. But he then indicates that there's another place where he would much rather be: in his love's intimate embrace and in his own bed. And so we somehow gather that he's a traveler of some sort who is far from where he belongs (both where he belongs emotionally—in his love's embrace; and physically—in his own home, his own bed).

These four lines manage to concentrate intense longing and misery and the bittersweet pain of imagining a better place where we could be—a pretty universal human situation. Most of us have experienced homesickness; and when you add loneliness, physical discomfort, and longing for intimacy, you achieve real intensity. But the narrative? It's almost nonexistent—there's no action at all (except the wind and rain doing their thing). What we have is the dramatic context of a situation that is so subtly and briefly sketched that it seems best to refer to it is as a ghost-narrative hovering behind the poem's lyric language. Yet that sense of dramatic context is crucial to grounding lyric emotion in poetry. And we *get it*; we can see and feel all we need to know of the speaker's situation in "Western Wind" in order to connect to the feelings it bodies forth in words.

LYRIC UNDER THE PRESSURE OF STORY

Lyric poetry can be said to seek *intensity* more than anything. Therefore it concentrates its situation and its emotion and seeks what I would call dramatic focus—it only names the most essential things or people necessary to generate a certain emotional intensity. Using the fewest words and phrases possible, it concentrates its meaning and power. We saw in Roethke's "My Papa's Waltz" how the mother was given a role (thereby expanding the story and nudging it toward narrative about a family's relationships), but a very limited one. Only two lines reveal her presence and attitude, as if she was allowed into the poem just to show how she wasn't actually a part of the exuberance and chaos of the son–father dance. If the mother hadn't been there at all, the poem would have had more dramatic focus on the son–father interaction, but it would have lost other emotional implications about a wider world of family relationships (mother to son, mother/wife to husband, husband/father to wife). In the next two poems, we'll see how the dramatic focus increases because there are only two people present.

With the topic of "lyric under the pressure of story," we've crossed the midpoint on the lyric–narrative spectrum and moved closer to the lyric pole. Now the power of lyric concentration takes over, and the story element becomes less prominent. When this happens, the emotional and subjective intensity becomes much more pronounced and the story element dwindles to ghost status, simply haunting the edges of the lyric. Let me give this sonnet by John Keats as an example:

Bright Star

Bright star, would I were steadfast as thou art—
Not in lone splendor hung aloft the night
And watching, with eternal lids apart,
Like nature's patient, sleepless Eremite,
The moving waters at their priestlike task   5
Of pure ablution round earth's human shores,
Or gazing on the new soft-fallen mask
Of snow upon the mountains and the moors—
No—yet still steadfast, still unchangeable,
Pillowed upon my fair love's ripening breast,   10
To feel for ever its soft fall and swell,
Awake for ever in a sweet unrest,
Still, still to hear her tender-taken breath,
And so live ever—or else swoon to death.

John Keats (1819)

We can assume the speaker is looking at a star (or has looked at one in a certain mood—of loneliness? solitude? alienation?). The poem opens with him speaking to the star as if it were a person or conscious being: "Bright star, would I were steadfast. . . ." There is a star quality he wishes to own: "steadfastness"—being steady and unchanging and unchanged by anything. He says all that in his opening line. But he no sooner expresses this wish than he shifts to aspects of being like the star that he *wouldn't want*: the star is detached, "hung aloft" above it all, existing in a "lone splendor." Keats's imagination makes the star into a hermit (an Eremite), cut off from the world of people but connected to them by a strange task: to always look down from the sky and watch things happen on earth from a great distance (a detachment?). This hermit/star watches the ocean wash the shore (again a metaphor: the waves are priests; the shore is all humankind being absolved of sin and suffering). Keats doesn't want to be that sleepless watcher; he doesn't want to gaze down from on high and see the landscape become covered with snow as if it had put on a mask to cover its face ("Or gazing on the new soft-fallen mask / Of snow upon the mountains and the moors").

These metaphors of detachment—of what the speaker doesn't want from his connection to the star, and his longing to have *some* of its qualities (e.g., the unchangeableness)—are woven together with lots of repeated vowel sounds. Repeating and varying vowel sounds was one of Keats's favorite poetry pleasures: listen to the *oo* sounds (as in a cow's *moo*) that link these two lines—"The moving waters at their priestlike task / Of pure ablution round earth's human shores"—and then leap ahead to close out and connect up the poem's first scene with the *oo* sound again in *moors*. Keats's poem is full of such sound-weavings and vowel music. I'll say more about this in the Singing chapter of Part Three, but here I want to concentrate on the poem as lyric with a ghost-narrative hovering in its background.

So far in the first eight lines, Keats has presumably looked at a star and longed for one (human?) ideal quality that he thinks it possesses and that he wishes to possess, and he has rejected other qualities that he imagines go along with being that detached body in the night sky. Keats uses the traditional structure of a Petrarchan sonnet to order his poem: this sonnet form calls for a rhyme scheme, but also for a shift or "turn" in the poem somewhere around line 9—a shift that signals a new direction of the poem's imagining. Keats signals his shift by repeating his rejection of the star and yet also repeating his longing for that first quality he spoke of: "steadfastness." "No" he says, emphasizing the rejection, only to then immediately say "yet" he still can't stop longing for this one aspect: a steadfastness that is now also "unchangeable."

Then suddenly the next four lines bring us to a new landscape of physical intimacy: Keats imagines resting and sleeping on his beloved's breast. There is a weirdness in this shift also—the sense of vast, uninhabited spaces (night sky, oceans, mountains, moors) in the first eight lines, and then a *zooming in* to the intense human intimacy of a couple in physical contact, presumably in a room. Keats takes us from cosmic vastness to almost claustrophobia, just like that. Instead of the hermit (who denies himself the pleasure of human company) or the priest (who is sworn to abstain from bodily pleasures of sexual intimacy), we have the poet desiring a sensual connection of his body with hers. She's asleep in the poem, so it's not as if he wants to talk with her or have ordinary intimacy—he wants to sleep "pillowed" on her "ripening breast" (he doesn't necessarily want to "sleep with her" in a sexual sense, though the poem is rather sexy especially by way of its sound texture).

But it's hard to say if this situation is real—either the star or the beloved's body. It's almost as if the speaker has conjured both the star and the beloved out of thin air, conjured them into this situation with the sounds of his poem. The poem is almost a "wish" poem (as people used to make a wish on the first star they saw in the night sky, repeating a little folk-magic language charm as they did so: "First star I see tonight, I wish I may, I wish I might, have the wish I wish tonight.") This is what I want, says the intensely yearning poet: "To feel for ever its soft fall and swell. . . ." And if I can't have that, I'd just as soon be dead, just as soon pass out of this world entirely: "swoon to death."

But really, there is no "action" in this poem, no narrative activity. In fact, the speaker is really quite passive. If you read a few Keats poems, you'll see that this passivity is characteristic—he feels very strongly in his poems, but he doesn't do much in them, which is one reason we think of him as a deeply lyric poet. What the poem presents is only the evocation of mood and longing and yearning (all of it pretty intense, of course, as the longing for intimacy can be when one is young and alone).

The structural element of tension between two characters in story-making focuses emotion. The emotion of lyric makes story matter, gives it urgency. The two impulses, tension in story and emotion of lyric, work together in many poems. Here's another example of a poem with two figures. The event or action in this poem by Gerard Manley Hopkins is so minimal that it's hard to even call it a ghost-narrative, but the meaning (as we would expect in lyric) emerges from the emotional responses that concentrate around the scene. Here's the poem:

Spring and Fall

to a young child

Margaret, are you grieving
Over Goldengrove unleaving?
Leaves like the things of man, you
With your fresh thoughts care for, can you?
Ah! As the heart grows older   5
It will come to such sights colder
By and by, nor spare a sigh
Though worlds of wanwood leafmeal lie;
And yet you will weep and know why.
Now no matter, child, the name: 10
Sorrow's springs are the same.
Nor mouth had, no nor mind, expressed
What heart heard of, ghost guessed:
It is the blight man was born for,
It is Margaret you mourn for.   15

Gerard Manley Hopkins (1880)

What is the situation that this poem creates and explores? It's tucked into the epigraph, "to a young child," and developed in the opening two lines. We're given the information that the language is addressed to a female and that she is young. We're given an action: Margaret is "grieving" over some leaves falling in a grove of autumn trees (a cluster of trees the poem calls "Goldengrove")—she's crying and he's responding to her, so we have the pressure of two characters and a third thing also: the trees letting their autumnal leaves fall. Here we can clearly see how (as in many lyrics) the story tension makes use of a third thing to reveal the characters' feelings and attitudes (Margaret, speaker, and the trees). We saw this "third thing" at work in Hayden's poem with the "good shoes"; in Roethke's poem, the dance was the "third thing" that revealed differing attitudes and emotions; and in the poem we're about to consider, it is a grove of trees in autumn.

Watching the leaves fall, the two characters (the speaker and Margaret, a young girl) do not share the same feelings about the event they're witnessing. The child sees the leaves falling and cries, thinks it's sad—perhaps she thinks that the trees are dying. The speaker responds to the child's response. At first, he seems to talk down to her, as if to say: "You think you can care for these, you'll get used to it, you'll harden emotionally" ("the heart . . . will come to such sights colder / By and by . . ."). But at line 9 there's a small event, a turn: rather than stopping her crying, the child keeps on weeping ("And yet you will weep and know why")—the child's grief hasn't been stopped by his rather harsh adult wisdom; instead, he's forced to reconsider his earlier attitude. (Notice that I say "at line 9"—as in Keats's "Bright Star," we're looking at a sonnet structure with its "turn," although "Spring and Fall" is a "sonnet" of fifteen lines rather than the traditional fourteen.)

At this point, the speaker tries for a deeper and different understanding of the girl's continuing grief. Her ongoing sadness leads him to see that her grief isn't just about the trees, but has something to do with us humans. But that "something" is mysterious—our mind doesn't quite get it and our mouth (language) can't quite express it, but our heart (emotion?) has heard of it and our "ghost" (soul?) has guessed what it's about. What is it? In the last lines of the poem, the speaker thinks he's finally figured it out (and now he's much more sympathetic to the child's grief than he was at the poem's beginning). What is this mystery that the child is encountering and weeping over? Something humans and trees (and all living things) share: a "blight" (vegetation disease)—a blight that we were all born into and must suffer: the blight of being mortal, of knowing ("what heart heard of, ghost guessed") that we will also die, just like the trees seem to do in fall. The falling leaves speak to Margaret directly about her own inevitable death, and her response is deep and mysterious and appropriate (unlike the speaker's scolding in the opening lines). But what is the narrative action of the poem? What happened in the plot? A few leaves have fallen; a young girl has wept at the sight and been saddened by it; an older person has (perhaps only in his mind) first scolded her mildly, then felt and thought and imagined more deeply about the situation until he recognized that the child was right to intuit this connection between tree and human self and had responded appropriately from the beginning.

Yearning in Keats's poem; grief and confusion in Hopkins's poem—these are emotions that have the power to concentrate all the language around them. The sketched scene (a man looking at or thinking about a star; two people looking at leaves falling) is enough of a story to ground and support the intense emotion that the lyric seeks to express.

There is minimal action in both poems. Could the lyric go further and convey nothing but the thoughts, feelings, perceptions of a single speaker, a single voice talking? Yes, but that's not a great idea for poetry—even for lyric poetry, which is most interested in the responses of the speaker (the *I* of the poem). Why? Because such a speaker talking aloud to himself or herself can drift and become lost quite easily. However, if there's another thing (star, beloved's breast, child weeping, leaves falling) for the speaker to focus on, then there's relationship and focus and the possibility of increasing intensity (all of which are lyric goals). There are poems in which a single consciousness directly expresses its thoughts and feelings, but they can quickly become boring or pretentious or unanchored to the world we live in. There are poets who can write this sort of poem well, but not many. Especially when we're just starting out in poetry, such unfocused monologues are wisely avoided, even though they're tempting, since they seem to offer a great opportunity to say exactly what's on our minds. Paradoxically, we can more quickly and efficiently achieve self-expression or self-revelation when we focus attention (our language) on some thing *other* than ourselves—another person, a creature, even a tree. When we respond to some thing or person outside ourselves, we become more conscious of our own feelings and attitudes. And that other person, creature, or thing (or landscape) allows us to focus our language and attention, and thereby intensify our emotional response or clarify our attitude.

LYRIC AND STORY COMBINED: SECTIONED POEMS AND THE LYRIC SEQUENCE

Story gives us an awareness of self and other. It enables us to discover how action and interaction can engage both ourselves and our readers and also open up a sense of a larger world where people act and interact. There's a lot to be said for this approach, since it resembles the way we as individuals move through the world, acting and reacting to things and people and events. Lyric, in contrast, focuses on a single moment or situation and intensifies it to reveal its emotional essence. As I've mentioned, poets often tend to favor either the narrative or the lyric end of a lyric–narrative spectrum, depending on which approach seems the truest and most interesting way to dramatize what matters most to them. But what if we poets could make use of the virtues of both approaches: the scope and real-world accuracy of narrative, and the emotional intensity and "inner-world" focus of lyric?

Why not combine the two? Why not write a poem that has narrative scope and continuity through time and yet keeps the pleasures of intensity that lyric concentration provides? One way to do this is by writing something called a lyric sequence. The simplest form of lyric sequencing is something I'll call a sectioned poem. It may be that you've tried to write poems about an important figure in your life—for example, your paternal grandfather. Maybe you've tried to write about him more than once, and each time you've gotten some words written, but what you've written doesn't seem to hold together as a single poem and doesn't adequately dramatize how significant (for better or worse) he is in your life. What if you took five or six of these attempts at writing about this figure and found you could put them together in some form?

In a sectioned poem the poet is free to write lyric units, but then he or she links the lyric units in a loose overall connection. This type of poem might have an overall title and then present a series of num-bered sections, or each section might have its own subsidiary title so as to re-orient the reader to the topic or situation that each (lyric story) section is focused around. A sectioned poem offers a way of experi-menting with a loose unifying principle. If the individual lyric calls for a highly unified poem organized around a single image, emotion, or action, then by contrast a sectioned poem can present a loosely linked series of lyric units and thereby accommodate more discontinuity and dynamic disorder. For example, if the poet had some experience of a particular geographical setting, she could use that place to create an "umbrella" title (e.g., "Edisto Island Poems" or "Coney Island Poems" or "Philadelphia Summer"), and then what follows might be lyrics loosely connected to that place and written with different subjects or scenes as their primary focus. For instance, one lyric unit section might describe a natural scene on the island, another might draw a lyric portrait of a person there or a local character, another might express the poet's personal connection to that place or an experience she had there, and another might present the landscape in a particular season. All of these "Edisto Island Poems" or "Coney Island Poems" or "Philadelphia Summer" poems would be held together by the fact that they take place in the landscape or setting of the title.

Likewise, you could write a poem with the umbrella title "Grand-father Poems" and include in it five or six poems about your paternal grandfather, each focusing on some different moment in or aspect of his life. One section might, for example, either imagine his youth or tell a family story about his youth. A second section might focus on (or imagine) the speaker's (your) first memories of the grandfather.

A third section might focus on physical characteristics of the grandfather or a favorite activity of his; yet another on the grandfather's relationship (or lack of relationship) with his spouse (is he a widower, divorced, in a harmonious relationship?). Another section might speak of a recent encounter or situation involving both you (the speaker) and your grandfather.

One way of generating the material for such a sectioned poem is to sit down and give yourself permission to write as many memories and scenes as possible that have to do with this figure—*just let the language flow and jump where it wishes; let it follow its own path until you have four or five pages of material.* Then consider if there are any "centers" of subject matter or scene within this flow of words—centers that might form individual lyric sections within the overall poem's sequence. Once you've isolated a group of such scenes or moments, revise them to bring them into dramatic focus. You may end up with eight grandfather-related poems or parts of poems.

One of the good things about a sectioned poem is that a "partial poem" or fragment can still function as a section of the overall sequence—it doesn't have to resolve into unity the way an individual poem does. Let's suppose you've circled eight scenes or centers in these four or five pages, and you've worked them until they seem to dramatize their content as successfully as they can. A next step is to realize that if you have eight little lyric sections, *you can arrange them in various orders*—you don't have to follow, say, a chronological order. You're free to move them around and determine the most dramatically effective arrangement. You'll quickly see that the order you arrange the sections in has the power to change the meaning of the overall poem. The first section will be important because it introduces your reader to the figure; the last section will be important because (like the final line of a poem) it has the power of being the last words the reader absorbs from your poem. Last sections, like last lines, are doubly important and have a stronger impact than anything else in the poem except the opening section.

It may be that the first section of your sequence comes earliest in chronological time (grandfather's childhood in our example) and that the last section comes later in time (your grandfather as an old man, say, or as someone dead who exists as a photo on a living room wall); but that's not the only order that might make your sequence lively and interesting. What really matters in a sectioned poem is that it feel to the reader (and writer) as though each section is a piece from the same jigsaw puzzle. This "same puzzle" requirement might even cause you to remove one of the sections even though it seems interesting in itself; you'll want to include it in your sectioned poem *only* if it feels in some way part of the same puzzle. (Maybe that discarded piece belongs to another puzzle—one still to be written and focusing on some other figure or topic.)

To continue the puzzle analogy, one of the most exciting things about a sectioned poem or lyric sequence is the *missing pieces*, the gaps. A sectioned poem isn't a puzzle in which all pieces fit neatly together (that would be boring, I suspect). As long as the pieces feel like they're from the same puzzle, and as long as the reader's imagination can leap the gap between sections, then for your reader the missing pieces are almost as interesting as the brightly colored pieces (sections) that they're reading.

A LYRIC SEQUENCE BASED ON MYTH OR FAIRY TALE OR MOVIE

It may be that you aren't quite ready to write a sectioned poem based on your own themes or experiences from an *I* point of view. Such a project can be quite challenging, especially when you're a young poet—it might make you feel too self-conscious. But there's another way to write a lyric sequence that shifts the attention away from yourself a bit, but still yields the pleasures and revelations of lyric as well as those of narrative. And it has a huge advantage: you yourself don't have to make up the narrative plot or sequence of events. It's ready-made.

Here's what you do. Choose a myth or fairy tale or movie. Write a

sequence of lyric poems that follows the narrative; but instead of tell-
ing the whole story, only write the five or six (or ten or three) scenes
within that story that most interest you. You write those scenes or
situations as lyric poems spoken by one or another of the characters in
the myth or tale or movie. You start with a big and useful assumption:
that your readers *already* know the storyline or plot (this is one reason
it helps to choose a well-known story), so you only write the scenes or
situations that most matter to you. Your readers won't be reading out
of curiosity over the plot (as they would be in a narrative you made
up)—they'll already know how the fairy tale of, say, Sleeping Beauty
or Cinderella turns out. Instead, they'll be reading out of curiosity
about how you will re-tell the story and what personal quirks, twists,
or insights your version will reveal.

Let me slow down here and go back over this project now that
you have the general idea. Myths and fairy tales persist over time,
get remembered from generation to generation because they're
stories that seem to capture and dramatize basic human relationship
patterns and mysteries about human nature. They wouldn't sur-
vive or continue to interest us if they didn't touch on some essen-
tial themes. For example, we know that fairy tales often featured
a cruel stepmother (think of the tales of Hansel and Gretel or
Cinderella).

The story of a rejecting or hostile maternal figure and how it affects
a young girl is a compelling one that has personal relevance for many
women, and they can feel a deep response to such a figure and her
destructive actions in the stories. In addition, we could add the insight
of novelist and poet D. H. Lawrence, who said that myths were "inex-
haustible" and could be told and retold infinite times, because they
were *symbols of heart mysteries* that have the power to engage some-
thing in us that persists throughout time. This doesn't apply to all
myths (or fairy tales), but many of them do seem to encode deeply
psychological material into their storylines.

Here's an exercise based on this notion of lyric sequence.

■ ■ ■

LYRIC SEQUENCE EXERCISE

Remember that the most important part of this exercise is picking a myth or fairy tale or movie that you personally love or are haunted by. If you wish to make this kind of poem work, you must choose a story you care about. Otherwise there won't be deep links and deep discoveries—lyric discoveries. It's good to realize that there are unlikely to be narrative discoveries, because the narrative is already written and (presumably) known to the reader as well as to the poet. I'm not saying that you have to understand your connection to the story at a rational level—one that you could talk about and analyze. Quite the opposite: what's important is that the plot engage you emotionally and imaginatively, that you welcome the chance and challenge to dramatize it in your own words.

The next step after you've chosen a fairy tale (or myth or movie) is to pick scenes from it, moments from it that you wish to "speak from." You probably aren't going to tell the whole plot (that would be straight narrative), but you should choose scenes—individual moments in the story's flow—to dramatize for their lyric intensity. For example, let's say you choose the story of Hansel and Gretel. Which character do you most identify with? Perhaps Hansel. You might decide to tell the whole tale as a series of scenes spoken by Hansel and presenting his point of view. Or you might begin the sequence with a poem in which Hansel speaks just as he begins to suspect that he and his sister have been abandoned in the forest by their woodchopper father—but he hasn't decided to tell Gretel his fears yet. Into the sequence you might add another poem in which they first see the witch's gingerbread house (either Hansel or Gretel is speaking); you could describe the house or, maybe, not describe the house at all but only tell what it felt like to stumble upon it—did the child feel wonder, fear, or joy? Maybe you'll add a poem in which the witch speaks about why she lures in inno-cent children. (Possible point of view: everyone feels justified in their actions—even child-eating witches. What is her side of the story?) You might also add a poem from the father's perspective at some point in the story.

The possibility of what scenes you choose to dramatize is only lim-ited by your imagination and your emotional connection to the story. One goal might be to have enough individual lyrics to sketch in the arc of the whole story, but I know poets who started out to write a ten-poem lyric sequence about a myth and then ended up just using a single one from the series—because somehow that one poem captured best what moved them about the story and its characters, somehow that single scene fully dramatized the emotional and imaginative bond they had with the original story.

Here are a few other suggestions for such a project. Once you've chosen a myth or tale or movie, resist the temptation to begin by read-ing or rereading a plot summary of the story. Instead, start first with your *memory* of the plot and the different scenes. What *you* remember (or misremember) is what matters most. Your own version of the story, your own emphasis, is what's most lively—where memory, imagination, and self braid together into the mystery of why you love what you love. Respect your own version of the plot, because that's the lyric–emotional link. By the same token, feel free to choose only the scenes that inter-est you, and ignore those that don't—that increases your chances of caring about what you're doing. (Remember Frost's wisdom about how readers will only care if the poet cares: "No tears in the writer, no tears in the reader. No surprise for the writer, no surprise for the reader.") Let me put that last suggestion a different way: write as many scenes and viewpoints as you can imagine as individual lyrics; and then later look them over and decide which ones are fresh or real to you, and consider eliminating those that don't seem interesting or successful. Since your reader already probably knows the plot, you don't have to be too dutiful in filling in the storyline. However, if you've chosen a fairy tale that isn't very well known, then you may want to figure out how to fill your reader in on the essential plot and character elements without becoming dull.

I strongly urge you to take the opportunity to speak from other characters' viewpoints, not just, say, Cinderella's. This is a thrilling freedom. You may identify with the main character or hero of the myth or fairy tale, but being confined to that viewpoint can make your poem boring and predictable. It can limit the discoveries that await you.

CHAPTER SIX

Some Basic Issues

ORIENTATION, INFORMATION, AND LOCATION

Here's an odd but obvious fact: a poem can be set in ancient China, or on the moon, or in the poet's backyard. What power and freedom poets feel in that fact! But for the poet, responsibility goes with that freedom. When writing a poem, we sometimes forget that our readers will only know where the poem is taking place in time or space *if* we give them that information early on. Even when we first begin writing a poem, *we* probably already know who is speaking and where the poem takes place. As we work longer on our poem, we often carry in our minds an increasingly clearer sense of "where and when and what." But our readers only know what the words of the poem on the page tell them—this is an obvious but crucial fact. Informing and orienting readers has to happen early in the poem, at the very outset, because if they're confused about where the poem takes place or who's talking, then they can't pay attention to the poem or enjoy it. Often, the title itself can do a great deal of informing and orienting. Here are a few titles that give readers a clear sense of location, information, and orientation:

> *"Meditation at Lagunitas" (Robert Hass)—we're told that the poem*
> *takes place at a specific geographical location and that it will*
> *possibly follow the flow of someone's thoughts (meditations).*
> *"After Apple-Picking" (Robert Frost)—we're oriented to a particular*
> *rural event (apple-picking; a late summer or autumn activity) and*
> *that this poem takes place after that task has been completed.*
> *"homage to my hips" (Lucille Clifton)—we're told that the poem is a*
> *celebration ("homage to"), that it's personal ("my"), and that it's*
> *oriented toward an aspect of the speaker's bodily being ("hips").*

Sometimes a title can convey information that would be rhythmically clunky or awkward to integrate into the poem itself, as when Wordsworth entitles a poem "Lines Composed a Few Miles above Tintern Abbey, on Revisiting the Banks of the Wye during a Tour, July 13, 1798." Wordsworth's title certainly orients the reader, but it would be an ugly mouthful to pronounce in the body of the poem itself. Once he's gotten his (clunky) title out of the way and given the reader a sense of where the poem takes place and that he's been there before ("Revisiting"), Wordsworth can be confident that the reader is "with him" in the landscape and situation that the poem's words will create, describe, or ponder.

Sometimes a title can be a general orientation, which the opening lines clarify and bring into focus. Such is the case when William Butler Yeats entitles a poem "Among School Children" and then begins:

> I walk through the long schoolroom, questioning.
> A kind old nun in a white hood replies;

Already we have a location (school), a protagonist (*I*), a person the protagonist interacts with (a nun/teacher), and a relationship (the protagonist is visiting the school, being shown around). Already an entire dramatic context has been sketched out and we know where the poem's story begins (though not where it will go, of course).

Even a poem with a more general title like Sylvia Plath's "Tulips" moves quickly to sketch in its main character, her situation, and her location by the end of line 7:

> The tulips are too excitable, it is winter here.
> Look how white everything is, how quiet, how snowed-in.
> I am learning peacefulness, lying by myself quietly
> As the light lies on these white walls, this bed, these hands.
> I am nobody; I have nothing to do with explosions.   5
> I have given my name and my day-clothes up to the nurses
> And my history to the anaesthetist and my body to surgeons.

Plath's poem also reminds us that the characters that interact in a lyric don't always have to be people. In her poem, the relationship of the speaker to the tulips is the main source of dramatic tension, and such human figures as the surgeons and nurses in the hospital ward will turn out to be passive and peripheral, merely objects that denote the speaker's situation but not her crisis. In contrast, her relationship with and response to the tulips will dramatize her emotional state with lyric-expressive power.

When creating the world of a poem, we have to orient our readers in it, or they will become anxious and distracted—as anyone would be who enters a strange room in which things can't be clearly discerned. I'll speculate that this responsibility for orienting and informing is addressed in 95 percent of all poems that get written, and it's a truth that a young poet needs to remember. However, in poetry all truths also have countertruths, so I'll say that in 5 percent of poems written now the poet consciously wishes the reader to be disoriented for one reason or another. Certainly, this is true for "A Piano," the experimentalist poem written by Gertrude Stein and published in 1914 in a collection called *Tender Buttons*:

> If the speed is open, if the color is careless, if the selection of a strong scent is not awkward, if the button holder is held by all the waving color and there is no color, not any color.

As a reader beginning Stein's poem, I have a strong sense that she feels no responsibility to orient me; on the contrary, my disorientation seems to be what she's aiming at for some reason. Perhaps to wake me up or to have fun with my confusion?

I argue that orienting and informing your readers (and yourself) constitutes the most effective and essential act in poetry-writing, but there's room for disagreement. The issue, finally, is one of intention. If a poet consciously intends to disorient her readers for some purpose that furthers the ambitions of her poem, then she can rightly proceed, though always at the peril of losing most of her readers. If you write a poem that confuses and disorients all your readers, only your best friends can be expected to read it all the way to the end.

THE CONTRACT BETWEEN POET AND READER, POEM AND WORLD

Closely related to the issues of orientation, information, and location is something I'll call the Contract. It is an understanding established by the poet with her or his readers about how language will sound and function in the poem they're about to read. In the Contract, the poet makes certain agreements with the readers. Specifically:

- how the poem will sound to the readers, and
- how language in the poem will relate to the world of experience—how its words will connect (or not connect) to the world as the readers know it.

The Contract is a binding promise that the poem will live up to by being consistent from beginning to end. This consistency is one of the most powerful and persuasive ways of making a poem feel whole and cohesive, which is a chief pleasure that poems provide. This contract will include tone—the emotional weight or slant of the voice, which is hugely important as a unifying force in a poem. A poem's tone can be sad or ecstatic or angry—it can express the whole range of human emotions; but for the purposes of giving a sense of unity to the piece, consistent tone is essential.

Consider the tone of the opening lines of Sylvia Plath's "Daddy":

You do not do, you do not do
Any more, black shoe . . .

It's an urgent voice whose intensity is amplified by incantatory repetition and rhyme. Plath is saying to us: this is how I'm going to "speak" in this poem, this is what you can expect—intensity, density of sound (frequent internal and end rhyme), and metaphor (it will be quickly apparent that the "black shoe" isn't an actual piece of footwear, but a metaphor for Plath's father). The poem's title indicates that she's speaking of or addressing her father. Use of the word *Daddy* as the title also orients us toward the child-nature of the speaker, or a certain tone of relation; that tone would have been different if she'd titled the poem "Father," for example. In Plath's contract with us as readers, urgent metaphor occurs even before the father is present in any recognizable human form—he is a "black shoe" and soon will be other things: "a bag full of God," a "ghastly statue," and so on.

For contrast, we can consider the contract that William Carlos Williams establishes with his readers in the opening lines of his brief poem "This Is Just To Say":

I have eaten
the plums
that were in
the icebox . . .

The voice is quiet. The poem's title is casual ("just to say"), and by poem's end it's clear that the model for the poem (what the poem is "pretending to be") is a note left to someone else in the household—a note that's intimate, quiet, matter of fact. Williams's poem highlights another aspect of the Contract: how language in the poem will relate to the world. In the Williams poem, the language is simple and the words relate in a straightforward way to the material world: *eat* means to chew and swallow; *plums* are the fruit we know by that name; *icebox* is mildly archaic (the poem was published in 1934) but is the ordinary term in its time for a refrigerator. We need only recall Plath's rapid metaphoric transformations of the father for contrast.

Here's a third contract established by a poem in its opening lines, from "A Box" by Gertrude Stein:

Out of kindness comes redness and out of rudeness comes rapid same question, out of an eye comes research, out of selection comes painful cattle.

Stein's contract with us as readers says that her language use will be at a certain level of organization (the repeated phrase "out of . . . comes") that will propel the poem forward and give it a rapid momentum. But while as a reader I can understand each individual word, the phrases don't seem to make any easy sense (at least to me), and as a reader I'm being informed that I'll be reading a poem whose references to the world or a dramatic situation won't in any way be obvious to me. If I choose to read on, I can only expect more of the same, and I'll have to surrender to it in order to discover any meaning or pleasure her poem might have for me.

Here are a few other contracts established by other poems:

From the opening of "You Can't Have It All" by Barbara Ras:

But you can have the fig tree and its fat leaves like clown hands gloved with green. You can have . . .

In Ras's poem the title orients me toward a proverbial expression popular in our culture, "You can't have it all," which is often said when someone complains about feeling deprived or shortchanged and is being encouraged to accept the situation. The opening line of the poem announces that it will be organized as a further statement of consolation, one that lists things that "you can have"—and that the list will comprise things that are present in the physical landscape presumably inhabited by the speaker (and reader): fig trees, for starters. The repeated phrase "you can have" indicates that the poem will be a list of alert consolations (Wake up! The world is right here in front of you; look at it, look at those odd leaves on the tree). "Wake up and see what you *do* have" is presented as an answer to the daydreaming of wanting to "have it all."

From the opening of "Animal Graves" by Chase Twichell:

The mower flipped it belly up,
a baby garter less than a foot long,
dull green with a single sharp

stripe of pale manila down its back . . .

In Twichell's poem we're oriented in a general sense by the title, "Animal Graves"—places where animals (as contrasted with people) are buried. The opening lines that establish the poem's contract indicate that the speaker will talk directly and matter-of-factly about a situation (*mower* for lawnmower; *garter* for garter snake, a harmless snake). Accuracy and alertness of observation and reporting will characterize the poem's way of talking: the snake is a "baby" "less than a foot long," "dull green" "with a . . . stripe" It's almost as if the speaker were a neutral but alert reporter of events (a lawnmower mangling a small snake concealed in the lawn).

The contract between reader and poet essentially serves as an invisible preamble to each poem that reads: "I, the poet, hereby indicate this is how I will use words in my poem and this is how I'll sound as a voice speaking from the page to you. You can insist (or at least expect) that I will consistently sound this way and use language in this way throughout my poem. In fact, my consistency of tone and language use will be a powerful unifying factor in my poem and will help you to feel that all my words cohere in a vital way."

The advantages of living up to the Contract are obvious: when we listen to someone speaking to us, we value consistency—it inspires *confidence and trust*. For the most part, the poet's contract with the reader is an indication that he or she is in charge of the poem and can be relied upon—"I am the presiding intelligence, and I've brought these words together in a consistent way that I hope will engage you." Of course, as poets most of us don't deliberately break our contract with the reader; we simply fail to live up to it. And perhaps that happens most often because we don't pay attention to its terms. Without quite realizing it, as we write our poems we may wander off into another way of using words. In such a case, we jeopardize our reader's confidence in our poem.

■ ■ ■

The Contract isn't something you deliberately invent in order to begin your poem. Quite the contrary; most poets agree that many of their poems tend to "just start happening"—the language starts to flow and unfold, or a phrase excites them and they start putting words on the page, hoping that more words and phrases will keep coming (remember our early chapters' discussion of giving yourself permission). It's as if the poets are (rightly) responsible for the terms of the contract but didn't necessarily originate them. Perhaps this is what is meant by the "given" that so many poets say starts their poems—some phrase or sentence that seems to promise that if the poet listens to it and follows it, a real poem will happen. Although the Contract is one important part of the bond between poet and reader, it's worth remembering that it's there first and foremost for the poet, and only later for the reader. The Contract can guide the poet as she or he writes the poem.

If, by accident or negligence, the poet breaks the Contract in the course of writing (say, you lose the thread of the original inspiration or phrasing that first lured you into writing the poem), it can signal one of two things. Either the poet would be well advised to go back to the poem's beginning and get a renewed feel for the contract that initiated the poem, or the poet may want to "rewrite" the Contract. Perhaps that unexpected break in the Contract signals a different way that the poem wants to sound. Maybe the poet should use the "new" model to revisit the poem's contractual unity and make changes accordingly. (By the way, that's easier to say than to do.) But the important thing is this: the poet must realize that she or he is entering into a contract with two important parts—the first is between poet and language, and the second is between poet and reader.

■ ■ ■

One strong motive for writing a new contract for each poem is to discover and explore new ways of using language. Let me give some examples of how different contracts from the same poet might sound as they announce themselves in the opening lines of various poems.

Thomas Hardy (1840–1928) is best known as an English novelist, but his first love was poetry (although he didn't publish his first poetry collection until he was fifty-eight years old!). Here's the opening section of a nine-sectioned lyric poem called "To Lizbie Browne":

> I
> Dear Lizbie Browne,
> Where are you now?
> In sun, in rain?—
> Or is your brow
> Past joy, past pain,
> Dear Lizbie Browne?

The poem announces to us that it is using language as direct address—the poem is speaking out loud to another person, asking questions of her (and we're invited to eavesdrop on this one-sided conversation). It's language that's modeled on speech, on how someone might talk; but it also tells us that it's very compressed speech—not slack and casual, but lively and focused (and rhymed). The opener also announces that the poem will talk about serious subjects in a kind of glancing and indirect way, almost in a jaunty tone: "Or is your brow / Past joy, past pain?" the poet asks, wondering whether Lizbie is even still alive. The speaker's affection for the person addressed (he calls her "Dear") is further reinforced by using her nickname ("Lizbie" for "Elizabeth") and by returning to her name to close out and frame the first section of the poem. Hardy will keep this tone of jaunty compression and the beginning/ending frame of her name for nine more six-line sections. It's the contract he's made with us in this poem.

But in another poem, titled "Wessex Heights," Hardy's contract is completely different. Here's the first stanza of this long-lined poem:

There are some heights in Wessex, shaped as if by a kindly hand
For thinking, dreaming, dying on, and at crises when I stand,
Say, on Ingpen Beacon eastward, or on Wylls-Neck westwardly,
I seem where I was before my birth, and after death may be.

Here again, we might say that the contractual model for the poem is speech—someone talking aloud. But is the speaker talking directly to us or just thinking out loud? There are clear indications that the poem's speech tone will be modeled on "real" speech; the third line especially, with its use of "say," is an imitation of the way someone actually pauses in speech to say something like "for example." It's not what we expect in a sharply focused poem. Likewise, in line 3 the speaker mentions a specific location ("Ingpen Beacon") but then says "or on Wylls-Neck" as if to indicate that the musing is casual and drifting as it considers this landscape, even as it also drifts across human topics—"thinking, dreaming, dying on." The tone and commitment to the specific names of certain geographical high places, combined with the way the speaker links them to a matter-of-fact way of talking, open toward a quiet but serious set of life possibilities ("crises") and more mysterious implications (a place "where I was before my birth"). As readers, we expect to hear how a landscape and an individual human life are braided together in some profound but quiet way.

In yet another poem, "The Garden Seat," Hardy's contract with us is to use quiet and precise language to observe an object—a rather worn-out and broken-down garden seat:

> Its former green is blue and thin,
> And its once firm legs sink in and in;
> Soon it will break down unaware,
> Soon it will break down unaware.

The language is simple and descriptive and matter-of-fact. The only thing a bit odd about it is the repetition of the third line. We're in the real world of ordinary things, and some voice is speaking impersonally about this object. The contract here is that language is simple and descriptive and tone is calm and detached, although the speaker is observant. As the poem continues, the tone will allow the speaker to say ordinary things in a way that hints at the extraordinary, or to speak of supernatural things as if they exist alongside of and interact with natural things. And so the speaker goes on:

> At night when reddest flowers are black
> Those who once sat thereon come back;
> Quite a row of them sitting there,
> Quite a row of them sitting there.

Sure enough, red flowers in the dark of night *don't* seem red, they seem black. This is an ordinary but slightly odd point. Then, with equal casual authority, some humans enter the poem's calm, descriptive flow: ghosts. But the Contract is being kept. The poem isn't spooked or excited by these supernaturals; it just notices (in its final stanza) that they are weightless as they sit on the bench, immune to the weather, being just ghosts (but lots of them):

> With them the seat does not break down,
> Nor winter freeze them, nor floods drown,

For they are light as upper air,
They are light as upper air!

In each of these poems, Hardy uses language differently, enters into a different contract with us, and then honors it throughout the poem.

■ ■ ■

For the most part, the reader will accept (or reject) any kind of contract—acceptance or rejection is an initial act of faith and interest on the reader's part. This is what Samuel Taylor Coleridge called the reader's "willing suspension of disbelief"—a trust the reader puts in the poet and in the poem. But just as orientation and information go a long way in easing the reader toward that willing suspension, the Contract (when followed) maintains it through the whole poem.

■ ■ ■

I've claimed that it's rarely useful or effective to change the Contract partway through a poem. Having said that, I want to give one example of a poet's decision to suddenly alter the Contract being exactly what makes a poem unusual and successful. It's a poem we already considered in Part One, D. H. Lawrence's "Song of a Man Who Has Come Through," but it's worth revisiting in this new context:

Song of a Man Who Has Come Through

Not I, not I, but the wind that blows through me!
A fine wind is blowing the new direction of Time.
If only I let it bear me, carry me, if only it carry me!
If only I am sensitive, subtle, oh, delicate, a winged gift!
If only, most lovely of all, I yield myself and am borrowed   5
By the fine, fine wind that takes its course though the chaos of
    the world
Like a fine, an exquisite chisel, a wedge-blade inserted;
If only I am keen and hard like the sheer tip of a wedge

Driven by invisible blows,
The rock will split, we shall come at the wonder, we shall find the
    Hesperides.   **10**

Oh, for the wonder that bubbles into my soul,
I would be a good fountain, a good well-head,
Would blur no whisper, spoil no expression.

What is the knocking?
What is the knocking at the door in the night?   **15**
It is somebody wants to do us harm.

No, no, it is the three strange angels.
Admit them, admit them.

                               D. H. Lawrence (1917)

Up through line 13, the language is consistently that of rapture and use of metaphor (and metamorphosis) to evoke the speaker's exhilarated state. The speaker begins with a denial of his achievement ("Not I, not I"), but the voice is excited and even boastful in a backwards kind of way. The title claims the person speaking has "come through"—has passed through something and arrived. Come through what? Arrived where? Instead of answering these questions, the speaker denies that it was he who "came through": no, it wasn't me; it was "the wind," a special wind, and all I did was "yield" to it, let myself be "borrowed" by that wind and carried along like a winged seed (think maple seed or thistle or milkweed here). Our speaker is a seed, and then he becomes the sharp edge of a chisel that's "Driven by invisible blows." We might ask if the wind, the hammer, is driving this chisel-self. We might wonder how a person becomes a winged seed and then a chisel edge. We might ordinarily wonder that, *except* that the Contract has established that we're listening to a hymn of ecstatic, even mystical or magical, experience—the story of someone who "shall come at the wonder" by being borrowed and by splitting the rock.

The Contract is of breathless excitement about wondrous experience, and it moves rapidly and consistently through most of the poem. True, there are hints that the speaker is perhaps not quite as far along on this magical journey as the title claims: there's the phrase "If only" that occurs twice in line 3 and then begins lines 4, 5, and 8. What exactly does this phrase mean in the poem? It might mean that "these are the conditions I achieved—the only thing I had to do is let myself be borrowed"; but it might also mean that "these are the conditions I *will* have to meet to 'come through.'" In this second sense, the speaker may be hinting that the magical journey isn't complete yet. And sure enough, in line 10 we find "we *shall* come at the wonder"; that "shall," combined with the earlier uses of "If," hints that this whole thing is (possibly) a process not yet completed.

Why does this matter—this uncertainty of exactly where the (excited) speaker is on the mystical or mysterious journey toward "the wonder"? The slight uncertainty matters for one reason only: *because* in line 14, the poet breaks the Contract, and suddenly there's a complete change in the way language is used. Suddenly the *language use shifts* away from rapturous phrase repetition, magical transformations (person to seed to chisel edge), and mythical landscapes. Suddenly we're hearing an ordinary human voice in a human context charged with anxiety, if not downright paranoia:

What is the knocking?
What is the knocking at the door in the night?
It is somebody wants to do us harm.

This is the voice of a person speaking directly and emotionally to another person. Yes, it's slightly stylized speech, but it mimics the way someone would talk who is startled or frightened by a knocking on the door in the middle of the night. The poem is not just completely reoriented in terms of location (not "the Hesperides" or the wind "blowing the new direction of Time," but an ordinary house or apartment with a door); it's also changing in terms of tone and language use.

Now we're hearing an ordinary, vulnerable person talking—not an entranced, jazzed-up mystic. It's not just that we've gone from rapture to terror in tone, but the language is now realistic speech. Of course, this break in the contract of Lawrence's poem is in the service of the poem's drama—it's exactly how he gets to the strange (and deeper) mystery of the last two lines in which some voice (speaking the stylized and reality-oriented speech of the "new contract") responds to the speaker's fear and says with calm authority:

> No, no, it is the three strange angels.
> Admit them, admit them.

By breaking the Contract with these last five lines, Lawrence dramatizes not just the ecstatic joy of "coming through" but also the risks that could be involved—the moments of panic and paranoia when the speaker loses his nerve and his ego is suddenly frightened and vulnerable.

■ ■ ■

Still, most poets are well advised to establish and honor their contract about how they will use language in a poem and how it will relate (or not relate) to the language of experience. Readers count on this. The consistency of voice and language use strengthens poems and helps make them feel whole. Let me give an example of a poem that breaks its contract partway down the page and is not successful in that it doesn't seem likely to serve a dramatic purpose; it will only puzzle or confuse the reader. Here's the (would-be) poem:

My Last Poem

> I wrote it just for you.
> I turned the photographs,
> Face to the wall.
> I closed all my books

And unplugged the tv   5
In order to concentrate
Only on you.
                I thought
Of all the objects
Lost, left, loaned   10
And forgotten—
Corsages dropped
After the prom.
Or worse: creatures
Forsaken—   15
Dogs beaten and left
In the street,
Bagged kittens tossed
In a river—litany
Of misery, of life   20
Gone wrong
And the longing
For someone
To blame or explain.

In "My Last Poem," the contract the poem enters into with its open-ing lines and title introduces a flat, speaking voice addressing another person as "you" and suggesting an intimacy of connection ("Only on you"). The speaking voice is matter-of-fact but earnest; the nouns are simple and create the sense of a house or living space (*wall, books, tv*). This tone continues up through lines 6 and 7, where the speaker again repeats the importance of the "you" ("In order to concentrate / Only on you."). The next stanza begins with the same voice—"I thought / Of all the objects"; but as the sentence continues, there's a percepti-ble shift to alliteration ("Lost, left, loaned"). In fact, the sound echoes among words in this new stanza become more concentrated (the *r* and *o* sounds that bounce off each other starting with *objects* and continu-ing with *forgotten, corsages, dropped, prom, worse, forsaken* and the vowel rhyme of the long *e* sound in *creatures, beaten,* and *street*). There is also an accumulation of words beginning with *l* that occupy final word position in this part of the poem: *left, litany, life,* and *longing.* And there's the off-rhyme, or vowel rhyme (long *a* sound), of *blame* and *explain* in the final line. All in all, there's a quiet but real change in how language sounds and is used in lines 9 through 24.

Suppose our poet rereads the poem and recognizes this shift. There seem to me to be three possible ways the poet could respond. One would be to ignore or deny the shift. Not a good choice for a poet wanting to improve his or her poem. A second choice would be to commit to the opening contract of lines 1 through 7. To do this, our poet might return to the opening and reconnect with the original tone and language use (and also perhaps bring the "you" back into the poem; it has disappeared in the later lines). The poet could return to the beginning, follow along to where the poem went off the track, and try to extend the initial contract further down the page. As a third option, the poet could think of the break at line 7 as a sign that a *new* subject and a *new* contract are announcing themselves and want the poem to take a new direction. In other words, the poet could see the break as an opportunity.

How would the poet respond to this new opportunity? One approach would be to start with the new contract (the new voice) and see where it leads; in other words, treat the break not as a rupture or failure, but as the possible beginning of a new and different poem. And then experiment with beginning the poem there:

I thought of all
The objects
Lost, left, loaned
And forgotten—
Corsages dropped
After the prom.
Or worse: creatures
Forsaken—

Dogs beaten and left
In the street,
Bagged kittens tossed
In a river—litany
Of misery, of life
Gone wrong
And the longing
For someone
To blame or explain.

Is this a poem? Does it need more? Does it need, for example, some other thing after the corsage line and before the creatures—some other inanimate object that's connected indirectly to human situations of caring or sociability and yet is discarded like the prom corsage? Come to think of it, *discarded* would be a word that might fit into the new poem—it echoes sounds in *corsage*. Maybe a line could be "Corsages discarded after the prom" or "Corsages dropped after the prom," and we could add something new like "Letters read and then discarded." So our poet might have this to work with:

I thought of all
The objects
Lost, left, loaned
And forgotten—
Corsages dropped
In the wastebasket
After the prom,
Letters read
And then discarded.

Or worse: creatures
Forsaken—dogs
Beaten and left
In the street,

Bagged kittens
Tossed in rivers—
Litany of misery,
Of life gone awry,
Gone wrong.

And always the longing
For someone
To blame or explain.

Who knows? You can see I've fiddled around even more with this new version, adding a few repetitions and new words, changing line breaks (to place verbs at some line beginnings in order to give them a bit more emphasis). But there's a sense (to me at least) that this second half wants to go to a different place and use language that's different from that of the original eight lines that came before it in the first draft. The sound of these later lines is more lilting, and the references to things in the world is more various (the original opening seemed confined to naming things inside a house). And the focus has shifted as well, of course. The "you" to whom the original poem was addressed is no longer part of it at all; nor does the old title, "My Last Poem," seem related to this new direction. If the poet kept on with this, he or she would probably have to come up with a new title that makes more sense in relation to the lines of the poem.

REVISING AND REWRITING POEMS

In discussing implications in shifts in the contract of a poem, we've backed into a big topic that I might as well mention now: revision. It's the general wisdom of poets that poems come into completion as much through rewriting as through writing. Poems can and usually do get better through revision. That's a simple fact.

A simple fact, but nevertheless a complicated topic, and one that can be tangled up in real confusion and anxiety for a poet starting out. It certainly was for me when I was a beginning poet. I say "beginning poet," but I had been writing poetry for five years with real dedication and excitement (though not under the guidance of any mentor) before I was able to even begin to learn to revise my poems. Back then, I didn't have a clue as to how to make changes in the poems I was trying to write. Back then, if I felt a poem I had written didn't work, or if someone I showed it to had the slightest objection or question about any part of it, I'd simply abandon the effort and go on to the next poem, hoping it would somehow turn out better. I didn't enjoy giving up on my poems, but I felt oddly powerless to change them; confused about how to do it, and overwhelmed with anxiety and frustration. To put it mildly, I wasn't relaxed and flexible. If people had told me the poet's wisdom about revision—that poems are not written, they are rewritten—I wouldn't have believed them or understood the point of the remark. But there it is: the poem that can't be improved and made more effective by some changes is a very, very rare beast.

But how to revise? How to change something you've written? Before I begin, let me repeat a basic belief I have about starting out as a poet. It's more important to give yourself permission to put words down on a page than it is to labor long and hard over making a poem "perfect" by fiddling with it endlessly. It's more important for a beginning poet to explore subject matter and different ways of using language than it is to complete any given poem. This isn't an absolute statement, only an emphasis. And having reiterated that emphasis, I'll try to mention a few things about revision.

The first thing I would say is that I was cured (slowly and painfully) of my inability to revise poems in the first workshops I took, but those workshops didn't take place until I was in graduate school in my twenties. Over the course of a lifetime, I've learned to enjoy revising, and now, fifty years on, I find revising almost as much fun as beginning a new poem. But I don't expect to cure any reader of reluctance or trepidation about revising by anything I say here. All I'll try to do is present a few scattershot observations in the hope that they might be useful.

■ ■ ■

One of the worst feelings for a poet is to sit and stare at a blank page. Perhaps the next worst thing is to try to have the poem "perfect" or "all figured out in your head" before you start to put words on the page (or laptop, or however you write). So give yourself permission to write, and to write too much or too crazy or too off the subject (turns out we don't always know what the "real" subject of our poem will be). Let the words and your own imagination lead you—just follow, writing as fast as you need to in order to keep up. Later, when the first flow or first several flows of words are over, then you can begin to revise. But the most important thing is to trust the words on the page and not judge them or be self-conscious about them.

One of the smartest pieces of advice for a writer I ever heard was D. H. Lawrence's comment to "trust the tale, not the teller." What that means for a writer is simple: trust your own words more than you trust your conscious intentions for your words. Trust that the flow of language out of your imagination has its *own* intentions and purposes and its *own* idea of what the poem is about. We poets need to trust that some part of our minds is connected to language in a way that's more mysterious and vivid (and honest, perhaps) than we are consciously aware of. Thus, poets will sometimes say: "How can I know what I feel until I see what I write?" When, several pages back, looking at the earliest version of "My Last Poem," we noticed that the Contract shifted partway through, we were also noticing that the tale had decided to go off in a different direction from what the earliest lines suggested. Here are some of the structural questions that shift raised: Should the poem follow the new direction indicated by the language shift, or should it try to take control and go back to the original plot and language use of the opening lines? Should it return to the direction and tone of the opening lines (perhaps the speaker's original intention), or should it follow the tale that emerged later on as language use became more lilting and the poem's location shifted from inside a house to a larger world outside? I've heard that novelists often let their characters lead them deeper into their narrative plots—that the characters take on a life of their own. With poets, it's often language itself that seems to have a life of its own and leads the poet into the poem and down the page.

So the first thing is to give yourself permission and not judge what emerges. Then comes the shaping. For me, the best experience is to have too much (language, story, whatever) to begin with and then to cut back by crossing out stuff that the poem (and reader) doesn't really need, stuff that doesn't seem exciting or that seems "off the track" of the poem. Emily Dickinson wrote her great poems mostly in isolation from any response and any advice about revision. When she first sent some of her poems to a professional poet and editor and he wrote back with suggestions as to how she might improve them by removing some material, she answered in her next letter: "Thank you for the surgery." Surgery isn't fun or painless; nor is eliminating words or phrases or whole passages of a poem you wrote—lines you might be very fond of. When you decide to revise by crossing out a word or line in a draft, you're deciding that the wholeness of the poem is more important than any single word or line. This notion of sacrificing a part (word or phrase or image) for the sake of the whole (the poem) isn't always easy to accept when starting out in writing. But surgery is often essential for the health of a patient, and revision by surgery can strengthen a poem.

Let me give an excellent example of surgical advice for revising a poem. The first draft of T. S. Eliot's poem "The Waste Land" was almost twice as long as the published version. It came out in an anguished rush, and there's no doubt that it was essential that all those lines got written down. Shortly after finishing that first draft, he showed it to his friend and fellow poet Ezra Pound. Pound went through Eliot's draft, crossing out half the lines (and writing in the margins the reason he was crossing out this or that passage). The original draft began with a long, rambling narrative anecdote about a group of guys carousing, getting drunk, and then heading off to a bordello. It went on with one of these characters giving an account of their behavior for fifty-four lines. When Eliot showed this version of his poem to Pound, Pound drew a red X through the whole first section and told him to start with line 55. That new starting line is an excellent example of forceful and cryptic Saying (a way of using words that we'll discuss in Part Three). So forceful and intriguing was that line that it became one of the most famous opening lines of twentieth-century poetry:

April is the cruelest month . . .

In fact, without Pound's radical surgery throughout the poem, "The Waste Land" would never have been so important and compelling a poem as it turned out to be when it finally appeared, and for decades thereafter. Eliot's poem ended up being half as long and twice as strong because of Pound's deletions of what wasn't necessary or interesting. Pound had a gift for empathetically reading and responding to other poets' poems with helpful advice; he had a generosity of spirit that enabled him to put aside his own ego when commenting on other poets' poems and suggesting revisions. Here's what Eliot himself had to say on the subject:

[O]ne of the temptations against which I have to be on guard, is trying to re-write somebody's poem in the way I should have written it myself if I had wanted to write that poem. Pound never did that: he tried first to understand what one was attempting to do, and then tried to help one do it in one's own way.

The history of poetry confirms what the anecdote about Eliot's poem tells us: poets can help other poets rewrite and revise their poems. Can we get good advice about our poems from friends who love poetry and read a lot of it, but don't write themselves? It's a good question. It helps a great deal if your reader-critics have firsthand experience of the joys and difficulties of writing poetry. Those who are only readers of poetry might have the right amount of detachment to look at your poem from "outside" and compare it to other poems they've read; but unless they've also written poems, it's harder for them to read your poem from "inside" in the empathetic but astute way that Pound read Eliot. Even when you're getting critical advice and revision suggestions from a fellow poet, it helps a great deal if there are basic sympathy and shared values in the relationship. When there is no such connection, it can be frustrating and even potentially destructive to you as a poet.

William Blake had this to say on the subject in his "Proverbs of Hell": "The eagle never lost so much time as when he submitted to learn of the crow." Never mind if eagles are "better" than crows— Blake's point is that crows know about being crows, and that's all they can teach. An eagle needs to learn what eagles do (presumably, hanging out with other eagles might teach our eagle something). I had an older teacher once who meant well and wrote his own kind of poem and knew a fair amount about poetry, but he was completely different from me and had no real sympathy with my own (incoherent but genuine) ambitions for my poems. Nor did he care much for my generation in general (though he claimed to like me). His advice about my poems was based completely on what he liked and what he valued in poems. If I had taken every suggestion he made about my poems, they would have sounded just like his (and not like my own). Finally, he couldn't resist the temptation that Eliot spoke of: "trying to re-write somebody's poem in the way I should have written it myself." I don't doubt that my teacher meant well with his comments, but they weren't useful to me.

Lyric and Narrative Styles of Revision

Earlier I suggested that narrative poems are like the modeling method of sculpture, whereby the artist slaps handfuls of clay onto a skeletal structure and gradually builds the piece up into the desired shape; and that lyrics are similar to the carving method of sculpture, whereby the artist cuts away from the stone to find the smaller, essential form hidden within. These different aspirations suggest that there are different ways to revise lyric and narrative poems.

Narratively inclined poets whom I know often say "we need more here," pointing to some spot on the page. They want more information, more detail, more description. Narrative poets aren't afraid to *expand*: they learn by growing their work sometimes, by adding details and pushing actions or events further. Or by filling in some part of the poem that is too sparse, too unclear, or lacking in detail. *For the narrative poet, more is more.* That seems common sense, of course, but it's not that simple. *For the lyric poet, often* less *is more.* You'll recall that I mentioned that a lyric poet uses language and imagination to locate and evoke some central emotion or emotionally charged scene or situation. The lyric poet (as Robert Browning said) "digs where he stands." It doesn't have to be a wide hole, but a deep one could be interesting. But it's still a hole. (I guess a narrative poet could be seen to dig a trench extending across a landscape—as if creating a space in which to lay the pipe for narrative flow.) A lyric poet often revises by *challenging* every word in her poem. "Do I really need this adjective? This line? This phrase?" A narrative poet *cherishes* the words she has and often wonders if adding more wouldn't be fun or interesting. Look at the pleasure Elizabeth Bishop has in elaborately describing the fish in her poem "The Fish" (you can find it online). A narrative poet might seem to be fascinated by the outer world and enjoy using words and phrases to make it *vivid and real*. By contrast, a lyric poet seeks *intensity*, and one way of doing that is by concentrating her poem into the fewest possible words.

When I was a kid, there used to be a show on TV called *The Adventures of Superman*. (It was quite hokey; you can probably find episodes of it on YouTube.) In the episode I remember best, Superman came to the rescue of a tribe whose idol had been desecrated by thieves who stole the huge diamond that was set in the idol's forehead. The thieves fell into the volcano when they tried to escape the island (served them right!), but the diamond disappeared with them. Superman (in his disguise as Clark Kent) saved the day by squeezing a lump of coal in his fist with such force that it was transformed into a (huge) diamond (which he pretended to find in the shrubbery and quietly placed back where it belonged). Coal and diamonds—both are the same element: carbon; but a diamond is a lump of coal transformed into crystal. That's the lyric poet's dream: to put language under such pressure that it changes into a faceted, radiant, and mysterious thing—something that's small enough to hold in your hand and that flashes out dazzling rays when you hold it up to the light at different angles. A narrative poet might enjoy the silly (though deeply ethnically condescending) tale of the thieves and the volcano—enjoy it to the point of drawing it out, elaborating its details and actions; but a lyric poet lives for that single moment when language under pressure turns from coal to diamond.

Back to practical advice: if your poem is headed toward the narrative end of the lyric–narrative spectrum, might more details or actions make it more vivid or interesting as a story? If your poem is lyrically inclined, is there any word or phrase you could remove to make it stronger? Twenty-five hundred years ago, the Greek philosopher Aristotle noted that if you remove something from a poem and no one notices that anything is missing, then it was never a part of the whole in the first place, never an essential element in the artistic unity of the poem. That's the way lyric poets think. The elimination of what you don't need. If the reader doesn't miss it, it didn't belong. I love the fact that Aristotle figured that out and stated it thousands of years ago and yet it's still valid and useful to poets today. Of course, there are poets (and poems) that thrive on excess (I think of Allen Ginsberg's Beat anthem "Howl")—poets who need space and detail and excess to make it work. But mostly, writers go overboard, saying more than they need to say.

Narrative Extends, Lyric Surrounds

What is the danger with lyric revision by surgery? You'll need to "surround" your whole poem in the earliest drafts, because you'll end up with less material if you choose to revise by the cutting-out method. However, such surgery creates concentration and dramatic focus. William Butler Yeats, the great Irish poet, had a lyric strategy that he used in revising: if he had two or three metaphors in his early draft, he deliberately crossed out all except one. The effect was to draw further attention to the one he kept—to focus the drama on that single metaphor rather than disperse it over several imaginings. Of course, that one metaphor had best be a good one—and probably should come near the end of the poem, for maximum dramatic impact.

Where Poems Begin and End

Where poems begin and end is a fascinating topic to poets. Often, in early drafts of a poem it can be as if the poet is talking his or her way into the topic, warming up to the theme or even discovering it in the first several lines. But when the poet steps back and looks at the poem from "outside," he may realize that a reader doesn't necessarily need that warming up—a reader will probably be happiest jumping into the poem once it's ready to take off. It's hard to talk about this warming up abstractly, but there's a practical trick to discover if your opening lines are simply a warming up or if they're essential to the poem. Ask yourself this: "If I cover up the first line or several lines, is there a more interesting or exciting place where the reader could jump in and be carried along by the current of the poem?" Needless to say, the warming up in Eliot's first version of his poem was huge (fifty-four lines!); but often in shorter poems the "real" beginning can be found hidden a few lines down the page.

With endings of poems, it's even more intriguing. Endings and beginnings are the two most important parts of a poem (though, since it's poetry, all lines matter). If every line in a poem matters, then the last line matters twice as much. Sometimes as poets we think it's smart to save our best for last, and we're right. Endings of poems are crucial. I often think of them this way: it's as if the last line of every poem were written entirely in **bold type**.

But the obvious importance of endings can make me self-conscious about where to stop my poem. I even have a term for it: anxiety of ending. How do I know when and where to stop? What's the most dramatically effective, structurally effective place to stop? I often worry that as I approach what I sense is the final part of my poem, I can't tell whether I've made the poem's meaning clear (even to myself)—I worry that the reader won't "get it." As a result, I'm often tempted to write too much—as if I feel I need to spell out my meaning to the reader, or try to sum up the poem's whole theme, its big truth, in the last lines. Of course, it's easy to get abstract and pompous in this end-of-poem situation; it's easy to yield to the temptation to write on *past the (dramatically effective) true end* in a desperate effort to make sure I've communicated.

The good news is that there's an easy way to revise the endings of poems. The first step is to just write it and see what you choose to end with, where you choose to stop. Then ask yourself this question: Is this the best and most dramatically effective place to end? The way to answer that question is equally easy. Cover up the last line or last several lines of your poem. What you're trying to determine is this: How would it sound if it ended earlier? Would it be too abrupt or cryptic? Or would it have more impact and still be understandable to the reader? Often, we poets go on too long at the end, as if we don't trust the reader to intuit the significance of a climactic gesture or image and, instead, feel we need to "translate" our poem into abstract statements or deep-sounding claims. Perhaps we imagine this kind of language will impress the reader with our wisdom or intelligence. Not a good idea—most readers would rather reach for a meaning than be condescended to by the poet.

While we're on the subject of errors that young poets are prone to make about endings, here's another one. When starting out as poets, we often save our best line for last, or else we simply recognize that our last line is a kind of compressed essence of our poem's meaning. This may or may not be correct, but it can cause us to make a beginner's error (I did this when I began): using our last line as the title of our poem. Let's say we wrote a poem that concluded with the line "beauty is a ragged daffodil." That may not be a great ending (I'm certainly skeptical), but we can make it even worse with the "bright idea" of using the line as our title. "Beauty Is a Ragged Daffodil," we announce at the top of the page. What's wrong with this impulse? After all, we think it's a neat line, the best in our poem—that's why we have it as the final, climactic line. Here's what's wrong with the idea: it overlooks the essential fact that a poem is a *dramatic structure*, or it is *language structured for dramatic impact*. One basic rule of drama is this: don't give away your ending, or it won't have impact on the audience. If readers of our hypothetical poem get to the end and see "beauty is a ragged daffodil," it's not new and surprising—it falls with a thud on their ear and their mind. No surprise; no startle. Assigning the title "Beauty Is a Ragged Daffodil" is an easy mistake to make (especially since titling poems isn't easy for most of us), but it's an even easier error to correct through the crossing-out method.

Here are a few more notes about revision.

Not Putting It All in One Poem

Don't try to say "everything" (about anything important) in one poem. Feel free to try to say everything on a topic or theme or person in the first draft, but then consider narrowing it for purposes of dramatic focus. Often, lyric poems are structured around dramatized relationships between a speaker and some other person or thing. By dramatizing that relationship in a certain time and place, the poem creates meaning. Thus, we have Plath dramatizing her relationship to her father in "Daddy," and Roethke dramatizing a moment in his life in relation to his father and mother in "My Papa's Waltz." But important relationships are multiple and complex, and they change over time. So when you write about a significant relationship, don't try to cram all your feelings and attitudes into a single poem. Consider your relationship with your parents—how can you reduce such a complex thing to a single poem? "My mother and me," summed up in twenty lines—not likely. "Me and my dad," summed up in twelve lines—don't count on it. Once you realize you can (and often should) write about such relationships, it's tempting to jump to a wrong conclusion: that you can get the story down on the page once and for all and be done with it.

But that isn't realistic about poetry or about people. Nor should we as poets be upset by this. Why shouldn't we feel lucky that there are ten (or thirty) poems we can (or need to) write about our mother? Why not dramatize in one poem how irritating she is, or used to be; and then in another poem, write about the time when she said or did something that made us love her totally (where, when, what—the situation; the details; the metaphor; the action and reaction of story that reveals aspects of both you and your mother). Seen from this perspective, even the quietest of relationships is full of moments and incidents that we can transform into poems—be they praise or lament, elegy or rant.

Pronouns and Intimacy and Revision

There's an easy method to experience the way in which lyric intimacy differs from narrative distance. It can also be an interesting part of your revision process with some poems. Simply take a poem of yours that uses *he* or *she* (or even *one*) as the main character, and try turning that third-person pronoun into an *I* throughout the poem. Shifting from the third-person (narrative) pronoun to the first-person (lyric) pronoun will quite probably give you a shock of intimacy. The first time you do this you may feel an existential shiver, either as a thrill or a threat. But beyond that initial thrill or threat, see if the sudden closeness makes the poem more urgent.

You can try the same thing in reverse. Take a lyric *I* poem, and substitute *he* or *she* for the first-person pronoun throughout—suddenly you'll get a different perspective on your poem, and perhaps even on the subject matter. This narrative distance may make it easier to work with the material (sometimes the *I* poem is too close to the subject matter, too "dangerous" or anxiety provoking for the poet to craft comfortably). In the course of writing and rewriting a poem, I often find myself changing pronouns back and forth, searching for the right distance. Sometimes the distance of third person makes me feel safe enough to add (or remember) more details or see the dramatic situation and actions more clearly, and I end up expanding the poem a bit. Sometimes when switching to the intimate *I*, I can see or feel that certain details or events are extraneous and dilute the lyric (emotional) urgency of the poem. However it finally turns out, it's always an interesting experiment and easily done.

A Final Remark on Revision, Workshops, and You

It is a basic premise of this book that the writing and reading of poems constitute an important and pleasurable creative possibility for individuals in our culture. Anyone can write a poem and, given a willingness to work at it, can learn more about this expressive art that is at once both complex and simple—learn enough to make its challenges and gratifications a part of their ongoing lives. The teaching of poetry-writing in America has become institutionalized over the course of the twentieth century into something we call a workshop. In most workshops, a group of students are guided by an older teacher/poet mentor who provides lessons on craft topics, example poems, and writing assignments that emphasize craft issues while also encouraging the students' overall impulse to write.

Usually, a central aspect of such courses is a group critique of student poems. The teacher guides and directs these discussions to varying degrees. In a sense, when you submit a poem to such a workshop discussion, you're turning it over to the group so that others can collectively respond to your work and suggest revisions in order to improve it—to gain advice as to how it can communicate or express your intentions more effectively. Submitting a poem to a group critique can be a very complicated experience. You're inherently vulnerable to the varied responses you receive, and that's not always fun. I believe workshops can and should help poets grow. Ezra Pound's helpful revisions to Eliot's "The Waste Land" should be ample proof that poets can help their contemporaries to improve their work.

Having said that, though, let me add an overall warning about some limitations of the workshop process. Lyric poetry is an individual art form, and it has various ambitions and pleasures. The fact that it's so rich and various (as rich and various as individual personalities?) is one of the qualities that makes it so valuable to us. When we submit a poem to a workshop critique, we turn it over to the social world of other people's opinions, tastes, knowledge, and needs. So remember this: you ultimately need to keep possession of your own poem. If you get too many responses to it too early in the process of creation, you risk losing connection to it. You may be overwhelmed by so many (well-meaning) responses that you stop caring about your poem and see it as a "thing" outside you, alienated from your original impulse and connection to it.

Writing poems calls for a fine balance: you want enough detachment in rewriting that you have the freedom to be honest with yourself and also the freedom to change things in the poem that don't seem to work. In a workshop situation, you want enough detachment to be able to listen to a well-meaning and empathetic reader who points out places where your poem isn't working in the way you hoped. But you don't want to become so detached from the poem that you lose all connection to it. I've frequently noticed that the vulnerability we experience when our work is discussed aloud by others combines with the inevitably contradictory messages of a group response to leave us confused or even bruised. We're grateful for the attention our poem has received, but it may take us a while to reclaim the poem and feel that it is ours to write, rewrite, and bring to its fullest and most effective form. The more we can learn on our own about revising our poems, the more confident we can be when they're critiqued by others.

One trick, of course, is to write it and work on it as long as it engages you in a single session, then put it away for a short time (say, three days or a week) and then read it again with a fresh eye—as if you yourself were a reader of the poem, rather than its writer. It's then, for example, that questions of successful or inadequate orientation and location can leap out at you and be easily fixed. Perhaps you assumed that the reader knew who the *you* was in the poem, but now you see that you don't really make the identity of the *you* clear until line 7.

Finally, the more techniques of revision we can learn to use on our own, the more we will feel in charge of our own poem as it evolves toward its fullest and most forceful or persuasive form.

Part Three

WORDS COMING
ALIVE IN POEMS

CHAPTER SEVEN

Words Coming Alive in Poems

Words, language—that's what poems are made of. It's so obvious a fact that we tend to pass over it quickly, which is a very bad idea in relation to poetry. In our everyday lives, we tend to think that language is pretty transparent and user-friendly—we don't think much about it; we just speak it. We say we read a newspaper or an article on Wikipedia, but often what we're really doing is skimming it, zipping across the surface of meaning rather than deeply registering language and phrases. And that's fine for day-to-day purposes, up to and including schoolwork or research. But language in poetry calls for our full attention. Faced with the obviously complex use of language in poetry, it's easy to become confused and even intimidated.

The raw material of poetry is words, is language. In order to take in the implications of that fact, it might be good to step back from the topic a bit. Let's imagine for a moment that we wanted to be a painter or a sculptor. We'd learn pretty early on that paintings have traditionally been made out of oil paint applied to canvas or wood panels with brushes or other tools; that the raw material of sculpting is often clay or some kind of rock and tools to work with it. Oil paint, clay, stone—these are the materials of those arts (at least in their traditional terms in the West). It's hard to imagine a painter who doesn't have a gut pleasure in fooling around with paint, or a sculptor who doesn't experience pleasure feeling clay beneath her hands or chiseling away at the surface of stone. Poets, too, are deeply connected to the *materiality* of language—they love to give their tongues over to the sounds that words make. And I'd advise young poets, shy though they often are, to permit themselves to sound aloud the poems they love and the poems they're trying to write. Give yourself over to that pleasure of making sounds and rhythms, and know that it is inseparable from poetry's power to matter to us.

FOUR CATEGORIES OF LANGUAGE USE IN POETRY

But there's more than just the pleasure of sound-making, because language is more complex a phenomenon than paint or stone (though I mean no disrespect to painters or sculptors). Let me return to the analogy with a young artist working with pigment. When it comes to painting, there's color (the hues the artist places on the canvas) and there's the theory of color. Without understanding color theory, it wouldn't be possible for a painter to mix all her colors out of a basic few. When I say "color theory," I don't mean anything fancy. In fact, the color theory I'm thinking of is so basic that most of us learned it in third grade art class, where the teacher informed us that out of the three primary colors—red, blue, and yellow—we could make three complementary colors (red + blue = purple; blue + yellow = green; yellow + red = orange), and from there on we could further mix and blend to create a huge number of other colors. As I say, this is so basic that it's almost laughable, and it may seem even highfalutin to call it a theory. But words are as basic a material to a poet as colored pigment is to a painter. Yet we're never taught a simple, basic "theory of language" that we can use as poets or readers of poetry. So I'd like to propose one—a very basic "theory of language use in poems" that isn't intended to impress or persuade linguists or academics, but one

that I hope will serve to guide poets toward a better and more grat-
ifying sense of the wonder they experience when reading poems or
writing them.

For the purposes of this book, I want to set up four categories of
language use in poetry: Naming, Singing, Saying, and Imagining. If
we come to understand what these four kinds of language use sound
and look like and what they can do in a poem, then we'll have gone a
long way toward understanding how poems can so often delight and
disturb us in urgent ways. Let me offer brief explanations of each of
these terms before considering them at greater length.

Naming refers to the fact that we use specific, agreed-upon words
to refer to things in the world. In English, we say "tree" when we want
people to direct their attention (either their eyes or their mental atten-
tion) to a certain kind of vegetation. We might be standing with some-
one on a street and say, "Look at the way the wind is thrashing the
branches of that tree." The word *tree* directs our listener's (or reader's)
attention toward that object. If you say, standing on the same street,
"Look at the way the wind is thrashing the branches of that penguin,"
your listener would probably not know where to look, although I'm
guessing he would look mostly at your face and possibly step back away
from you a little bit until he could figure out whether your odd word
choice indicated something odd about you that he hadn't suspected
before. We live in a world full of material objects, and we use words
to name them and thereby orient ourselves among them. Likewise,
we use language in a naming way to describe actions; for example,
the movement of walking is different when it's named as "stumbling"
rather than "striding." We also have a more limited number of experi-
ences that are mental and emotional rather than physical, but that we
also have names for and use in a naming way: "grief" or "regret" or
"joy" or "loneliness" and so on.

Singing refers to the fact that words are sounds we make. Not all
sounds we make are words, but every word can be a sound, can be
pronounced aloud. When words are put together, they create a series
of sounds—and when spoken aloud, a rhythm. This aspect of language

in poetry is what Samuel Taylor Coleridge called "musical delight." He said that a poet had to be born with it, had to experience it as a primary pleasure. Not only must the poet experience this pleasure, but she or he must also have the power to make others experience it: "the sense of musical delight, *with the power of producing it*" (emphasis added).

We don't always say words aloud. Many people read poems silently to themselves, although they must be making those sounds inside their brains as they read them. But of course, when we sound words out loud, we can become aware of their qualities as sounds—harsh or soft or capable of making patterns such as rhyme or alliteration. Singing has to do with a poet's awareness of the sounds (and silences) involved in language use and the use of this sound aspect for expressive purposes. Where the Naming aspect of language clearly makes communication between people possible, the Singing aspect has a lot to do with emotional expressiveness and the pleasure we take in sounds and phrases. When I say "Singing," I don't actually mean what a person does with melody in a song—it's not usually that stylized a use of voice—but it's a metaphor for language that is alive to the pleasures and possibilities of sounds and sound patterns.

Saying refers to the way we use language to make statements and claims about ideas and concepts. Language in a Saying mode can have enormous authority because it gives a sense of real intelligence, conviction, and insight. When someone says something like "Friendship is at the heart of a good marriage," the listener does her best to bring together those two notions (friendship and good marriage) and test them against her own experience, but she's also persuaded by the tone of authority and confidence with which those words have been put together. A part of us hungers for and takes pleasure in assertions about experience and human nature that are expressed as ideas or insights. "A coward dies a thousand deaths; a brave man dies only once"—that's emphatic and worth considering as an idea. (There's also a bit of Imagining in that statement, since those "thousand deaths" of the coward are probably the *imagined* deaths the alleged coward undergoes as compared to the brave person who doesn't waste time imagining what awful thing might happen to him, but simply and bravely acts.) Saying is also complicated by the fact that even though we're impressed by the authority and confidence of Saying language, we sometimes resist the fact that it calls for us to accept the sayer's strong opinion. Many of us would rather be the source of Saying language than the person who's listening to it and yielding to its force.

Imagining refers to the very strange ability that humans have to compare one thing to another thing. I'm referring to metaphors and similes—to figurative language in general. People use metaphors and similes all the time, and we seem to derive pleasure from this kind of language use. "That guy is a trainwreck," I overheard someone say just a moment ago. Even dead metaphors like the one I just quoted have the power to enliven our daily conversations—how much more exciting it is to encounter the new and unexpected comparisons that poets specialize in.

Naming, Singing, Saying, and Imagining—these are things people do with words, with language. Poets are fascinated by what words can do when arranged into certain patterns and organized for certain purposes. Are we experts or specialists in language use? I don't know. Not in the way that I think that advertising writers or political speech writers are. We aren't necessarily specialists in manipulating our readers with different kinds of language. Or, if manipulation is a temptation for anyone who uses language a lot, then I would say that we as poets are partly protected by our sheer love of words. If manipulators of language (and people) use words and phrases to put their listeners under a spell, then poets are people who are themselves under the spell of language. We poets are the first to be spellbound by the magic of language, and if we're lucky, we pass along that magic to our readers in the form of poems.

Naming, Singing, Saying, Imagining. These four kinds of language use are layered or mixed into poems in varying proportions depending on the poet and the poem, so that what results is the rich complexity of meaning and sound that we recognize as a poem. Different poets emphasize one or another of these powers—they give their loyalty to, or feel excitement about, one or two qualities of language more than the others, perhaps. But no good poet is unaware of all four of these qualities, and many of us use them all in varying proportions in order to make our poems strong. These qualities are not totally separate things, and the terms I'm giving for them are my own, though I hope they're simple enough to be understandable and useful to someone eager to make words into poems. My presenting these four qualities as distinct aspects of language is a calculated misrepresentation in pursuit of a clearer sense of the wonder of language in poetry. In fact, these qualities can be roughly distinguished from one another; yet in actual language use they aren't distinct, but mingle and braid and overlap in the rich flow of speech or writing.

I want to make one final thing clear before I begin discussing these four powers of lyric language. They aren't part of a formula for a sure-fire poem. I'm not saying there's a recipe for poetry that goes like this: "add one passage of Saying to three lines of Naming and top off with one dollop of Imagining; season with Singing and simmer for three-quarters of an hour in a half-baked brain." Nor do I think any poet has ever constructed a good poem according to any formula or recipe like that. Here's my point: I think these four qualities account for some of the marvelous things language does in poems, generating the concentrated power and liveliness that are at the heart of it. If you recognize and respond to the presence of these forces in poems you love, then that recognition will make it easier for you to release similar forces in your own poems. I'm speaking here about intuition and (imitative) love, not analysis. If you can use these qualities analytically to study a poem or write an essay about one, and if they help you to gain insights into the ways the poem works—the way energy manifests and moves through a poem—that's wonderful. But if these four qualities give you insight into poems you love and inspire you to experiment with making similar language—that's even better.

NAMING AND SINGING: A BASIC DUALITY OF WORDS

I've just claimed that words are powerful in a fourfold way in lyric, but I want to approach this fourfold nature by first discussing a primary duality of words that concerns all poetry: Naming and Singing. Most words designate something—some object or action in the world as we know it. Not all words designate or name, but it's an essential function of language. Likewise, every pronounced word is a sound, a noise we can make. The word *bridge* is a sound in English, but it also designates an architectural structure—it's not just a sound. The word *bridge* on a road sign that says "Warning: Bridge is out" indicates clearly the absence in the world of the thing it names, and a reader of that sign is alerted to a real danger.

Words are often used to point toward things (Naming); words are also sounds (Singing). This is a basic duality of language. It's sometimes interesting to ask young poets this: If you had to choose, would you choose accurate language (the language of precise naming) or pleasurable and emotionally evocative language? Would you rather write lines that are precise in their naming, or would you rather create lines that are a rich unfolding of sounds and rhythms? Of course, we probably want both in our poetry (though not all poets do), but you can see that the inclination or preference is a real one. A poet could decide to value Singing above Naming, or Naming above Singing—and the poems that result from this preference would be different and distinct.

CHAPTER EIGHT

Naming

NAMING AND THE PARTS OF SPEECH

Naming has to do first of all with nouns and secondarily with verbs. Using only nouns and verbs, we can begin to create a world out of words and then set it in motion, start it moving as a story: "The deer crossed the field . . ."; "The car skidded off the road . . ."; "The boy loved the girl. . . ." This is a world that our readers can enter. The right nouns and verbs give us vividness and precision—they can both ground us in the world we live in and also bring that world alive inside our reader's brain, make it appear before the "mind's eye" (William Butler Yeats's term for the imagination).

If I say "table," the chances are that most listeners and readers would see a similar object in response to that naming. It would probably have four legs and a flat top. Some might "see" a table made of wood, others one made of plastic, metal, or stone. Some might see something quite grand—on which a banquet is served; others might see something smaller and more modest—where a lamp or a laptop rests, or where people eat in a kitchen. If, however, I say "beauty," it's difficult if not impossible to predict with any certainty what people would "see" in response to that word. They might see hugely various things: a person, a place, a creature, an object in nature or in a museum—or they might see nothing at all. We may no longer (did we ever?) agree on what "beauty" looks like, what objects or things or creatures it conjures up to the mind's eye. Beauty is an abstract concept, an idea.

Naming in language suggests that while it may no longer be possible to assume that we all have shared values that can be expressed in conceptual language, we *do* share a world of objects. Especially when we're young poets, we're tempted to use abstract nouns like *beauty* because we sense that they're value words we may wish to associate with our poem or ourselves. We feel that if we can use them in our poems, then our poems might sound (or be) more important, more grand, more meaningful. It's an important humility in poetry-writing to start with the world of our own sensory experience and the power of simple Naming.

■ ■ ■

Nouns connect us to the world through Naming, and that connection is a source of wonder and delight. You can see it in its naïve glory and glee in the face of a two-year-old who's just learning language and shouts "doggie! doggie!" whenever that creature enters the room.

■ ■ ■

The variety of images brought before the mind's eye by the naming of things is rich and varied. Think how each of the following nouns summons a different bird image: *sparrow, egret, pigeon, chickadee, robin, eagle, swan, swallow, parakeet, penguin, finch.*

Or consider the accuracy of verbs. Think how each of the following verbs names a different way a person might move down a sidewalk: *amble, stride, stumble, race, stroll, run, sashay, hobble.*

How much precise information the right nouns and verbs convey!

Oddly enough, adjectives are less useful to poets, less important to poetry than they are to prose. Maybe this has to do with poetry's desire to compress and focus the reader's attention in order to get to the heart of something right away. After all, we usually don't have twenty pages in which to create a world in poems; we have to move quickly and efficiently, trying to capture the essence of that world. But it isn't only that nouns and verbs are more efficient than adjectives; there's also the issue of a lazy writer bullying his or her readers with adjectives. When someone says "the amazing dog" or "the beautiful dog" in writing, the language is telling the reader rather than showing. And there's another issue with the use (or misuse) of adjectives. We've been taught since grade school that to enlarge our vocabulary is to show that we're smart; that as we proceed in our education, we can accumulate all sorts of elaborate adjectives (e.g., *munificent, audacious, intriguing, scabrous*) that might turn up on vocabulary quizzes or statewide tests. We're also told that this large vocabulary of adjectives will make our writing richer and more various—and for all I know, that might be true about writing prose. But for poets, the main goal is often to focus on the heart of a scene or situation with precise nouns and verbs; elaborate and showy adjectives can clutter our lines and distract our readers.

The one big exception to this advice concerns color adjectives. For some reason, color words have a vividness that even poets respect. Almost inexplicably, the phrase "the blue truck" provides a more vivid image than "the truck." Maybe the reason for this is obvious, maybe not—but many poets appreciate what color adjectives can accomplish.

It can be hard to realize that Naming and describing are different. Naming seldom involves description, which can be extremely important in prose writing but can be clumsy and awkward in poetry. Naming is succinct. Using precise and accurate Naming, lyric poets hope that they can conjure up not only the thing they're naming, but also its mystery and wonder.

■ ■ ■

NAMING TO ORIENT IN A LANDSCAPE

Naming is important when it concerns the things and characters in your poem, but there's also a corollary that involves the poem's setting. When writing a poem that inhabits a *landscape* of some kind (urban, suburban, rural, wilderness, indoors, a yard in a town), you should orient your reader or characters in that landscape and keep track of where they are in relation to it. You, as the poet, may know what your character is doing at any given moment, but the *reader* will only know if you use orienting words, which are often simple nouns (*stairs, door, tree, street, path*), to locate a character precisely and to keep track of that character as she or he acts or reacts in that setting. Think again of the title and opening line of Yeats's poem "Among School Children": "I walk through the long schoolroom, questioning"; here he not only names "school children" and "long schoolroom" but also gives us "walk through" and "questioning," both of which orient us in that world and name it more clearly.

■ ■ ■

When William Carlos Williams says there should be "no ideas but in things," he represents a movement away from abstraction in poetry in English that happened in the early years of the twentieth century. Ezra Pound pointed the way when he urged young poets to "go in fear of abstractions."

Naming worked well for Williams for a number of reasons—he wished to set his poetry solidly in America and to write in American speech rhythms. (Both Pound and T. S. Eliot had left America for good as young poets, and even Robert Frost went to live in England for three years.) To Williams, it was an ethical as well as an aesthetic issue. Working as a pediatrician in suburban New Jersey, he incorporated into his poems the speech rhythms of his patients and the landscapes and objects he encountered. (That famous "red wheel / barrow //

glazed with rain / water // beside the white / chickens" wasn't on a farm, but in a back alley in the city of Paterson that Williams drove down one afternoon on his way to see a patient.) Williams was only following Walt Whitman, who walked the streets of New York with joy and tried to name as much of what he saw as he could enliven in his poems. The premise behind such Naming is that we share a world of objects, and this sharing can be the basis of connection between poet and reader or listener. The rapper Jay-Z proposes the same thing as Whitman and Williams when he writes in his memoir, *Decoded*:

> New York has a thousand universes in it that don't always connect but we do all walk the same streets, hear the same sirens, ride the same subways, see the same headlines in the *Post*, read the same writings on the walls. That shared landscape gets inside of all of us and, in some small way, unites us, makes us think we know each other even when we don't. (pg. 92)

The power of Naming is based on what Jay-Z calls a "shared landscape," even though he is right to point out that the uniting takes place "in some small way" and that the sense of knowing each other is sometimes an illusion.

■ ■ ■

NAMING AND THE FIVE SENSES

To cherish the language force of Naming is to stay connected to the vividness and reality of our own five senses, which are the first and most essential sources of our knowledge and understanding. Let me give a crude example. If we were to hear a spiritual authority (preacher, priest, imam, or rabbi) give a sermon about "the necessity of acting with love" on one day, and the next day we saw that person walking down a sidewalk and pausing to kick a cat, would we place our faith in the noble words or in what our own eyes had seen? Naming helps us to stay in close contact with the world of our senses, and to value that world.

■ ■ ■

Walt Whitman, Abstraction, and the Reality of the Senses

The human mind has the ability to think abstractly and to use language abstractly. Probably the most abstract use of written symbols that humans use is mathematics. Much of the world we live in uses the language of mathematics: computers, obviously; and mathematics is at work when we try to balance a checkbook or handle a credit card. Isaac Newton, the great seventeenth-century scientist whose discoveries profoundly affected science and technology, once said: "We have discovered the language that Nature speaks: it is mathematics." Newton came to understand the world through experiments, scientific formulas, and charts expressed in the language of mathematics; but many of us still speak a different language, the language of our five senses.

Here's a poem by Whitman that acknowledges the world of science and abstract diagrams, but that also is a critique and satire of it. He knows the astronomer is respected ("much applause"), but he also knows that he's bored by these abstractions ("How soon unaccountable I became tired and sick") and needs to return to the reality of his senses—the simple act of gazing at the stars:

When I Heard the Learn'd Astronomer

When I heard the learn'd astronomer,
When the proofs, the figures, were ranged in columns before me,
When I was shown the charts and diagrams, to add, divide, and
    measure them,
When I sitting heard the astronomer where he lectured with much
    applause in the lecture-room,
How soon unaccountable I became tired and sick,
Till rising and gliding out I wander'd off by myself,

In the mystical moist night-air, and from time to time,
Look'd up in perfect silence at the stars.

Walt Whitman (1865)

Even as I write this primer, I worry about becoming the boring astronomer. I've taught and lectured for most of my life, and I use abstractions to teach (think of the concepts of "order and disorder"), yet I believe that the heart of poetry is somehow the effort to share human experiences and affirm their value—to speak of the world in a way that communicates (names) something as basic as "Look'd up in perfect silence at the stars." As if to show us that adjectives' careful and sparing use can have a strong impact in a poem that mostly comprises nouns and verbs, we can note that *mystical* and *perfect* are essential to the impact of Whitman's brief poem.

■ ■ ■

No poet was greater at naming things in the shareable world than Whitman. We could say that his skill at Naming came out of his training and work as a newspaper reporter and editor, jobs that required a focus on facts and details. A journalist must be observant, precise, and economical with language; must quickly translate the scene before his eyes into words that will go on a (newspaper) page. Naming is the heart of it. But is to name to celebrate? It's an interesting question. Certainly, Naming and celebration of self and world and others was the heart of Whitman's great moral vision as realized in *Leaves of Grass*. True to his belief that poetry should be based in both pride (in self) and empathy (identification with others and with not-self), Whitman named in order to celebrate. In what was a scandalous breach of good taste for his time, Whitman claims very early on in his "Song of Myself" that he prefers being naked in the open air, where he can admire and celebrate his own physical body and its sensations:

Houses and rooms are full of perfumes, the shelves are crowded with
perfumes,

I breathe the fragrance myself and know it and like it,
The distillation would intoxicate me also, but I shall not let it.

The atmosphere is not a perfume, it has no taste of the distillation, it
    is odorless,
It is for my mouth forever, I am in love with it,
I will go to the bank by the wood and become undisguised
    and naked,
I am mad for it to be in contact with me.

The smoke of my own breath,
Echoes, ripples, buzz'd whispers, love-root, silk-thread, crotch
    and vine,
My respiration and inspiration, the beating of my heart, the passing
    of blood and air through my lungs,
The sniff of green leaves and dry leaves, and of the shore and dark-
    color'd sea-rocks, and of hay in the barn,
The sound of the belch'd words of my voice loos'd to the eddies of
    the wind,
A few light kisses, a few embraces, a reaching around of arms,
The play of shine and shade on the trees as the supple boughs wag,
The delight alone or in the rush of the streets, or along the fields and
    hill-sides,
The feeling of health, the full-noon trill, the song of me rising from
    bed and meeting the sun.

from "Song of Myself," section 2

Later he namingly celebrates others—creatures and people and anything that populates the world around him. According to Whitman's radical mystic vision of democracy, all genders, all races, all ethnicities, all occupations, all creatures and things should be named and celebrated; nothing was beneath his notice. Sometimes he extends his Naming into a brief scene or sketch—a vignette, really. Notice how the first three naming sketches in the following lines are a quick "tour" of three major human mysteries: birth, sex, death. After that, the poem's attention moves out into a busy, urban street and gets more random in its listing or Naming:

The little one sleeps in its cradle,
I lift the gauze and look a long time, and silently brush away flies
    with my hand.   *[birth; my parenthesis]*

The youngster and the red-faced girl turn aside up the bushy hill,
I peeringly view them from the top.   *[sex]*

The suicide sprawls on the bloody floor of the bedroom,
I witness the corpse with its dabbled hair, I note where the pistol has
    fallen.   *[death]*

The blab of the pave, tires of carts, sluff of boot-soles, talk of the
    promenaders,
The heavy omnibus, the driver with his interrogating thumb, the
    clank of the shod horses on the granite floor,
The snow-sleighs, clinking, shouted jokes, pelts of snow-balls,
The hurrahs for popular favorites, the fury of roused mobs,
The flap of the curtained litter, a sick man inside borne to the
    hospital,
The meeting of enemies, the sudden oath, the blows and fall,
The excited crowd, the policeman with his star quickly working his
    passage to the center of the crowd,
The impassive stones that receive and return so many echoes,
What groans of over-fed or half-starved who fall sunstruck or in fits,
What exclamations of women taken suddenly who hurry home and
    give birth to babes,
What living and buried speech is always vibrating here, what howls
    restrain'd by decorum,
Arrests of criminals, slights, adulterous offers made, acceptances,
    rejections with convex lips,

I mind them or the show or resonance of them—I come and
    I depart.

from "Song of Myself," section 8

Read also this, the beginning of section 15 of "Song of Myself":

The pure contralto sings in the organ loft,
The carpenter dresses his plank, the tongue of his foreplane whistles
    its wild ascending lisp,
The married and unmarried children ride home to their
    Thanksgiving dinner,
The pilot seizes the king-pin, he heaves down with a strong arm,
The mate stands braced in the whale-boat, lance and harpoon
    are ready,
The duck-shooter walks by silent and cautious stretches,
The deacons are ordain'd with crossed hands at the altar,
The spinning-girl retreats and advances to the hum of the big wheel,
The farmer stops by the bars as he walks on a First-day loaf and looks
    at the oats and rye,
The lunatic is carried at last to the asylum a confirm'd case,
(He will never sleep any more as he did in the cot in his mother's
    bed-room;)
The jour printer with gray head and gaunt jaws works at his case,
He turns his quid of tobacco while his eyes blur with the manuscript;
The malform'd limbs are tied to the surgeon's table,
What is removed drops horribly in a pail;
The quadroon girl is sold at the auction-stand, the drunkard nods by
    the bar-room stove,
The machinist rolls up his sleeves, the policeman travels his beat, the
    gate-keeper marks who pass,
The young fellow drives the express-wagon, (I love him, though I do
    not know him;)
The half-breed straps on his light boots to compete in the race, . . .

from "Song of Myself," section 15

It's as if the Naming that is so extensive in Whitman's long poem is the evidence that will support his larger, more philosophical claims about the perfection and beauty of the material world and those who dwell in it. These larger claims are made in the language of Saying, and I'll talk about them and how they sound later in this chapter.

■ ■ ■

Haiku as a Poetry of Sensation

The Japanese poetry form known as haiku adheres to the strictest principles of Naming. It is a poetry of sensation—it demands that the poet present in seventeen syllables some scene or object or action, but it is against the form's rules to editorialize or emotionalize in any way or to make use of any abstract nouns. Here are a couple by the seventeenth-century haiku master Bashō, in which I haven't attempted to keep the syllable count, but only the observational spirit, the clarity and alertness this kind of poem cherishes:

Summer's End

Fall starts now:
Sea and rice fields—
One, single green!

Suma Beach; Autumn

When each wave recedes:
Tiny shells revealed,
And shreds of beach clover
Mingled with them.

The fact that haiku are about accurate and alert observation does not imply that they aren't intended to evoke a complex emotional and intellectual response in the reader. Quite the contrary. But a haiku does so by strictly avoiding any abstractions or concept words and limiting itself to simply and precisely naming what the poet sees or hears or smells or tastes or touches. Again and again, haiku poets are urged to return to their senses and to gather knowledge directly from experience. "Learn about the pines from the pine," says Bashō (who was also a teacher of poets)—go and see and smell and listen and name.

■ ■ ■

Knowing and Naming in Poems

It's important that we as poets know the world we're talking about— the world of our poems and what's in them. This often means knowing about the world we live in. You don't need to know everything; but if it's a poem about fish, or streams, or basketball, or recreational drugs, or driving a car, or gardening, you should know the words that are appropriate to that experience or activity, and you should use them with accuracy and precision. It will go a long way toward making your poem believable, credible, persuasive.

■ ■ ■

"Learn about the city block from the city block." The American poet Galway Kinnell has a great early poem called "The Avenue Bearing the Initial of Christ into the New World," which is structured as an exuberant walk along Avenue C in the Lower East Side of New York City—an area famous for its history of absorbing various immigrant groups and ethnicities into its crowded streets and tenements. The poem wants to notice and celebrate and name everything that it can about the neighborhood. At one point in the poem, a woman opens her window to set two potted plants on the window ledge: "tic tic" the poem says, perfectly naming the sound that a soil-filled terracotta flowerpot makes when it's set down "terribly softly" on a stone windowsill.

■ ■ ■

TWO NAMING EXERCISES

Naming alone doesn't constitute a poem, but it situates you in a world and in a context in that world. And Naming has the power to bring something before your (and your reader's) imagination. Recall that when you did the "I Remember" exercise in Chapter 1, you turned word-less memory images into words that named what you remembered. Some of those "I remembers" stirred you up emotionally. If you were to reread your list (which is now a naming list), would it lead you back to those memories and even to those or other emotions? One aspect of the power of Naming in poems is the possibility that Naming leads to emotions—not just in the poet, but in a reader also. Can the words and Naming that evoke emotions in you also evoke them in a reader? It's hard to know, but Naming in poetry often aspires to such an outcome.

What I'm proposing here is more a meditation on language and how it connects you to the world than it is an exercise designed to lead to a poem or a draft of a poem. Consider this: If you can't name something, do you really notice it, are you really aware of it?

In other words, do Naming and noticing and having knowledge make you more aware of your world and more connected to it (or alienated from it, if that's where the noticing leads)? Connection and an alert awareness of alienation are both significant human experiences—countless poems have been written from those experiences. Which is to say, countless moments of heightened consciousness have been brought about when language in a poem names the world a person inhabits.

■

Here's the first exercise. Go somewhere (e.g., to a room, a streetcorner, a park, a field), and name what you encounter. Make a list that names what you see, hear, smell, taste, and touch. Is the number of things that surround you surprising? Do you notice some things that you can't name, don't have names for? Sit or pause in a place (e.g., room, park bench, stoop, under a tree, coffee shop), and try to notice and name twenty things that you see or hear or smell. Write them down. Can you circle four or five that give the most vivid sense of the place or that would most effectively orient a person reading them in that world you're trying to evoke?

As the second exercise, do another naming list. This time, take something you know and care about—something you enjoy or are deeply involved in. Name the things that are part of it, the sensations that are involved with it. It needn't be the obvious choice of a sport or hobby or skill you have; it could be anything (good or bad) that you're experientially familiar with (e.g., a kind of music or a favorite spot). Try to come up with around twenty things you can name that are part of your involvement—objects, actions, sensations—and when you're done, circle the four or five that seem most vivid and essential to you. Again, as with the "I remembers," the key is to give yourself permission to remember, know, and name.

■ ■ ■

NAMING AND CLAIMING AND TAMING

A crisis can occur when the nouns (the Naming) available to a person aren't adequate to the reality that he or she is facing. Imagine being a young English boy eighteen years of age in 1914, when World War I broke out; he might well have responded to that event by writing an excited poem about how he was looking forward to the heroic adventure of battle. Wilfred Owen was just such a boy. Eager to enlist in the army, he wrote a short poem about how thrilled he felt at the prospect of being a soldier among his comrades and perhaps dying a hero's death:

O meet it is and passing sweet
To live in peace with others,
But sweeter still and far more meet,
To die in war for brothers.

Wilfred Owen (1914)

Owen used the vocabulary—the Naming—that was available to him at the time. His little poem is abstract and sentimental; it uses old-fashioned "poetic" language (*meet* is an archaic word for "fitting"—no one, even in Owen's day, would have used it in ordinary conversation). Neither young Owen nor anyone else at the time had any idea of what this first "modern" war was going to be like for soldiers. No one yet knew how to name what was going to happen, because World War I changed warfare forever by introducing a whole new set of "things" (nouns, names) into experience: poison gas, machine guns, barbed wire, trench warfare, airplanes that dropped bombs from the sky, the area between the two front lines that would come to be called no-man's-land.

The war that young Owen soon joined as a front-line officer had new and horrible realities to show him: horror upon horror of trench warfare, and hopeless charges across the desolation and through the churned mud of no-man's-land under ceaseless artillery barrages. The destruction was on a scale that was impossible to comprehend. In the Battle of the Somme, the British lost 55,400 soldiers on the first day of their attack. By the time the battle finally ended five months later, the British had suffered 415,690 casualties, the French 200,000, and the Germans 434,500. And the battle with its unimaginable carnage changed nothing—when it was finally over, the front lines had shifted a scant and meaningless seven miles.

Embedded in this mathematical hugeness of horror were Owen's own particular experiences. After leading a charge, he was pinned down in a shallow hole for seven days of artillery fire before being relieved. During that time, he watched his men being blown up, right and left. He himself suffered a breakdown (what we'd now call post-traumatic stress disorder) and was shipped back home to recover briefly and then sent back to the front again. My point isn't about the trauma Owen suffered in the war, but about his response. After having been in battle and experiencing its horrors, he was determined to write a different kind of poem that named the new and terrifying reality he and countless other soldiers had experienced:

Dulce et Decorum Est

Bent double, like old beggars under sacks
Knock-kneed, coughing like hags, we cursed through sludge,
Till on the haunting flares we turned our backs
And toward our distant rest began to trudge.
Men marched asleep. Many had lost their boots
But limped on, blood-shod. All went lame; all blind;
Drunk with fatigue; deaf even to the hoots
Of tired, outstripped Five-Nines that dropped behind.

Gas! GAS! Quick, boys!—an ecstasy of fumbling
Fitting the clumsy helmets just in time;
But someone still was yelling out and stumbling
And floundering like a man in fire or lime. . . .
Dim, through the misty panes and thick green light,
As under a green sea, I saw him drowning.

In all my dreams, before my helpless sight,
He plunges at me, guttering, choking, drowning.

If in some smothering dreams you too could pace
Behind the wagon that we flung him in,
And watch the white eyes writhing in his face,
His hanging face, like a devil's sick of sin;
If you could hear, at every jolt, the blood
Come gargling from the froth-corrupted lungs,

Obscene as cancer, bitter as the cud
Of vile, incurable sores on innocent tongues,—
My friend, you would not tell with such high zest
To children ardent for some desperate glory,
The old Lie: Dulce et decorum est
Pro patria mori.

Wilfred Owen (1917)

In this and other fierce poems Owen wrote during his short life, the *Naming* of a new reality of war is powerfully insisted upon and the old patriotic "lies" about the glory of war are rejected. As in his early poem, *sweet* and *meet* are present in the Latin motto "Dulce et decorum," but now the sweetness and meetness are harshly ironic. Now Owen presents a new Naming that includes "flares" and the artillery shells called "Five-Nines" and the gas "helmets" and the horrible poison gas itself.

My point isn't about patriotism or war, but about language and Naming. If we can't name something accurately and bravely, then we can easily become a victim of experience. This holds true for the intimate traumas and civilian traumas of social life just as much as it does for something as vast and universal as warfare.

NAMING AND THE LIBERATION OF SELF THROUGH LANGUAGE

Paolo Freire (1921–1997) was a Brazilian educator and philosopher who had a lifelong belief that literacy—the ability to read and write—could be a powerful force in freeing people from political and economic oppression. According to Freire, political oppression is built into our teaching systems as a kind of indoctrination: children are taught to read and write in the vocabulary determined by the ruling groups in their particular culture. Learning the vocabulary, thought structures, and value words of the ruling establishment dooms students to a restricted freedom and an unconscious acceptance of "things as they are." If you happen to be a member of an oppressed or exploited group, then "things as they are" only confirm and continue your oppression. Freire believed that "true literacy," a literacy of self-liberation, begins when we learn to "name *our* world in *our* words."

In the course of developing his ideas about "naming *our* world in *our* words," Freire went back to "reread" his own childhood—that is, to revisit his childhood experiences in Recife, Brazil, and turn those memories into words. He remembered the birds and the weather, his fear of ghosts, the trees and the backyard of his family home. He called childhood's awareness of things an act of "reading the world." This world is *outer* (e.g., the trees in the backyard of Freire's childhood home, the weather, the cats and dog and rooms and birds), but also *inner* (e.g., his terror of ghosts, how at night the sounds seemed louder because he was more frightened). Reading and writing one's world is a way of claiming one's personhood. Following Freire's thinking, I would say that to *name your world is to claim your world*. You must claim your world before the world claims you (and renames you: person #3498345374). When Friere developed the notion of reclaiming his dignity and subjectivity by going back to remember his childhood, he was doing his own version of "I remember."

In a real sense, your impulse to write lyric poetry can also be understood as your struggle to become *fully* human: to name and thus lay claim to your experiences and feelings, and to derive your values and beliefs at least in part from these experiences and feelings.

■ ■ ■

A genuine personal literacy has the power to spread this doctrine of the assertive self. That the literate self can witness and affirm its own existence is the cause of both excitement and anxiety, as we see in these words from the contemporary American poet Dorianne Laux recounting her first time attending a poetry workshop:

I was in my late twenties, a single mother, working as a waitress at a small family restaurant. . . . I had been told to write about what I knew, and what I knew was my life, a life I wasn't sure was acceptable as a subject matter for poetry, a life that included instances of domestic abuse and sexual abuse. In Steve's workshop I was given permission to write about that life. I was working class. I was a woman. I was a mother. Could this mundane, ordinary world be a subject for my poetry?

from her Foreword to Steven Kowitt's
In the Palm of Your Hand, pg. 3

And, of course, the answer to Laux's question is yes. This is one of the important things poetry does for all poets—helps them lay claim to the life they live and turn it into vivid words that dramatize and dignify it. To bring us further into the contemporary world to a point at which literacy, lyric poetry, and the power of passionate personal testimony intersect, we have these autobiographical words from the Chicano poet Jimmy Santiago Baca on how he first came to write poetry as a young man in prison. First came reading poems late at night from an anthology stolen from a jail guard. His reading started as mere curiosity, but the more absorbed he became in the sounds and rhythms, the more he felt a pleasure that verged on happiness—even in that bleak place of confinement—as memories and emotions began to surface.

Shortly after experiencing the exhilarations and ecstatic release of reading lyric poetry, Baca discovered the even more dynamic liberating powers that come with writing poems. Propped on a bunk in his cell, with a notebook on his knees and a pencil stub gripped in his hand, he wrote his first words. As he did so, he realized that, prior to that moment, he felt as if his whole life had been spent swimming a shoreless ocean, but as he wrote he felt an island rising up under his feet—that the words he placed on the page were creating something solid and real: "As more and more words emerged, I could finally rest: I had a place to stand for the first time in my life. The island grew . . .

into a continent inhabited by people I knew and mapped with the life I lived" (from "Lock and Key," in *Working in the Dark: Reflections of a Poet of the Barrio*). For the first time, he discovers the power of shaped language to express and transform all he has endured and seen and felt into the complicated affirmation of individual being that lyric poetry can represent.

SILENCE AND NAMING

In the examples of Baca and Laux, the silencing is connected to cultural bias and the insecurity that social prejudice can induce in the self—the sense that one is unworthy of self-expresssion. There's another power Naming has: to say what has been silenced, what people are afraid to say out loud in conversation or in other social circumstances—say, in a family or among friends. Often, we discover that we can "say to the page" (write) what we wouldn't dare say out loud, even to (especially to?) those nearest us. Whether out of fear or shame or a sense of confusion, many things that are personally urgent to us can't be spoken in the day-to-day world we inhabit—the world of school, job, friends, and family. But there is nothing a person can't say to a page. That sense of freedom and liberation of the self isn't just one of being free of other people's judgments, but—even more important—one of being free of our own self-censorship and self-judging. To give ourselves permission to put words down on the page—what a delicious risk and thrill!

This discussion brings us back again to the crucial first steps of poetry-writing. First comes the decision to turn the world into words, to turn away from the ordinary world we inhabit and to speak openly to the page, without fear or shame or embarrassment. This is one of the great freedoms and adventures of poetry-writing. And it begins with Naming. Naming is the antidote to silence. To name is to speak truly and accurately—to name what is in us, or what we have seen or done or endured or yearned to do.

Many of those first words we come up with in the "permission phase" of poetry-writing will be clumsy or clichéd or confused, but it's important not to judge them; instead, trust the process of writing, and know that you're often moving toward trying to name what's important to you. By the way, in terms of what we have silenced in ourselves—it isn't just others we've concealed it from, but also often (and importantly) from ourselves. Another great reason for writing poems is to discover our own secrets. Poets have often and truly said: "How do I know what I feel until I see what I write?" Writing often reveals us to ourselves, lets us name what's important to us and what has been silent or silenced inside us.

HOW NAMING CAN MOVE INTO SYMBOL-MAKING

Classical Chinese poetry, like Japanese lyric, is full of Naming and focuses on the world of things and people. Here the eleventh-century critic and poet Wei T'ai tells why he (and all Chinese poets) consider Naming the essential element of poetry:

> Poetry presents the thing, in order to convey the feeling. It should be precise about the thing and reticent about the feeling, for as soon as the mind responds and connects with the thing the feeling shows in the words; this is how poetry enters deeply into us. If the poet presents directly the feelings which overwhelm him, and keeps nothing back to linger as an aftertaste, he stirs us superficially; he cannot start the hands and feet involuntarily waving and tapping in time, far less strengthen morality and refine culture, set heaven and earth in motion and call up spirits!
>
> from A. C. Graham, *Poems of the Late T'ang*, pg. 8

While Wei T'ei is encouraging us to name accurately and precisely, he is also presenting an argument for symbols. He warns us that direct statement of feeling in poetry ("I'm sad"; "I'm lonely"; "I'm happy") lacks resonance; it doesn't really affect us deeply. But an object presented (named) in a poem can sometimes go beyond its naming function to suggest multiple meanings and implications, some of which are emotionally expressive of the poet's being. When it does so, that object is on its way to becoming a symbol.

The role of symbols in the human mind and in poems is a dauntingly broad topic, but Wei T'ei's comment can get us started by emphasizing that symbols come into being out of Naming: the poet begins by naming the thing itself, and if he chooses the right object (or action), then feelings (and meanings) will attach to it, "shine up through it," and affect the reader. Recall the "I Remember" exercise you did in Chapter 1. Some of the things you remembered were rich with complicated feelings and meanings. Those were what I'd call private symbols—symbols whose multiple and complex meanings and implications only you could feel and intuit, because they were so embedded in the private information of your own life events.

When Robert Hayden wrote "and polished my good shoes as well" (see pg. 95), a symbol entered his poem. Those polished shoes were shoes—they were a Naming, but they were also symbolic of the father's selflessness. He offered them to his frightened and evasive son, just as a priest or a person attending church makes an offering in the context of a religious ceremony. The "lonely offices" that love performs, that the father in the poem performed toward the son and his family (the fires, the polishing of the shoes), hint at the depths of feeling and complexity of circumstance that the poem cannot say directly. If you are a poet for whom symbols do emerge, then you possess a kind of thinking and knowing that can be quite powerful in poetry. But symbols can't be invented or forced into being. They often emerge from a story as what seems like just one more detail, one more named particular; but then they become something more.

Let's try a "for instance" with personal memory (Naming) and the power of images to function as symbols. Suppose your father had a beer mug that he drank from every night—drank to excess, drank to the point of personality change and meanness and even violence. For you, that beer mug could well be a symbol of all the misery and terror and sorrow and regret that centered around your father's drinking; yet for another person it would simply be an ordinary beer mug. Is there any way that you could communicate to a reader the intensity of associations that you have with that mug in the short space of a poem? It's hard to say, but the answer should be yes. Unfortunately, there's no formula for how to do it. Here's an odd thing: you would probably have more luck with the richness of your personal associations with that mug by focusing on the mug with your words than by speaking directly of the misery and uncertainty of having a drunk father.

That may be one way symbols come into being in a poem—by focusing on the thing with your imagination and words, and trusting that the hidden meanings will somehow emerge from the indirect focus on the object itself. Recall, back on page 100, when you began the Story exercise by choosing a significant figure in your life and then having that person do something (e.g., "My Uncle Weeding His Backyard Garden"). What you chose probably wasn't just a "typical" action—your imagination seized on it because you intuited that careful attention to that action and subsequent actions would reveal the meaning of that relationship to you (or at least one meaning). That action was symbolic of your relationship with and attitude toward that figure. Symbols are a mysterious form of knowing, a mysterious way in which our imagination taps into the rich complexities and contradictions of our multifaceted emotional life.

CHAPTER NINE

Singing

By conscious art practiced with natural ease;
By the delicate, invisible web you wove,
The inexplicable mystery of sound.

T. S. ELIOT, "To Walter de la Mare"

To understand how language sings, we must consider rhythm. But before we move forward to an appreciation of rhythm, we must clear up a confusion between rhythm and meter. We are entering a genuinely complicated story with this topic, and it's essential that the relationship between the two terms be clarified. Rhythm is the broader term, the larger experience, and it includes meter as one of its elements. I have no idea if young people learning to write and read poetry today are introduced to the concepts of meter and rhythm in a way that makes sense of them, but I do remember my own confusion, and I hope the brief discussion that follows can be useful.

METER AS AN ELEMENT OF RHYTHM

Scholars and professors sometimes focus a bit too much on meter when they discuss poetry. When I was first trying to write poetry, I was also a student reading poetry in English classes, mostly in college. One of the first things my professors wanted to talk about was the metrical pattern of the poems (sometimes it seemed like that was the only thing that really interested them). I've come to feel that my professors' approach was unfortunate but understandable—teachers frequently seek some way to speak decisively and precisely about the mysterious, complex unfolding of a poem's sounds and silences. The poems I was reading in those classes usually had been written before free verse appeared in English in the early twentieth century—free verse being essentially poetry "free of" meter as a structuring element. My teachers would (it seemed to me) confidently analyze the poems' lines in terms of meter, and I was expected to do so also in order to properly understand the poems. I found this project of metrical analysis (called scansion) baffling and intimidating. It also seemed to me *not* get to the heart of the poems. If only I had known as a young poet and reader what T. S. Eliot (a famous poet whom even my teachers respected) had said in his essay "The Music of Poetry": "I have never been able to retain the names of feet and meters, or to pay the proper respect to the accepted rules of scansion. . . . But certainly, when it came to applying (them) to English verse, . . . I wanted to know why one line was good and another bad; and this, scansion could not tell me." But I didn't have Eliot on my side then, when I was in school and (mostly on my own) trying to learn how to write poems. That was many, many years ago.

Let me be clear: I don't want to give the impression that it's just professors and scholars who are powerfully attracted to meter. Many people at the outset of poetry-writing are attracted to meter, and also to rhyme, because both seem to offer stable rules and repeating patterns, and it's nice to feel that by following them one is becoming a poet. After all, the attraction of order, the need for it, is basic to a response to poetry. Another appeal of such apparent rules comes from an even deeper source: the impulse to poetry often emerges from an acute awareness of disorder in human experience, and it can be scary to feel that by writing poetry one is opening oneself to disorder. We wouldn't mind having some stable ordering rules handy as we begin to open up to experiential or emotional disorder, as we begin to approach our thresholds. I'm sympathetic to this perspective among beginning poets—very much so; but the fact is that if we resort too quickly and too insistently to a superficial ordering principle like meter, we may not open ourselves to the underlying, rich force of language itself that resides in Naming, Singing, Saying, and Imagining.

■ ■ ■

In order to get a better sense of the relationship of meter to rhythm, imagine a rock band consisting of six instruments. Meter is the drum: it keeps the beat and stabilizes the music, but no one would say that the experience of the band's song is contained in the drum line. Maybe meter and metrical scansion get so much attention in introductions to poetry because it's much easier to talk confidently about the drum line than it is about the total experience of a song played simultaneously by six instruments. In *Decoded*, Jay-Z talks about it as "the flow" that moves over, or around, or in various complex relations to a stable rap beat:

> It's been said that the thing that makes rap special, that makes it different both from pop music and from written poetry, is that it's built around two kinds of rhythm. The first kind of rhythm is the meter. In poetry, the meter is abstract, but in rap, the meter is something you literally hear: it's the beat. The beat in a song never stops, it never varies. . . . But the beat is only one half of a rap song's rhythm. The other is the flow. When a rapper jumps on a beat, he adds his own rhythm. . . . The flow isn't like time, it's like life. It's like a heartbeat or the way you breathe, it can jump, speed up, slow down, stop, or pound right through like a machine. If the beat is time, flow is what we do with that time, how we live through it. The beat is everywhere, but every life has to find its own flow. (pg. 10)

A Poet's Motive for Meter

Scholars and teachers aren't the only ones who can confuse rhythm and meter; poets have been known to add to this problem in their search for a simple answer. The poet Louise Bogan goes so far as to boldly declare "Meter is rhythm" in a 1953 essay on the pleasures of formal (i.e., metrical) verse. To which we must answer even more emphatically: no, meter is not rhythm. In fact, I'd rather risk an extreme assertion in another direction: "Rhythm is singing." But first we should briefly consider meter and its large and honorable historical function in the story of poetry in English.

Essentially, meter is a powerful ordering element—a regularizing power to which poets have recourse. The dominant metrical form in poetry in English is accentual-syllabic (which counts both the number of stresses, or accents, and the number of syllables in each line). It became an ordering possibility when Modern English emerged from Middle English around 1550 and the stresses involved in pronunciation of individual words became more stable. Stressing is nothing more than a voice emphasis on a syllable in a word. In speaking English, we stress or emphasize certain syllables in words of multiple syllables, and certain one-syllable words that are important to the meaning of a sentence. There are certain one-syllable words in English that you cannot stress and still sound like you're speaking meaningful English—try stressing the word *of* or *the* in the phrase "of the cat." Your voice simply can't do that and sound like you're speaking meaningful English. Accentual-syllabic meter tries to make a regular repeating pattern out of the syllable count and the stress count in each line.

The poet who wishes to work in meter usually chooses a single meter or a pattern of meters in which to work—say, iambic pentameter*— and once that meter has been established in the opening lines of the poem, it becomes a pattern that the rest of the lines conform to. For

---

* Iambic meter is a two-syllable pattern in which the first syllable is unstressed and the second is stressed. Each iamb (or other metrical pattern) forms what's called a foot. An iambic pentameter line consists of five (*penta* in Greek) feet of iambs—that is, it's a ten-syllable line that appears as five iambic (unstressed and then stressed) feet. An iambic tetrameter line is an eight-syllable line made up of four (*tetra* in Greek) iambic feet.

example, these lines from Samuel Taylor Coleridge's "Dejection: An Ode" aspire to iambic regularity:

> O Lady! We receive but what we give,
> And in our life alone does nature live:
> Ours is her wedding-garment, ours her shroud!

I say these lines "aspire to" iambic pentameter in order to emphasize a key aspect of meter: it can't (and shouldn't) be "perfect" in its pattern or regularity, because that would make a poem sound sing-songy and boringly predictable. If we were reading these three lines aloud, we might well sense the following pattern of stressing, where the under-line stands for a stress:

> O <u>La</u>dy! <u>We</u> re<u>ceive</u> but <u>what</u> we <u>give</u>,
> And in our <u>life</u> a<u>lone</u> does <u>nature</u> <u>live</u>:
> <u>Ours</u> is her <u>wedding</u> <u>garment</u>, <u>ours</u> her <u>shroud</u>!

The first line is (to my ear) a regular iambic pentameter line, and the third one is also, except that the first iambic foot ("Ours is") is "reversed," which is very common and acceptable in metrical poetry. But you can see and hear that it wouldn't be possible to stress the first three syllables in the second line ("And in our"). A metrical poet (e.g., Coleridge) might simply say that one of those three syllables is lightly stressed and so still counts as part of the metrical pattern. In other words, not all five stresses in an iambic pentameter line are equally emphasized (if you try reading lines that way out loud, it sounds very odd and unnatural). So meter is a kind of patterning, but in good poems it's not a rigid rule.

Besides accentual-syllabic meter, formal poets writing in English might choose accentual meter—a patterning that only counts the num-ber of stressed syllables in a line; it doesn't keep track of the number of unstressed syllables. In accentual meter, the line length may vary a good deal, but the pattern consists of a regular number of stressed syllables per line. Here's an example of a few lines describing the curious way an inchworm moves. (If you've never seen an inchworm, search for a video online.) In the first version, it's written in lines that each have three stresses:

> <u>Watch</u>ing this <u>inch</u>worm
> As <u>it</u> <u>works</u> its way
> A<u>long</u> a <u>dog</u>wood <u>twig</u>—
> <u>How</u> it <u>arch</u>es <u>up</u>
> In a <u>cos</u>mic <u>shrug</u>, <u>then</u>
> <u>Lifts</u> in <u>front</u> and <u>flings</u>
> Its <u>whole</u> <u>length</u> <u>for</u>ward
> In a <u>small</u>, <u>sing</u>le <u>lunge</u>.

Alternatively, a poem could present the same creature in lines with four stresses (a four-beat line) rather than with three:

> I <u>watch</u> this <u>green</u> <u>inch</u> <u>worm</u>
> As <u>it</u> <u>works</u> its <u>slow</u> <u>way</u>
> A<u>long</u> a <u>nar</u>row, <u>dry</u> <u>twig</u>—
> <u>How</u> it <u>arch</u>es <u>up</u> in a <u>cos</u>mic
> <u>Shrug</u>, then <u>lifts</u> in <u>front</u> to <u>fling</u>
> Its <u>whole</u> <u>small</u> <u>length</u> <u>out</u>
> <u>In</u>to the <u>wait</u>ing <u>emp</u>tiness a<u>head</u>.

Here's a strange truth: different poets can hear the same line differently in terms of stress. If you had four poets analyzing a poem in terms of its stresses, you could easily come up with three (or five or eight) different analyses (the same poet could hear it in two possible ways). We know that stressing is crucial in English pronunciation and that the accent marks shown in dictionaries indicate where the primary stress falls when correctly pronouncing a word of more than one syllable. But it isn't just the accent mark that gives a sense of stressing in a spoken sentence (or a written line of poetry); a voice reading that sentence aloud might stress different words and syllables in order to convey meaning. And stressing is subtle; not every stressed syllable in a line is equally stressed—that would sound wooden and unreal. For example, I stress both syllables of *inchworm*; but are they equally stressed, or is the first syllable given a bit more stress than the second? No good poet I know stays up nights worrying about such things. All we really need to say at this point is that in the example above, the three-stress lines sound noticeably less dense than the four-stress lines. All that's important is that the poet decided to use a stress count as a way of controlling and structuring (ordering) the lines as they move down the page, and the examples above show the result.

A third, far less common form of meter is called syllabic meter. In contrast to accentual verse, syllabic verse *only* counts the number of syllables. If a poet writing in syllabics desires an eight-syllable line pattern, then whenever the line length gets to eight syllables, she stops the line ("breaks the line," as poets say) and puts the next words on the following line. The odd thing about syllabic meter (and it's especially odd in English, which is aware of stresses but not really of syllables) is that it's a pattern that no reader's or listener's ear could detect. Thus, it's only useful to the poet if she decides that such an ordering principle is helpful in writing or rewriting the poem. It's very unlikely that the reader of a syllabic poem will be aware of the metrical ordering the poet has chosen.

■ ■ ■

Meter thus becomes a formal structuring principle that helps unify the entire poem. And when meter is combined, as it frequently is, with a rhyme scheme, then the poet is marshaling two powerful ordering principles against a poem's disorderings.

Historically, meter has been one of the defining elements of poetry in English. Probably 98 percent of all poetry written in English between 1660 and 1910 aspired to some form of metrical regularity, often in conjunction with a rhyme scheme and stanza regularity.

In addition, one could say that 80 percent of metrical poetry writ-
ten during that period is essentially one or another version of iambic
accentual-syllabic meter (e.g., iambic tetrameter, iambic pentameter).
Last but not least, even after the advent of free verse in the early part
of the twentieth century, a great number of major poets continued (and
continue) to write in meters—including Robert Frost, William Butler
Yeats, W. H. Auden, and Elizabeth Bishop.

Free verse became a powerful option in English in the early part of
the twentieth century; it was popularized by the American poet Ezra
Pound and by several poets whom he influenced. Free verse caught
on and quickly became a preferred way for poets to compose. What
the term *free verse* means is quite simple: it is poetry "free of" overall
metrical patterns. When a poet writes in meter, that chosen meter
determines where each line ends and the next one begins. In contrast,
in free verse the nature and length of each line is determined not by
any metrical pattern but by the "free" choice of the poet. He or she
determines where one line should end and a new one should begin.

Two catchy phrases can orient you to the issues of free verse and
meter as options in poetry-writing. Robert Frost, a poet who favored
meter, famously pronounced that "free verse is like playing tennis with
the net down." Tennis without a net probably wouldn't make much
sense and would be very confusing. Representing the contrary view-
point of free-verse poets is Ezra Pound, who counseled young poets
this way: "As regarding rhythm: to compose in the sequence of the
musical phrase, not in sequence of a metronome" (from *A Few Do's
and Don'ts of an Imagiste*, 1913). A metronome is a device that keeps an
inflexible tick-tock beat for musical performers in training; it roughly
corresponds to an iambic meter, say, or to Jay-Z's "beat" in rap, just
as the "musical phrase" that Pound endorses is very much like Jay-Z's
"flow." Pound, the earliest and most forceful champion of free verse in
English, wanted to eliminate metrical poetry in favor of something far
more flexible and expressive.

Rhythm's Reasons

Be not afeard: the isle is full of noises,
Sounds and sweet airs, that give delight, and hurt not.
                              Shakespeare, *The Tempest*

If meter and metrical schemes order and regularize language in a poem, then rhythm could be said to complicate the flow of language. Notice that I say "complicate" rather than "disorder." Rhythm does not function contrary to meter, but in a far more complex and expressive way that involves the totality of a poem's phrasing and sound effects.

Whereas the dominant meter in English (accentual-syllabic) involves the straightforward patterning of the stress element in words, rhythm is far more complex and involves a great number of different elements of language, including (among other things): duration; vowel pitch; such sound effects as assonance, consonance, and alliteration; phrasing and pauses; syntax; rhetorical devices; and incantation. These elements operate not in isolation but in relation to one another, creating the overall oral performance of the poem—the sense of "musical delight" that Coleridge rightly insisted was essential to poetry.

One last point before we begin. In order to take the knowledge of rhythm into our brains and our poems, we have to take it first into our bodies. We have to overcome shyness about voicing and performing the lines of poems. When I was a young person first drawn strongly to writing poetry, I was terrified of the sound of my own voice and would never have considered reciting out loud what I was writing, even if I was alone with my poem. Now, having spent half a century writing poems, I can't imagine writing or rewriting a poem without sounding it out in order to get a deeper sense of its rhythmic possibilities. The sooner we overcome any residual shyness about voicing, the sooner we move the mystery of rhythm out of the head and down into the mouth and breath and body, where it comes alive.

ELEMENTS OF RHYTHM

At this point, to try to give a sense of the rich complexity of rhythm, I'm going to highlight individual elements as much as I can. In doing so, I'll be separating out rhythmic elements that are really woven together in language, that are really not only an "inexplicable mystery" (as Eliot said) but also an inextricable one. Nevertheless, this brief survey that slips from one element to the next is necessary.

Let's begin with *duration*. This is a syllable-level phenomenon, and it refers to the length of time that's required to pronounce a syllable. The best analogy here would be one derived from music: how long a singer holds a note. Let me give an example. Say aloud two different three-syllable phrases: "bit of it" and then "fools of doom." Did you notice how much longer it takes to pronounce the latter phrase even though both are made up of three monosyllables and would "scan" the same in a line of accentual-syllabic verse? "Fools of doom"—your voice could prolong the first and third words in that phrase for ten seconds or more, and (though it might sound a little odd) you would still be well on your way to making sense and sounding like you were speaking meaningful English. "Bit of it"—when you try to extend or prolong any part of that phrase, you simply can't do it. However, you could go in the other direction—you could speak those three words very rapidly and still sound like you were pronouncing meaningful English. Try to say "fools of doom" very rapidly, and you won't have much luck. Duration: it's a cool element of syllables, and there it is again—the long sound of *cool* telling us about an aspect of musical delight.

Duration of syllables is largely a consequence of vowels—what we call long and short vowel sounds. But duration can also be a result of consonant clustering. Alexander Pope's long poem "An Essay on Criticism" (1711) was, among other things, a compendium of poetic effects. In the following couplet, the second line has an exaggeratedly slow rhythm as a result of his careful attention to syllable duration:

A needless Alexandrine ends the song,

That, like a wounded snake, drags its slow length along.

Part II, lines 156–157

Some of the syllables' duration comes from long vowel sounds in *wounded*, *snake*, and *slow*, but some also results from consonant clusters (as in the *ngth* of *length*).

In the following two couplets, Pope goes from extended duration in the first couplet to a short, rapid movement in the second:

When Ajax strives some rock's vast weight to throw,

The line too labours, and the words move slow;

Not so when swift Camilla scours the plain,

Flies o'er th'unbending corn, and skims along the main.

Part I, lines 370–374

Diction and Rhythm

The issue of duration as an element of rhythm can bring us to a second related topic: *diction* and rhythm. Modern English has its sources mainly in three earlier languages: Anglo-Saxon, Latin, and French (brought over by the Norman conquerors of England in 1066). Anglo-Saxon is a Germanic language; it is heavily stressed, and many modern English words derived from it are monosyllabic. In addition, it frequently clusters three or four consonants together. By contrast, Latin, like Greek, places less emphasis on how heavily stressed a syllable is and more on its duration—how long or short the syllable is when pronounced. Also, Latin typically consists of multisyllabic words with only one or two consonants in a row. The French language is derived from Latin and has similar characteristics.

The best way to become aware of the contrast between Latin and Anglo-Saxon is to compare similar English words derived from these two distinct sources:

Anglo-Saxon derived	Latin derived
words	vocabulary
smell	odor
room	chamber
leaves	foliage
birth	nativity
speech	articulation

Latinate language (i.e., words derived from Latin) tends to be used for abstract nouns and adjectives: for example, *ambition, concentration, spiritual, rational, information, occupation* all come from Latin. By contrast, a number of the most physical of English words are derived from Anglo-Saxon nouns and some of them have no real Latinate equivalents: *death, earth, water, sun, moon, mother, father, child, foot, bone, blood, breath, hair, tooth, sheep, cow, tree.*

The short, lightly stressed syllables of Latinate English tend to be far more quickly pronounced; hence they speed up a line of poetry. Consider the following five syllables. One is a single Latinate word; the other is a phrase consisting primarily of Anglo-Saxon derived words. Say them aloud:

representation
thick, dark clumps of earth

The longer length of time it takes to say the second example is a result of duration (in this case, caused by consonant clustering). But we should mention that *stressing* affects the rhythm of these syllables also. Words in English tend to receive a single primary accent, or stress, on one syllable and perhaps, in a long word, a secondary stress of much less emphasis. Thus, the word *representation* receives its primary stress on the fourth syllable and a secondary stress on the first syllable:

rep' re sen <u>ta</u> tion

What you have here is five syllables and one heavy stress. By contrast, you have to stress four out of five syllables in order to pronounce the phrase "thick, dark clumps of earth."

Since rhythm is strongly affected by the concentration of stressed syllables (the more concentrated the stresses, the more intense the rhythm), a Latinate word has the effect of diluting or "flattening" a poem's rhythm. This isn't necessarily a bad thing—it depends on what effect you're after. *But* a concentration of Latinate words has the definite effect of flattening out the rhythm, as in this example of twenty-five syllables:

> *typical, intensified concentration of registered institutional*
> *representatives*

You might recognize the above phrase as the sort of language used in government or academic reports—it sounds intelligent even as it puts your ear to sleep. It's hard to make the preceding line sing, or even dance. And remember that dance, the tapping of feet to the beat of language, is part of what poetry is about, part of its primary pleasure.

Since every word with two or more syllables has one syllable stressed, *and* since we stress significant words in pronouncing English, it follows that a line of Anglo-Saxon derived English will have more and stronger stressings than a Latinate line of an equal number of syllables. For example, this passage from Theodore Roethke's "Root Cellar" has the same approximate number of syllables (twenty-four) as the preceding Latinate line:

> Roots ripe as old bait,
> Pulpy stems, rank, silo-rich,
> Leaf-mold, manure, lime, piled against slippery planks.

When you pronounce the two passages aloud, one after the other, you're immediately aware that the second passage has an immense number of stressed words when compared with the Latinate line. This fact dramatically thickens the rhythm. In addition, you can see that syllable duration has helped to slow down Roethke's lines and altered the rhythm.

Of course, the Roethke lines are as rich and thick with stressing and duration as the situation they describe is dense with smell. Few poets would (or could) work consistently with such an intensified rhythm. Nor would any sensible poet put together anything as flat as the twenty-five Latinate syllables in my example. I'm giving two extremes of American English possibility. Most poems mix kinds of language to suit their need, but it's important to see how profound an effect diction has on rhythm.

Vowel Pitch and Assonance

Now, with Roethke's rich monosyllables still in our mouths, might be a good time to consider another element: *vowel pitch*. Here we again make use of a musical analogy. If duration can best be understood as how long we hold a musical note in singing, then vowel pitch can be understood as where a note is located on a musical scale.

Vowel pitch is one of several neglected elements that complicate rhythm and create musical delight in English. When John Keats, one of the great masters of rhythm in English poetry (despite the fact that he died at the age of twenty-six), confided to his friend Benjamin Bailey that he had discovered the "principle of melody" in English poetry, he was in large part referring to rhythmic effects achieved by vowel pitch:

> One of his favorite topics of discourse was the principle of melody in Verse, upon which he had his own notions, particularly in the management of open & close vowels. . . .Keats' theory was, that the vowels should be so managed as not to clash one with another so as to mar the melody,--& yet that they should be interchanged, like differing notes of music to prevent monotony.
>
> Hyder E. Rollins, *The Keats Circle*, pg. 277

Here's an example of Keats letting his "theory" loose in the opening
four lines of his poem "To Autumn":

Season of mists and mellow fruitfulness!
    Close bosom-friend of the maturing sun,
Conspiring with him how to load and bless
    With fruit the vines that round the thatch-eaves run;

from "To Autumn" (1819)

What do these four lines mean? What would they be saying if
you turned them into prose? Not that much. They're addressed to
a personified Autumn as if the season were a goddess who worked
well with the sun ("conspired" with him) to make fruit ripe—some
kind of vine fruit, grapes maybe. But try saying these lines out loud.
See how your mouth and tongue must travel a wild, roller-coaster
journey—one that slows down (the duration of the long *e* in "season
of mists" and the prolonged hiss of "mists") and speeds up ("thatch-
eaves run" happens fast when I sound it out) as on a roller-coaster, up
and down and around. It's a mouth-opening, tongue-twisting sound-
journey that goes on at this concentrated intensity for another thirty
lines, only to end with a little catalogue of sounds that happen at dusk
in this rural setting:

Hedge-crickets sing; and now with treble soft
The redbreast whistles from the garden-croft;
    And gathering swallows twitter in the skies.

■ ■ ■

Vowel pitch is a quality of words that affects how a line of poetry
sounds. Essentially, the human voice is a flexible instrument, and
when it comes to vowel sounds (present in all words), we make
them by varying the pitch (sound frequency plus overtones) of the
sound. To make the various vowel sounds, we breathe out and
change the shape of our open throats, the placement of our tongues,

and the shape of our lips. There are five main simple vowels (*a, e, i, o, u*) that can be either long or short (the long *e* of *need* and the short *e* of *bed*); there are also lots of vowel sounds called diphthongs that are combinations of single vowel sounds like the *ow* in *sound*. Altogether, there are about fifteen of these sounds that our hearing can identify.

What's interesting and important for us as poets is that these sounds can seem like notes on a musical scale. There are vowel sounds like the *oo* of *food* that are low-frequency vibrations and could sound like low notes on a musical scale, and there are vowel sounds like the long *i* of *fine* or the long *e* of *bead* that are high-frequency vibrations when said aloud and could sound like high notes on a scale. Our voices are instruments; words spoken aloud are a kind of singing, especially in relation to vowel sounds for which the speaker's voice vibrates higher or lower, depending on the sound in the word. When these vowel sounds repeat themselves, we get the effect called assonance, or vowel-rhyme. But when the vowel sounds both repeat and vary (as in Keats's formula), the poet is playing the line of the poem (and its voicing) like a melody of varying notes in a song. Variety and pattern of vowel pitch constitute just one more source of richness and Singing in the lines of a poem.

■ ■ ■

Consider this vowel scale arranged by pitch so that the low-frequency vowel sounds are on the left and are rising toward the higher-frequency sounds on the right. A word example of each vowel sound appears in parentheses after the sound:

(high-frequency vowel sounds)

long *e* (*flee*)

long *a* (*flay*)

long *i* (*fry, sigh*)

(medium-frequency vowel sounds)

short *i* (*fit*)

short *e* (*bet*)

short *a* (*fat*)

short *u* (*r*) (*bird*)

short *u* (*bum*)

(low-frequency vowel sounds)

ah (*far*)

ow (*fowl, foul*)

oi (*boy, foil*)

aw (*fought, claw*)

oo of (*book*)

long *o* (*phone, bone*)

oo of (*fool, pool, through*)

Here's the final line of Gerard Manley Hopkins's poem "Thou Art Indeed Just, Lord," which makes remarkable use of vowel pitch to enact its distinctive Singing:

Mine, O thou Lord of Life, send my roots rain.

If we were to "translate" or isolate the vowel sounds in this line to show their variety, we'd come up with the following:

long *i*, long *o*, *ow*, *u(r)* of *Lord*, short *u* of *of*, long *i* of *Life*, short *e*, long *i* again in *my*, *oo* of *roots*, and long *a* of *rain*

This business of vowel pitch isn't linguistic science (whatever that is) when it concerns poetry. It's simply this: one more source of sound pattern and variety that registers as pleasure, whether we're voicing it ourselves out loud or hearing someone else voice it. I doubt any poet would compose lines thinking consciously about vowel pitch, but it's just part of the density of sound pleasure that language in poetry offers. What does it mean for a beginning poet? Just to know that it exists, and to notice it in poets who especially like to make what I'd call vowel music—like Theodore Roethke, John Keats, and Dylan Thomas. (Other poets, like John Milton and Robert Lowell, like to make what I'd call consonant music.)

When a poem has an elaborately varied vowel pitch, the reader's or reciter's voice will follow the vowel lead up and down a musical scale. This is the mouth moving around, making music. You can only do that by pronouncing the lines aloud. You can do it in private, but doing it silently inside your head misses half the fun and half the music. Let your voice loose, that instrument of the Singing force of words. Choose passages you like in a poem, and then sound them aloud so that your mouth can discover some of the sources of the poem's hold on you. Do that to find out what kinds of music and sounds you most like in poems. (And keep this fact in the back of your mind: different poets and readers like different kinds of Singing; you'll want to learn what *you* love most.)

■ ■ ■

I say that Keats's "melody" in large part concerns vowel pitch, but another vowel-determined rhythmic effect is also at work in this quote: *assonance* (sometimes called vowel-rhyme). In the Hopkins line we just considered for its variety of vowel pitch ("Mine, O thou Lord of Life, send my roots rain"), there is a clear example of assonance: the repeated long *i* sound in *Mine, Life,* and *my* that helps create a sound continuity in a line that is characterized by such variety of vowel pitch sounds.

Assonance is a form of *sound clustering* that affects the rhythmic texture of a poem. When similar sounds occur near one another in a passage, our ear and mouth recognize their connection. They form a pattern of sound that hovers slightly outside the temporal unfolding of the passage, as if a part of our ear lingered back, gathering up and connecting the rhyming vowels. This lingering back and gathering up has a genuine and mysterious impact on the forward momentum of a poem's rhythm.

Consonance and Alliteration

The same kind of sound recognition can take place with consonant sounds. *Consonance* is at work in the passage from Roethke recently quoted (pg. 195):

> Roots ripe as old bait,
> Pulpy stems, rank, silo-rich,
> Leaf-mold, manure, lime, piled against slippery planks.

The *p* sounds in *ripe, pulpy, piled, slippery,* and *planks* create an obvious pattern of consonant sounds. And then there is the closely related sound-cluster effect called *alliteration*, as with the *r* sounds in *Roots, ripe, rank,* and *rich.* (Most poets feel that alliteration speeds up the rhythm of a line, but certainly in the Roethke passage any speeding-up effect runs into the slowing down created by the variety of vowel pitch, the consonant clusters, the syntax, and the heavy stressing of the Anglo-Saxon derived monosyllables.) And while we're at it, we could note the powerful effect of *internal rhyme* in *old/mold* and *rank/planks*; and the vowel rhyme/assonance of the long *i* sound in *ripe, silo,* and *piled*; or the short *i* sounds of *rich* and *slippery.*

■ ■ ■

A SINGING EXERCISE

Write a poem using the following eight words:

> *willow* (use as noun)
> *swallow* (use as either verb or noun)
> *lame* (adjective)
> *disdain* (use as either verb or noun)
> *flame* (use as either verb or noun)

> *green* (adjective)
> *sway* (verb)
> *gave* (verb)

Here are the rules:

> The poem must be ten to twelve lines long.
> You must use all the words.
> You can use them in whatever order you wish.
> You can't use more than one of the listed words in each line (i.e., you must space the designated words throughout the poem—you can't jam several of them into the same line).

Hint: If you find yourself aware of the sound echoes and effects that these eight words suggest, feel free to use words of your own choosing that continue, or expand on, or play off the sounds you're responding to in these eight words. Doing so will heighten and possibly alter the sonic texture of your poem.

If you don't care for the preceding eight words, then try following the same rules (create a ten- to twelve-line poem) with these words instead:

> *grave* (use as either noun or adjective)
> *face* (noun or verb)
> *vein* (noun)
> *argue* (verb)
> *far* (adjective)
> *voodoo* (noun)
> *sinew* (noun)
> *mar* (verb)

■ ■ ■

Incantation

Moving up from the level of individual syllables and words to whole phrases, we can consider *incantation*, the formulaic repetition of phrases or words for rhythmic effect. Here's an example from "Marina," a poem by T. S. Eliot:

> What seas what shores what gray rocks and what islands
> What water lapping the bow
> And scent of pine and the woodthrush singing through the fog
> What images return
> O my daughter.
>
> from T. S. Eliot, "Marina" (1930)

Here we have the word *What* repeated again and again, repeated so often and oddly that it breaks up the sense of the lines yet adds somehow, mysteriously, to their emotional intensity. Does incantation operate as an ordering principle here, the way meter both orders and patterns stresses? It's not that simple. Incantation is a complex rhythmic phenomenon too little understood despite its frequent use in poetry in English.

Here's another example from the opening of "They Feed They Lion" by the contemporary poet Philip Levine:

> Out of burlap sacks, out of bearing butter,
> Out of black bean and wet slate bread,
> Out of the acids of rage, the candor of tar,
> Out of creosote, gasoline, drive shafts, wooden dollies,
> They Lion grow.
> Out of the gray hills
> Of industrial barns, out of rain, out of bus ride,
> West Virginia to Kiss My Ass, out of buried aunties,
> Mothers hardening like pounded stumps, out of stumps,

> Out of the bone's need to sharpen and the muscles' to stretch,
> They Lion grow.
>
> from Philip Levine, "They Feed They Lion" (1972)

In Levine's poem, incantatory repetition creates a sense of relentless momentum. If I were a scholar, I would add that the particular kind of repetition Levine uses with his eleven repeated uses of the phrase "Out of" in only eleven lines is a device called anaphora, a structuring technique that involves repeating a word or set of words at the beginning of a line.

Anaphora and numerous other complicated verbal devices involving repetition and patterning of sound and phrases were catalogued by ancient Greek and Roman rhetoricians two thousand years ago. In ancient Greece and Rome, speeches were both an art form and an important aspect of political life, so people were trained to organize spoken language into emotionally and/or intellectually compelling patterns. Western poetry has inherited this trove of possible orderings, although not all are used now and seldom are they studied and given their ancient labels, except by scholars.

Putting the issue of labels to the side (there are too many of them, anyway), we can say that contemporary poets often spontaneously use these rhetorical patterns for their rhythmic ordering possibilities. For the purposes of our discussion of rhythmic elements, the notion of *repetition* will suffice, along with the related phenomenon of *incantation* (for its connotations of magic and the possible supernatural power associated with repetition).

Before moving on, I'll add one more effect that incantation produces. When a poem repeats a line or phrase exactly as Robert Hayden does in "Those Winter Sundays" ("What did I know? What did I know . . . ?") or as Robert Frost does with the final two lines in his famous "Stopping by Woods on a Snowy Evening," then a curious fact about language and speech is revealed. It turns out that when faced with an exactly repeated phrase, the human voice is reluctant to pronounce it the same way the second time. I find this fascinating.

The reader or reciter seems to seek out a different emphasis in the
lines, as if intuiting that the same phrase, pronounced differently, can
reveal different nuances of meaning. We know this from our own
conversations—if we choose to repeat a phrase exactly (something
we tend to do *only* in emotionally charged circumstances), we tweak
the repetition to bring out some further meaning. Imagine yourself
repeating the plea "I didn't mean it; I didn't mean it." Odds are, the
second time you say the phrase aloud you might draw out the word
mean to indicate that what occurred was unconscious or uninten-
tional. Or you might introduce another variation to stress some other
meaning latent in such a powerful phrase. A theater director would
say that there are half a dozen ways that an actor could pronounce
"Yes, I agree," several of which would probably indicate the opposite
of actual agreement.

And then there's the almost terrifying power of incantatory repeti-
tion of the word *never* that we hear released in Shakespeare's *King Lear*
when Lear holds the corpse of his beloved daughter and realizes she
will never breathe again:

> No, no, no life!
> Why should a dog, a horse, a rat have life
> and thou no breath at all? Thou'lt come no more,
> never, never, never, never, never.
>
> from *King Lear*, 5.3

Nor would a discussion of the strangeness of incantatory repetition
be complete without mentioning the phenomenon many of us have
experienced whereby repeating a word enough times in a row sud-
denly makes it become meaningless, and a kind of existential vertigo
occurs as the connection between sound and meaning comes unstuck.
I like Emerson's account of it:

> I remember, when a child, in the pew on Sundays amusing myself
> with saying over common words as 'black,' 'white,' 'board,'

etc, twenty or thirty times until the word lost all meaning and
fixedness . . .

from *Journals* (August 22, 1841)

So far, we have been glancing at various sound effects that help
create rhythm in poetry; but a whole other aspect of rhythm is
silence—the pauses created by *syntax, phrasing,* and *line breaks.* The
punctuation, pauses, transitive momentums, and clausal subordinations
of syntax have an enormous impact on rhythm. Again, saying a poem
aloud is the only really effective way of realizing this fact.

Syntax and Rhythm

One of the most basic ordering principles of language that poetry
makes use of actually precedes the idea of poetry—namely, syntax. As
defined by *The Random House College Dictionary,* syntax is "the pattern
and structure of the word order in a sentence or phrase." Syntax is so
fundamental that its profound effects on poetry are often overlooked
entirely (e.g., the reference book *The Princeton Encyclopedia of Poetry
and Poetics* doesn't even discuss the topic). Since, in written language,
syntax is the primary regulator and orderer of meaning, it seems log-
ical that in poetry it almost always functions as a formal ordering
principle.

In the poetries of certain cultures, this ordering power is so high-
lighted that complex patterns of syntax function in much the same
way that meter and rhyme serve as a fundamental structural device in
the poetries of other cultures. For example, the Chinese in their *shih*
(lyric) poetry of the Tang dynasty (618–907 CE) not only required a
set number of characters per line and a set number of lines (eight), but
they also imposed an elaborate syntactical requirement: the four lines
in the middle must form couplets that are syntactically parallel even
as they are conceptually and tonally contrasting or even antithetical.
Here's a translation of an eighth-century CE Chinese lyric by Du Fu

(also known as Tu Fu) that shows the complex way in which syntax structures the poem:

A Traveler at Night Writes His Thoughts

Tall bank grasses, light breeze bends them.
A single mast, it pokes up into night sky.
All those stars shining down over the fields.
The moon rising up, floating on the river.
Fame—I doubt my poems will bring me that.
Job status—I see old age and sickness nixing that.
Fluttering, fluttering—where's a stable image of me?
The sky, the ground, this one gliding gull.

Du Fu (eighth century), translated by Gregory Orr

Even in this free translation, I've kept the skeletal structure of syntactical parallelism that governs this kind of Chinese lyric poem: it's made up of couplets in which the first three couplets form units that are similar in sentence structure, but with a slight variation as well. For example, line one names multiple things standing upright (the grass); line two presents a single thing standing upright (the ship's mast) that doesn't sway or bend. Line three has lots of stars shining down; its companion, line four, has one thing (moon) rising up. Lines five and six begin with big ambition words ("fame" he hoped to get as a poet; "job status" he hoped to achieve working for the emperor as almost all poets did in his time and culture)—but both these ambition words are followed by a line that expresses his sense of defeat and quiet despair.

My point isn't to comment on the poem's meaning (whatever that might be—I'd say it's mostly an old person's lament and expression of defeat and isolation), but to point out that Chinese poets writing in this classical lyric tradition ordered their poems largely through couplets with parallel syntax—a steady pattern that involved sameness and variety.

■ ■ ■

Hebrew poetry of the Psalms likewise relies on the formal principle of several sorts of syntactical parallelism rather than on rhyme or meter:

> Lift up your heads, O gates!
>> and be lifted up, O ancient doors!
>> that the King of glory may come in.
> Who is the King of glory?
>> The LORD, strong and mighty,
>> the LORD, mighty in battle!
> Lift up your heads, O gates!
>> and be lifted up, O ancient doors!
>> that the King of glory may come in.
> Who is the King of glory?
> The LORD of hosts,
>> he is the King of glory!
>>>>> from Psalm 24, Revised Standard Version

Again, we see the repeated phrase structures with slight variations serving to create patterns. "O gates" in the first line becomes "O ancient doors" in the next, and so on through the first nine lines with a phrase or image stated and then repeated in a variant way, but with the same sentence structure.

We can also examine this ancient Hebrew poem known as the "Song of Songs," which is also called the "Song of Solomon." Here the metaphor of the speaker as a "rose" and "lily" varies the flower image but repeats the sentence structure: ("I am a rose . . . [I am] a lily") and later the initial phrase repetition of "As a lily" and "As an apple":

> I am a rose of Sharon,
>> a lily of the valleys.

As a lily among brambles,
     so is my love among maidens.

As an apple tree among the trees of the wood,
     so is my beloved among young men.
With great delight I sat in his shadow,
     and his fruit was sweet to my taste,
He brought me to the banqueting house,
     and his banner over me was love.
Sustain me with raisins,
     refresh me with apples;
     for I am sick with love.
            from "Song of Solomon," King James Version

■ ■ ■

By its very nature, syntax is *the* ordering principle of language. But because the word order of a sentence is flexible, syntax can be both an ordering and a disordering element in a poem, depending on how it's handled. Let me illustrate. One of the most straightforward syntactical arrangements in English is the transitive sentence. For example:

The dog bit the man.

Subject, verb, object of verb occur in that order. A poem composed entirely of transitive sentences would be highly ordered, highly regular. But it would also be rhythmically boring and repetitious.

Imagine that on a spectrum of syntax we draw a line running from Order to Disorder:

Order ←——————————————→ Disorder

If a transitive sentence is highly ordered and belongs way to the left at the Order pole on this spectrum of syntax, then more flexible uses of syntax will be closer to the Disorder pole.

Let me give an example of a more flexible use of syntax that has the power to disorder a poem and thereby decisively affect its rhythm. In 1916, the great Irish poet William Butler Yeats (1865–1939) experienced a breakthrough in his poetry that he later expressed in these words:

> I began to make it [a language to my liking] when I discovered some twenty years ago that I must seek . . . a powerful and passionate syntax, and a complete coincidence between period and stanza. Because I need a passionate syntax for passionate subject matter I compel myself to accept those traditional meters that have developed with the language.
>
> from "A General Introduction to My Work" (1937)

Note that Yeats no sooner celebrates his use of an expressive, disordering ("passionate") syntax than he counters it with the formal orderings of traditional stanzas and meters, instinctively sensing that the dynamic tension of their power to introduce both disorder and order is central to his poems. That "passion" is disordering is an essential theme of Yeats's work, whether it be love's passion or the violent political passions that constantly rend his Irish homeland.

Frequently, Yeats's use of "passionate syntax" creates elaborate suspensions of meaning. This is evident in the following example from "Lapis Lazuli," in which a dependent clause almost three lines long separates the subject ("handiwork") and predicate ("stands") of his sentence:

> No handiwork of Callimachus,
> Who handled marble as if it were bronze,
> Made draperies that seemed to rise
> When sea-wind swept the corner, stands;

Note also how the sound echo of subject and predicate (*handiwork, stands*) helps to bridge the distance that the clauses create.

Yeats sometimes unfolded his lines so cryptically that the feeling arrives before or almost in spite of the meaning that should be revealed by the syntax. For example, consider the disordering power of syntax in this final stanza of "Crazy Jane and Jack the Journeyman," where Crazy Jane speaks of her dead lover:

But were I left to lie alone
In an empty bed,
The skein so bound us ghost to ghost
When he turned his head
Passing on the road that night,
Mine must walk when dead.

Moving from the contortions of Yeats to the dislocations and deeper entanglements of the American poet Hart Crane (1899–1932) is a journey toward the more profoundly disordering rhythmic possibilities of syntax.

One of Crane's ambitions was to be up-to-the-minute modern in his poems: "New conditions of life germinate new forms of spiritual articulation," he stated in the essay "General Aims and Theories" (1925). If conventional syntax is guide and guardian of a sentence's logic, then Crane's ambition called for "an apparent illogic (that) operates so logically in conjunction with its context in the poem as to establish its claim to another logic, quite independent of the original definition of the word or phrase or image thus employed" (as stated in a letter to Harriet Monroe written in 1926). When we consider Crane's fascination with the ocean (poetry's primary concrete image for disorder), as well as his assertion (again from "General Aims") that "language has built towers and bridges, but itself is inevitably as fluid as always," we can't help but wonder if these notions and preoccupations gave rise to his eccentric, expressive efforts with syntax. Do they account for the disordering power of his syntax and the emotive power of his Singing?

Sometimes the simpler dislocations in Crane's poems have simple explanations. The inversions of the first sentence of "At Melville's Tomb" allow him to have two meanings:

> Often beneath the wave, wide from this ledge
> The dice of drowned men's bones he saw bequeath
> An embassy.

Wishing to keep a grip on meaning, and feeling the pressure of clause piled on clause, the reader's mind first tries to complete the sentence by seizing the probable subject at the first opportunity and getting this possible meaning: "Often he saw the dice of drowned men's bones" (using *he* as the subject and *saw* as the predicate). But the verb *bequeath* breaks the syntax of the sentence open again and is absorbed as: "Often he saw the dice of drowned men's bones bequeath an embassy." Fine. We can see that Crane has made here a complicated and flexibly singing syntax; but if we sort it out slowly, we can decide that it's a comprehensible sentence that has a meaning (or two).

But what happens when we step off the shore's ledge and give ourselves over to the oceanic "unfettered leewardings" of this passage that opens section 4 of Crane's poem "Voyages"?

> Whose counted smile of hours and days, suppose
> I know as spectrum of the sea and pledge
> Vastly now parting gulf on gulf of wings
> Whose circles bridge, I know, (from palms to the severe
> Chilled albatross's white immutability)
> No stream of greater love advancing now
> Than, singing, this mortality alone
> Through clay aflow immortally to you.

"Amen," we say (uncertain what else to say). I'm not claiming that this passage is immune to explication or that it is anti-syntactical. But I would say that we're experiencing an extremely expressive use of syntax, one that mocks the skeletal parsing of sentence with an image of fleshly, ecstatic flowing. If I were placing Crane's passage on the order–disorder spectrum, it would be pretty far over to the right:

Order ←———————————————×——→ Disorder

When Crane lets himself go as he does here, language becomes a flowing medium that severely disorders syntax and heightens rhythm in the service of theme—one that sings and hymns rather than speaks. I would also add, just to be clear about this, that I'm not really able to make any ordinary sense out of these lines, even though I think they're rather amazing and (once you decide you like Crane's strange music) fun to try saying aloud.

Free Verse and Rhythm

Notice that we haven't yet considered *meter* in terms of a poem's rhythm. Meter is, I remind you, an imposed pattern of regular stresses (and certain variations) that persists throughout a poem. An important fact to remember is that while meter in poetry always tends to be an ordering element, rhythm can be either an ordering or a disordering element, depending on the particular poem or passage of a poem.

In *free verse* the order of meter is abandoned, and in its place the poet substitutes an expressive, various *rhythm*. You'll recall I mentioned earlier that free verse gets its name from exactly what it is "free of"—meter. Depending on your attitude toward free verse, you might say that the use of free verse shifts the emphasis from rigid metrical patterns to the larger sphere of rhythm, and that this shift gives the poet more flexibility in expressing her or his subjectivity in looser and more various combinations of stressing and unstressing. Or, if you aren't a fan of free verse, you might say that in free verse rhythm has lost an important anchoring and stabilizing element—that of a dominant, recurring pattern of stressed and unstressed syllables.

ELEMENTS OF RHYTHM UNFOLDING

Perhaps it's time now to consider some longer passages of poetry to give a larger sense of rhythm as a complex unfolding of sound and silence within a poem. It might also give us an opportunity to observe the interaction of meter and rhythm in several poems. In each of the next four examples, we'll look at only the opening four to six lines of a poem.

Here are four lines from a poem by William Wordsworth:

> From low to high doth dissolution climb,
> And sink from high to low, along a scale
> Of awful notes, whose concord shall not fail;
> A musical but melancholy chime,

from "Mutability" (1822)

In this example, the meter is iambic pentameter (ten syllables of alternating stress and unstress). In addition, the rhythm is rather flat or untextured. What rhythmic elements serve to complicate this iambic meter? For one thing, there's a fair amount of variety in vowel pitch—the long *o* sound of *low* occurs twice; the high note of the long *i* in *high* appears twice, and also in *climb*. We can even note a certain cleverness in that Wordsworth is using low and high vowel pitch to talk about a situation that he's comparing to a musical scale with low and high notes. However, Wordsworth's diction consists of a number of Latinate words (e.g., *dissolution*) and Greek-derived words (e.g., *melancholy*), whose relative lack of stressing adds to the rhythmic flatness.

For contrast, let's look at the first four lines of a poem by Wordsworth's close friend, Samuel Taylor Coleridge:

> In Xanadu did Kubla Khan
> A stately pleasure dome decree:

Where Alph, the sacred river, ran
Through caverns measureless to man . . . .

from "Kubla Khan" (1816)

Metrically, the lines are quite similar to Wordsworth's—both are iambic. However, these are tetrameter lines (four feet per line) rather than Wordsworth's pentameter (five feet per line). The difference in the number of feet per line has real consequences: a tetrameter line is likely to feel jauntier. But meter alone does not account for the vastly different rhythmical feel of these lines.

One of the most obvious differences has to do with the richness of Coleridge's sound texture as compared to Wordsworth's. We could begin by noticing the relatively simple devices of alliteration and consonance woven through these few lines:

> the alliterated k sound in Kubla, Khan, and caverns, supported by
> consonance in decree and sacred
> the d of Xanadu, did, dome, and decree
> the r sound coming to the fore with "river ran" but actually woven
> throughout the last three lines

We could then listen to the first line and notice that its sounds have a way of repeating so that a pair of rhyming syllables frame the line and enclose another rhyming pair:

In Xanadu did Kubla Khan

See how *Xan/Khan* frames the *du/Ku* rhyme? It's an odd effect, an unusual one, but our ear hears it, picks it up, and adds it to the odd sound pleasure of the line's unfolding. Of course, the *Xan/Khan* sound continues with the rhymes *ran* and *man* as well, heightening the texture even more. In addition, there is more internal rhyme: *pleasure* and *measureless* connect up across the line that separates them.

This rich *formal* texture of sound and repetition known as incantation helps create the magical-spell feel of the poem. In turn, the notion of magical spells is a central *thematic* concern of the work. (Later in the poem, the speaker will be shown to be disordered because of "visions" and will be suspected of aspiring to magical language powers.)

Both the Wordsworth and Coleridge lines are metrical—their respective poems aspire to a dominant iambic pattern. Yet their rhythms, as even a cursory oral performance shows, are entirely different. Some readers might experience Wordsworth's rhythms as stately and grand (i.e., as a positive thing); other readers might find them rather dull or plodding. Coleridge's rhythms in "Kubla Khan" are clearly intended to create a vitalizing and mesmerizing effect: to enchant, in the old, magical sense of that word.

If we were comparing the rhythm of the Wordsworth and Coleridge lines in terms of order and disorder, we would probably see the former as clearly more ordered than the latter:

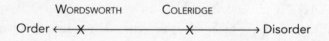

But what if we were considering rhythm in free verse poetry? Both Coleridge and Wordsworth wrote in the early part of the nineteenth century, but as we enter the twenty-first century free verse has become a dominant mode of writing poetry. Let's look at two examples of lines from free verse poems in terms of their rhythmic ordering and disordering.

Here is the opening sentence of a poem by William Carlos Williams (1883–1963):

Old age is
a flight of small
cheeping birds
skimming

bare trees   5
above a snow glaze.

from "To Waken an Old Lady" (1921)

If we were to begin to look at the rhythm here in terms of sound
patterning, as we did with the Coleridge and Wordsworth lines, we
wouldn't hear all that much. We could notice that the sentence is
framed at beginning and end with assonance; that is, the long *o* and *a*
sounds of *Old age* are repeated in *snow glaze* at the end of the sentence.
This is a subtle effect of pattern. (I say "subtle" because the sounds are
separated by a number of lines, and sound patterns only work when
the repeated sounds are fairly near each other in the poem and the
reader's ear still retains the echo of the initiating sound. If, say, ten
lines intervene between two repeated sounds, your ear wouldn't hear
them; they must be clustered to be heard.)

Since both *Old age* and *snow glaze* are pairs of monosyllables that
get more or less equal stress when said aloud, the sound pattern is
reinforced by the stress pattern. Punctuation adds to the effect: the
full stop of the period after *snow glaze* reinforces the phrase's impact.
We could also note that there's a repetition of the *ing* sound in *cheeping*
and *skimming*. Otherwise, in terms of sound patterns we would say
the vowel pitch is very various, with few repeating vowel sounds (the
long *e* of *cheeping* and *trees* being the main exception). The alliteration
is minimal: the *s* of *small, skimming,* and *snow.*

But we must remember that Singing consists of both sounds and
silences—in this case, the silences created by pauses and phrasing. The
rhythm in Williams's poem comes as much from the pauses and phras-
ing as from the sounds (this is quite often true about free verse). The
specific device creating the pauses in this poem is the *line break.*

In accentual-syllabic and syllabic metrical verse, the metrical pat-
tern of the poem determines where each line will end. In free verse,
the poet determines where each line will end, or "break." Since a line
break represents both a visual and an oral (or performance) pause, each

line break has an important rhythmic impact on the poem. A poem on a page can be understood as providing instructions for the poem's recitation, its oral performance. The line breaks in Williams's poem offer this instruction:

> Old age is   *[pause]*
> a flight of small   *[pause]*
> cheeping birds   *[pause]*
> skimming   *[pause]*
> bare trees   *[pause]*   5
> above the snow glaze.   *[longer pause of period]*

In speech, we pause naturally every once in a while for breath. Usually, we pause for breath at places where, in writing, we see punctuation marks. Punctuation organizes language into sense units, and so, conventionally, breath pause and meaning/sense pause correspond in both speech and writing.

Sometimes poets break their lines at such natural breath pauses. But Williams does not, especially between lines 1 and 2 and lines 2 and 3. When a line breaks in a spot where no breath pause is appropriate or indicated, we call it an *enjambed line*. Enjambment is another means by which poets control the poem's rhythm.

Enjambed lines represent dramatic pauses rather than breath pauses—they're part of a rhythmic effect in which the poet interrupts normal speech. Why? Often for suspense (a thematic concern). For example, the pauses at the end of both lines 1 and 2 have the effect of keeping the reader in intellectual suspense.

In line 1, the poem promises to give an authoritative definition of a state of being, to answer an unspoken "big" question: What is old age? The pause after "Old age is" represents the suspenseful pause of the good storyteller—a storyteller who draws out the story, knowing that listeners are stimulated by curiosity about what he or she will say next.

After *small* at the end of line 2, the poet could say almost anything.

What will he say? When our eye returns to the left margin to continue the sentence, we discover that he says "cheeping birds," but he could have said anything.

It is in this way that the suspense inherent in enjambed lines (in all poems, even metrical poems) introduces disorder into poems. Line breaks can enact (often in a minor way) the unknowability of the next moment. Here Williams plays with disorder, plays with bringing the reader up against disorder with these abrupt, suspense-oriented line breaks. When he chooses "cheeping birds" instead of "catastrophes," he's turning the poem (and the reader) away from the grimmest possibilities of disorder in his chosen subject of mortality.

But let's consider Williams's line breaks and rhythm one more time from a different angle. The rhythm of these lines is halting, hesitant. We see this rhythm *visually* as well as hear it aurally. In fact, since we see the poem before we speak it, we're immediately aware of the rhythm as a vital thing: we see that the poem consists of very short lines.

This *visual impact* of a poem is itself part of the poem's rhythm, but it's also part of the sense of disorder and order it conveys. A metrical poem in repeated stanza forms gives a sense of pronounced ordering. A reader has only to glance at a poem arranged in quatrains with lines of roughly equal length to feel the ordering behind them. Likewise with the three quatrains and a couplet of a Shakespearean sonnet. Relative to the visual patterning of metrical poetry in traditional forms or stanza patterns, free verse often gives a subliminal sense of visual disorder.

Let's now consider rhythm in another five lines of a free verse poem. Here are the opening lines of Theodore Roethke's "Root Cellar," a passage of which we considered earlier in this section:

Nothing would sleep in that cellar, dank as a ditch,
Bulbs broke out of boxes hunting for chinks in the dark,
Shoots dangled and drooped,

Lolling obscenely from mildewed crates,
Hung down long yellow evil necks, like tropical snakes.   5

                                    from "Root Cellar" (1948)

Although Roethke's lines are highly stressed, the syllabic stressing doesn't follow a pattern; and so, again, we're considering a free verse poem. But it's obvious that compared to the opening lines of Williams's poem, the texture of sounds and silences is far richer and more various.

Let's start with that most obvious of sound effects: alliteration. The clearest instance is of *d* sounds: *dank, ditch, dark, dangled, drooped, mildewed, down.* In fact, the *d* sound winds its way through each line like the sinuous spine of the poem's snake. *B* sounds powerfully alliterate the first half of line 2: *Bulbs, broke, boxes. L* sounds, mostly buried within the words, make a powerful claim on our ear or mouth: *sleep, cellar, bulbs, dangled, Lolling, obscenely, mildewed,* (and then three words in a row) *long, yellow, evil,* and (finally) *tropical.*

We might note that *crates* and *snakes* highlighted at their respective line ends are off-rhymes or half-rhymes.

Assonance occurs in the *oo* sound of *Shoots* and *drooped;* the short *i* of *ditch* and *chinks;* the long *o* of *Lolling* and *yellow;* and even more places.

In the second half of both lines 1 and 2, a particularly dense sound event happens: "dank as a ditch" parallels "chinks in the dark." Both phrases consist of four monosyllables in identical patterns of stress, unstress, unstress, stress:

<u>dank</u> as a <u>ditch</u>
<u>chinks</u> in the <u>dark</u>

In addition, three of the monosyllables alliterate on an initial *d;* two of them end with an *nk* sound and a third with an *rk* sound. The *ch* sound that ends *ditch* crisscrosses to start *chinks.*

If we shift from sounds to diction, we can note how many of the words are heavily stressed monosyllables derived from Anglo-Saxon. This predominance of monosyllables over the more polysyllabic, lightly stressed Latinates intensifies the rhythm of Roethke's lines. In addition, the thick consonant clustering characteristic of such Anglo-Saxon derived diction causes our mouth to work hard to get around each word—another rhythmic effect. These consonant clusters combine with the elaborate variety of vowel pitch to make a constantly changing and challenging music out of these lines. Say them aloud and then say aloud the Williams lines, and you cannot miss the differences.

But now comes a hard question. Is the rhythm of the Roethke poem more disordering than that of the Williams lines? Certainly, Roethke's rhythmic texture of sounds is richer and more various than Williams's. But is richer music more disordered or more ordered? And then there's the visual (and aural) rhythmic disorder of Williams's short, enjambed lines as opposed to Roethke's lines, which all break at natural breath pauses.

Maybe it isn't necessarily a good idea to compare rhythms across poems in terms of disorder and order. We can certainly compare the poems in terms of rhythmic richness or flatness of texture. But I think it would be best to keep discussions of whether a poem's rhythm plays a disordering or ordering role *internal* to the poem. That is, does the rhythm of Roethke's poem play an ordering or disordering role in the poem itself, relative, say, to its theme and to other formal elements?

For example, I would be inclined to see the rich confusion of the sounds in Roethke's lines as mirroring and adding to the dense, threatening confusion (disorder) of the plant life in the root cellar. These two disorders (one rhythmic and formal, the other thematic—i.e., the subject matter of describing the root cellar) are given some ordering by the simile that ends the sentence: "like tropical snakes." This simile brings the chaos of vegetation, sound, and syntax into a single visual focus (the image of snakes) and thus momentarily (the poem's not over yet) orders the disorder. Of course, the simile of tropical snakes is itself not without threatening (i.e., disordering) qualities.

Returning to the Williams lines, we can say that the unusual line breaks and brief line lengths are rhythmic elements that create a sense of mild disorder—the mild disorder, say, of suspense in an interrupted story. Set against that disordering is the rhythmic ordering of the assonance frame: "<u>O</u>ld <u>a</u>ge" and "sn<u>ow</u> gl<u>a</u>ze." In other words, rhythm in the Williams poem both orders and disorders.

Since rhythm (the totality of all sound textures and pauses in a poem) is so complex a phenomenon and consists of so many elements, we should expect that some elements of rhythm in a given poem will play a disordering role, others an ordering. Likewise, we might expect rhythmic elements to be predominantly ordering in one part of a poem and disordering in another.

Finally, the story of rhythm in poetry is frequently one of complication and complexity. What we must do is become familiar with the elements of sound and silence that create rhythm and then give ourselves over to them. And one of the best ways of doing this is by reading poems aloud, perhaps exaggerating the sounds and phrasing a bit more than we ordinarily would in order to bring out their richness and texture. As our voices and tongues grow more aware of poetry's myriad possible rhythms, our ears will too.

■ ■ ■

ANOTHER SINGING EXERCISE

Take a poem or poems of your own—or a poem by another poet, if you prefer—and locate, if you can find them, the following rhythmic or sonic effects: assonance (vowel rhyme), consonance, alliteration, syntax in action (i.e., word order in sentence creating an interesting or notable effect), rhyme, internal rhyme, diction (word choice) that is Latinate and, in contrast, diction derived from Anglo-Saxon sources of English. This isn't something you can do effectively on a computer screen. You'll want to work on a hard copy of your chosen poem—or even several, since this exercise can end up creating a complicated visual result. It will help to underline and circle things, to connect with drawn lines, even to use different colored inks to keep track of the texture that's being revealed. Also feel free to discover any other rhythmic or sonic effects that seem to occur in the poems, such as incantation. After making note of these instances of rhythmic and sonic effects, consider how they affect the poems.

■ ■ ■

CHAPTER TEN

Saying

Language in lyric isn't only Naming and Singing, no matter how powerful those forces may be. There's also Saying. What is Saying? *Saying is language that asserts—language in its assertive mode,* as used by the poet to make claims about the world of experience or about concepts and ideas. The power of Saying is related to our (secret) love of the tone of authority. "Beauty is truth, truth beauty—that is all / Ye know on earth, and all ye need to know" says Keats's Grecian urn. "Death is the mother of beauty" intones a voice in Wallace Stevens's "Sunday Morning." We are thrilled by bold claims about experience and human nature. We marvel at their audacity and scope. And yet they also have the power to disturb: "Every woman adores a fascist," announces Sylvia Plath in "Daddy." Rainer Maria Rilke writes a famous sonnet entitled "An Archaic Torso of Apollo"— the poem's last lines are an absolute saying: "for there is no place / that does not see you. You must change your life." In poems, as elsewhere, assertions and Saying indicate confidence and authority. And yet . . .

Probably the strongest forms of Saying aren't right or wrong, because Saying is really just the rhetorical assertion of an opinion. When W. H. Auden begins his famous poem "Musée des Beaux Arts" by claiming "About suffering they were never wrong / the Old Masters," how could a reader or listener possibly know—or, more to the point, how could Auden possibly know—if what he's saying is true or false? *Never* wrong? Not even once? Who even knew they wrote or stated opinions about suffering, these Dutch painters of the seventeenth century? Frankly, as far as we know, what they did is make paintings—all sorts of paintings, some of which might depict suffering; but really—"never wrong"? And suppose Auden's poem had begun this way: "About suffering they were never wrong, the cubist painters"? What if you substitute "the impressionists" or "the Chinese landscape painters" for "the Old Masters"? And what if art historians had chosen to call those painters something else instead of Old Masters? What if they were called the Dutch Fuddies or the Amsterdam Gang? Doesn't half the dignity and persuasive power of Auden's claim come from the word *Masters*? Doesn't *Masters* (especially capitalized) make them sound as if they were profound and authoritative individuals? And doesn't another part of its force come from the adjective *Old* as opposed to, say, the Young Masters?

■ ■ ■

Assertions are tricky. Though we may admire their confidence, many of us feel that we are manipulated by the power of large abstractions as used by politicians and others who would stir us up with rousing rhetoric. The twentieth-century French philosopher and mystic Simone Weil warned that the big abstractions so favored by politicians, those "words with capital letters," are like grim water balloons:

> If we grasp one of these words, all swollen with blood and tears, and squeeze it, we find it is empty. Words with content and meaning are not murderous.
>
> from "The Power of Words" (1937)

Or we could say "hot air" as we remark skeptically about political rhetoric of one sort or another that throws around words like *freedom*, *liberty*, and *justice*. We're often right to wonder whether these grand words that, in the right context, can captivate our minds are actually connected to the real, material and social world we inhabit. To recapitulate my example from the Naming section: think of the minister who speaks eloquently about "love" from the pulpit—what if, later that week, we observe him kicking a stray cat that crosses his path? Would we believe our Sunday ears or our weekday eyes?

■ ■ ■

Needless to say, ideas are hugely involved in the business of making order. We're often confused and uncertain about things, especially during adolescence when the world can seem large and bewildering and our own emotions volatile, if not chaotic. We can be so overwhelmed that we're eager to make large statements about the world in order to tame it—think again of Wilfred Owen, who had never even seen a battle at the age of eighteen and yet confidently announced (as we saw on pg. 174):

> O meet it is and passing sweet
> To live in peace with others,
> But sweeter still and far more meet,
> To die in war for brothers.
>
> Wilfred Owen (1914)

The effects of strong Saying can be very intoxicating for young poets. Often, we long to make abstract and profound statements that will order our poems and, indirectly, indicate (to our readers and ourselves) that we are smart and deep enough to order the world. We wouldn't mind sounding wise in our poems. We might even be happy to claim the authority that (the very young) Shelley gave to poets when he concluded his "A Defence of Poetry" (1821) with this sentence: "Poets are the unacknowledged legislators of the world." Shelley's claim is an odd one, but the appeal of its forceful Saying has proved enduring.

We may distrust rhetoric, but we also long for authoritative statements. W. H. Auden was critical of the saying power of poetry to enchant and intoxicate—he responded to Shelley's grand claim with this skeptical remark in an essay in *The Dyer's Hand* (1962): "the unacknowledged legislators of the world describes the secret police, not the poets." And yet a quick Internet search of Auden poems shows that he himself was famous for writing a poetry heavily invested in Saying and its power to engage readers.

How easily we are entranced by categorical and decisive statements. It's one of the many ironies of poetry that Auden, a master of Saying, turned against one of his most famous and important poems because he decided that what it claimed wasn't "true." The poem is "September 3, 1939"; the title situates it on the day that World War II began in Europe with the unprovoked German attack on Poland. The poem not only was famous (and famously loved) in its time, but it was one of the poems most turned to by Americans seeking articulation of their collective agony in the aftermath of the September 11 destruction of the Twin Towers in New York City. It's a wonderful poem that's completely unafraid to make large statements about the human condition:

> I and the public know
> What all schoolchildren learn,
> Those to whom evil is done
> Do evil in return.

Or later in the same poem:

> The windiest militant trash
> Important Persons shout
> Is not so crude as our wish:
> What mad Nijinsky wrote
> About Diaghilev
> Is true of the normal heart;
> For the error bred in the bone

Of each woman and each man
Craves what it cannot have,
Not universal love
But to be loved alone.

But it was one of the most memorable lines in a memorable passage
that Auden himself turned against:

There is no such thing as the State
And no one exists alone;
Hunger allows no choice
To the citizen or the police;
We must love one another or die.

After a certain point, Auden wouldn't allow his poem to be reprinted,
claiming that to say "We must love one another or die" was a lie—in
brutal fact, we all will die (we are mortal) whether or not we love one
another. It's hard to know what to make of Auden's rejection of his
own poem and his own rhetoric, but his stance represents an extreme
response to an important force of language in poetry. Most of us would
be pleased to be able to create such memorable formulations of asser-
tion about the human condition and would worry less than he did
about the moral implications of our Saying.

■ ■ ■

A SAYING EXERCISE

In this exercise, the goal is to savor the pleasures and risks of Saying
by inventing statements that make conceptual claims or assertions. In
order to get a sense of the territory of Saying, I urge you not to be
afraid to make sayings that are a bit outrageous or pretentious—that
claim something that either couldn't possibly be true or couldn't pos-
sibly be proved, even if a listener felt that it might actually be true.

Some opinion or claim that reaches for the extreme—that isn't afraid to say "everything" or "everyone" or "no one" or "we all know/think/fear/believe. . . ." It's important that these statements risk or claim a great deal of conceptual territory. Oddly enough, it might be best if the statements you make up *aren't* actually something you think or believe—because if they aren't, it might save you from getting tangled up in whether or not you're right to make such a claim. In other words, be outrageous and irresponsible and see what happens, see where you can go or what you might say.

Here are some examples I came up with:

No one knows what beauty is . . .

■

The preceding line gave me the nerve to try saying the opposite and see where that might take me:

Everyone knows what beauty is . . .
            it's the aftermath of sadness.

(or)

                    it's the foretaste of joy.

(or)

                it's what's left when joy recedes.

■

Only the dead understand beauty . . .

■

No one knows what truth is.

■

Everyone knows what truth is,
                it's the aftermath of sadness.

(or)

                it's the foretaste of joy

(or)

                it's what's left when joy evaporates.

(or)

                it's what death can't digest.

■

The trees understand the universe.

■

Everyone knows what beauty is
But they're afraid to say it . . .

■

The rocks think deep and hard,
But the trees believe
Whatever the breeze tells them.

■

A man is not half as smart as a rock.

■

Rocks hate their mothers
More than they hate themselves.

■

The mountain understands the weather
Better than the weather understands
The mountain.

■

A leaf gets death
In a way that rocks
Never will.

The point isn't to say something you believe is true and somewhat grand in scope. Instead, the point is to see how the language of Saying seems to grab a reader's attention with its claim to know something.

It might be fun to incorporate one of your favorite, made-up Sayings into a poem. I suggest this as a possible approach: find the one you like most or are the most interested by, and try using it as the opening line of your poem. For example, let's say I like "A man is not half as smart as a rock." Try to extend that phrase in the same way you extended your Story poem in Chapter 5 by asking, "What happens next?" Only here I suppose it would more likely be "What do I say/claim next?" Probably you'll need to continue with the main characters of your initial saying as you would in storytelling—in my case, "a man" and "a rock." Maybe I could say:

> *A man is not half as smart as a rock.*
> *Rocks learn from their mistakes,*
> *But I've never met a single man*
> *Who really sat back and thought*
> *(the way rocks do) and then tried*
> *Something different.*

(and then I'd try to keep it going further)

> *and then tried*
> *Something different. Women*
> *May or may not benefit*
> *From their errors. I've never*
> *Been too sure about that,*
> *Though many I've known*
> *Insist that.*

(and so on)

But I notice that what I'm saying is losing energy, getting off track, and that's not good. Probably, the same rule applies to this as to the Story exercise in Chapter 5—you always want your next line to be as good as (or as interesting as) or better than the preceding one. You want to keep the energy level of imagination or Saying or action as intense and interesting as possible.

Maybe I should take my initial line and move in a different direction:

> *A man is not half as smart as a rock,*
> *But he's twice as fast*

In any race that involves movement,
And, for the most part, he's almost
As good looking as the average stone.

I notice that the examples I've come up with are a bit on the silly side, and I don't know if that's because of the tone of the start-off statement. Perhaps if I'd chosen to work with "Everyone knows what truth is / It's what's left when joy evaporates" and tried to extend that into a poem, I might have ended up with something that sounded more serious. Try this exercise for yourself, and see where you end up. The journey might surprise you.

■ ■ ■

PROVERBIAL SAYING

Proverbs are a wonderful instance of the power of condensation that gives Saying so much force. Here are some of William Blake's "Proverbs of Hell," his gift to the world of an "infernal wisdom" that he hoped would counterbalance the assertions of traditional religious and secular authorities, which he considered repressive:

Exuberance is beauty.
Energy is eternal delight.

Sometimes proverbs mingle the power of Saying with the power of Imagining (metaphorical language), as this one from Blake does:

One law for the ox and the lion is oppression.

In other words, each creature deserves and follows the laws of its own distinct being, and to try to bring them under a single law is oppressive. Here are more from Blake:

The pride of the peacock is the beauty of God.
The lust of the goat is the bounty of God.
The wrath of the lion is the wisdom of God.
The nakedness of woman is the work of God.

In "Auguries of Innocence," Blake extends the form a bit into rhyming couplets:

Nought deforms the human race
Like to the armour's iron brace . . .

A Robin Red breast in a Cage
Puts all Heaven in a Rage

■ ■ ■

Half a century before Blake, Alexander Pope (1688–1744) perfected the heroic couplet (a pair of rhyming, iambic pentameter lines) as a form of wit—which was then a highly valued term for wise sayings elegantly phrased. In his long didactic poem "Essay on Man," Pope made it clear that what he had to say was that mankind should submit to God's will, that God conceals from us what will happen to us next or after death as a kind of mercy, so that we can live in this world with hope:

What future bliss, He (God) gives not thee to know,
But gives that hope to be thy blessing now.
Hope springs eternal in the human breast:
Man never is, but always to be blest:

You might recognize the line "Hope springs eternal in the human breast." Pope expressed his thoughts and opinions so eloquently that many of us quote his lines as if they were traditional proverbs rather than the products of a single poet's lucid eloquence:

To err is human; to forgive, divine.

Fools rush in where angels fear to tread.

This next one is commonly lifted from its context, as so many of Pope's witty sayings are:

A little learning is a dangerous thing;
Drink deep, or taste not the Pierian spring:
There shallow draughts intoxicate the brain,
And drinking largely sobers us again.

Or:

True wit is nature to advantage dressed,
What oft was thought, but never so well expressed.

■ ■ ■

It's interesting to see a Naming poet like Whitman linking his praise of the sensory world to concept language. In a Saying mode, Whitman was often eager to connect his beliefs to the natural world he loved to name:

I believe a leaf of grass is no less than the journey-work of the stars,
And the pismire is equally perfect, and a grain of sand, and the egg of
    the wren,   *[pismire = ant]*
And the tree-toad is a chef-d'oeuvre for the highest,
And the running blackberry would adorn the parlors of heaven,
And the narrowest hinge in my hand puts to scorn all machinery,
And the cow crunching with depressed head surpasses any statue,
And a mouse is miracle enough to stagger sextillions of infidels.
                             from "Song of Myself," section 31

But he was also eager to say out baldly and boldly his more provocative opinions—ones that shocked his contemporaries and still have the power to engage us with their freshness of expression:

I believe in the flesh and the appetites,
Seeing, hearing, feeling, are miracles, and each part and tag of me is
 a miracle.

Divine am I inside and out, and I make holy whatever I touch or am
 touched by,
The scent of these arm-pits aroma finer than prayer,
This head more than churches, bibles, and all the creeds.

If I worship one thing more than another it shall be the spread of my
 own body, or any part of it,
Translucent mold of me it shall be you!
Shaded rests and ledges it shall be you!
from "Song of Myself," section 24

If the overt self-centeredness of Whitman's pride in his own physicality unnerves us, we should note that he makes equally powerful claims for the counterbalancing principle of sympathy (empathy):

And whoever walks a furlong without sympathy walks to his own
 funeral drest in his shroud.
from "Song of Myself," section 48

■ ■ ■

Oddly enough, true large claims may not provide the shiver we crave, may not reach that part of us that both recognizes and longs for the outrageousness or the overreaching that may be part of Saying's power. Let me give an example. John Donne (1572–1631) has already begun with a certain impressive level of authority when he opens a sonnet by challenging a personified Death directly in his first line:

Death, be not proud, though some have called thee
Mighty and dreadful . . .

Donne keeps the pressure high all the way through his poem as he boldly ponders and debates the power death has over us. And he saves his strongest claim for the final line:

> One short sleep past, we wake eternally,
> And death shall be no more; death, thou shalt die.
>
> from "Death, Be Not Proud" (1609)

"Death, thou shalt die." That's about as strong a statement as we can imagine a mortal human making about the fact of mortality. But if a poem said "Life, thou shalt die," I doubt we would be thrilled or stimulated or pleasurably puzzled by the claim; I doubt such a statement, though probably true, would have the dramatic impact that Donne achieves. Wouldn't we perhaps just shrug sadly and say, "That's true, that's certainly true"? Saying in poems often gets power from the audacity or surprise of its claims.

■ ■ ■

It's possible to disguise powerful Saying, as William Blake does in his poem "The Tyger." Though Blake seldom hesitated to convey his radical notions through powerful and direct Saying, he constructs this particular poem out of nothing but questions—fourteen of them in twenty-four lines:

The Tyger

Tyger, Tyger, burning bright
In the forests of the night,
What immortal hand or eye
Could frame thy fearful symmetry?   [*fearful = terrifying*]

In what distant deeps or skies
Burnt the fire of thine eyes?

On what wings dare he aspire?
What the hand, dare seize the fire?

And what shoulder, & what art
Could twist the sinews of thy heart?
And, when thy heart began to beat,
What dread hand? & what dread feet?

What the hammer? What the chain,
In what furnace was thy brain?
What the anvil? What dread grasp,
Dare its deadly terrors clasp?

When the stars threw down their spears,
And water'd heaven with their tears:
Did He smile His work to see?
Did He who made the Lamb make thee?

Tyger, Tyger burning bright,
In the forests of the night,
What immortal hand or eye
Dare frame thy fearful symmetry?

William Blake (1794)

One impact of Blake's decision to make a poem out of questions is to understate the force of the assertions and the drift of the poem until he can surprise us with questions like this one: "Did He smile His work to see?" In theory Blake's questions are directed at the tiger; but in reality they're addressed to us, the poem's readers, and their difficulty startles us. Almost before we realize it, we are pondering the mysterious nature of a Creator God who made fierce and violent carnivores as well as peaceful creatures. Blake's poem is an excellent example of the way that questions, and especially rhetorical questions, can "smuggle" Saying into a poem without the reader quite realizing it. A poet's clever use of questions can make it so that the reader is not only the audience for an assertion, but almost an accomplice of the poet as he or she inserts a claim disguised by a question mark.

CHAPTER ELEVEN

Imagining

> The greatest thing by far is to be a master of metaphor. It is
> the one thing that cannot be learnt from others; and it is also
> a sign of genius, since a good metaphor implies an intuitive
> perception of the similarity in dissimilars.

ARISTOTLE, *Poetics*

I magining is a nonrational form of meaning-making. The basic
formula of metaphor is "A is B." Here's an example: "his cheeks
are roses." But logically, A can't be B—and even more obvi-
ously, his cheeks cannot be roses. Cheeks are part of a human face; a
rose is a flower. So why would anyone say such an untrue thing? Well,
perhaps the poet is after a heart-truth, some distortion or alteration of
reality caused by intense emotion—perhaps a truth that Naming or
Saying or Singing can't quite capture. And the poet chooses another
way: Imagining, metaphor-making.

IMAGINING AS METAPHOR-MAKING

Before we explore metaphor-making and the pleasures and insights
of Imagining, let's pause to take in again the radically unusual nature
of metaphor. As I say, the premise is "A is B." What if B in my exam-
ple of "his cheeks are roses" wasn't so easy to get or accept, didn't
fit into a history of comparisons and romantic compliments? What if
"A is B" were to read as "his cheeks are telephone poles"? From this
example, you can see that metaphor-making has the potential to be a

genuinely disturbing and puzzling use of language as well as a plea-surable one. For my part, imagining that someone's cheeks are tele-phone poles disturbs or confuses me far more than it could ever delight me. But let's get back to the main project of Imagining and successful metaphor-making.

■ ■ ■

Metaphor happens when the poet intuits connections between dispa-rate objects. Intuition is a way of knowing that involves the uncon-scious mind—you know something, but you don't know *how* you know it or even *why* you know it; you just sense the rightness of it. Intuition is distinct from rational, logical knowing—from analysis, which proceeds by dividing up into categories, and from synthesizing thought, which makes its discoveries by bringing things together. In intuitive thinking, most of the process of thought takes place uncon-sciously, and we're left only with the conclusion, not with the steps that led up to it. Metaphor seems to happen by means of this sudden "underground" linking of things.

Let's consider a few examples of metaphor and how they contain or radiate meanings. The poem "Zone," by the French poet Guil-laume Apollinaire (1880–1917), is set in Paris and begins by comparing the Eiffel Tower to a shepherdess, with the bridges across the River Seine as her sheep:

Shepherdess O Eiffel Tower your flock of bridges is bleating
    this morning

The poem is long and both jaunty and bittersweet in tone—its narra-tive involves the speaker of the poem wandering around Paris for one whole day and an entire night as well. It begins with the poet address-ing the Eiffel Tower in the morning and ends, several pages later, with the poet by now exhausted and somewhat depressed, witnessing the next day's dawn. This new dawn appears as a startling metaphor that is the entire final line of the poem:

soleil cou coupé

This line could be translated as "sun: severed neck." The metaphor compares the rising, red sun to the neck of someone who has been guillotined. The metaphor *concentrates* meanings in its comparison. It means more than one thing. The basis of the comparison is the sun's shape (round) and color (red), but the metaphor moves beyond those aspects to convey a feeling of despair and exhausted despondence that resolves the poem's several tonal possibilities.

■ ■ ■

Some poets, myself included, think that the Anglo-American poetic tradition is somewhat resistant to the lures of Imagining as a language force. No doubt this could be argued back and forth, but it's worth noting that the metaphor-making energy of romanticism in the nineteenth century flourished in France with Charles Baudelaire, the symbolists, and the surrealists. Surrealism, which started in France in 1924 and was deeply committed to the making of (strange/surreal) metaphors, spread far more quickly in Europe and South America than it did in the English-speaking world.

Here are two European poems in which the Imagining plays a decisive role. Because both poems have been translated out of their native languages, the Singing dimension has vanished and we are left with the bare bones of the poems. Images are the least vulnerable aspect of language, the least likely to get lost in translation. An image or metaphor can come across in another language more easily than Singing (I'm less sure about Naming and Saying—about how culture dependent they are). The following poem, by the contemporary Swedish poet Tomas Transtromer, begins with the consolations of music (playing Haydn on a piano after a long and tedious day) and ultimately leads to a marvelous metaphorical claim ("Music is a glass house") about the powers of beauty or art to resist destruction and desolation:

Allegro

I play Haydn after a black day
And feel a simple warmth in my hands.

The keyboard is willing. Mild hammers strike.
The sound is green, lively, tranquil.

The sound says that freedom exists,
That someone does not pay Caesar's tax.

I put my hands in my Haydn-pockets
And pretend to take a cool look at the world.

I hoist the Haydn-flag—it indicates:
"We won't surrender. But want peace."

Music is a glass house on the hillside
Where stones fly, stones crash.

And the stones crash straight through the glass,
But the house remains whole.

        Tomas Transtromer (1962), translated by Robert Bly

To me, Transtromer's Imagining of music (any music) as a (magical) house made of glass is something that feels instantly and absolutely right. When I first read it, my imagination said "Yes!" immediately, and it took a few more minutes for my brain to catch up and say: "Right, he's got it—music is an invisible but real structure, and when we're deeply enjoying it it's like we're inside a space the music makes, and yes, nothing can destroy or damage this (safe, emotionally sustaining) space because it isn't physical (it's made of sound, not something that can break)." My mind went on explaining to me how "right" Transtromer's Imagining was, but the fact is that some part of my consciousness had already said "Yes, that's it!" and so the explanation was just playing catch-up to the joy I felt immediately. I'm not saying that all metaphors work so quickly and decisively; but when they do, it's quite thrilling. (And imagine how Transtromer must have felt when the metaphor came to him—quite pleased, I'd suppose, to have made up something that feels completely "real.")

Here's a poem by the twentieth-century Greek poet Yannis Ritsos that seems to hinge on a single metaphor. I must admit that when I read the poem, I find its narrative plot to be quite cryptic. I'm sufficiently oriented by the poem's opening to know that a woman and a young officer (i.e., a soldier) are involved, that they interact in a room in a way that doesn't seem resolved or resolvable. But I'm pretty unclear about exactly what happens (or fails to happen, really)—something about the encounter goes awry, that's certain. But to me, the joy and mystery of the poem isn't in the story but in the one key figurative event—the comparison of "thin slices of lemon for tea" with the tiny ("Miniature" is the title) wheels of a magic carriage in a child's fairy tale. It's easy to see the basis for this comparison: the circular shape of both wheel and lemon slice; the radial spokes of the wheel and the comparable appearance of a sliced-open lemon. The metaphor fills me with wonder and enchantment and almost takes me back to the childhood it evokes—to that mind-set where such things as fairy-tale coaches are part of a story. I love the way the image inserts the mystery (often somber) of fairy tales into the middle of this awkward social scene that may also be a scene of thwarted intimacy:

Miniature

The woman stood up in front of the table. Her sad hands
begin to cut thin slices of lemon for tea
like yellow wheels for a very small carriage
made for a child's fairy tale. The young officer sitting opposite
is buried in the old armchair. He doesn't look at her.
He lights up his cigarette. His hand holding the match trembles,

throwing light on his tender chin and the teacup's handle. The clock
holds its heartbeat for a moment. Something has been postponed.
The moment has gone. It's too late now. Let's drink our tea.
Is it possible, then, for death to come in that kind of carriage?
To pass by and go away? And only this carriage to remain,
with its little yellow wheels of lemon
parked for so many years on a side street with unlit lamps,
and then a small song, a little mist, and then nothing?

Yannis Ritsos (1947),
translated from the Greek by Edmund Keeley

When I show this poem to most of my students, some like the image
of the lemon slice/carriage wheel and others reject it. For the students
who reject the image, the poem must fail, because if you don't give
your heart (and imagination) to that image when it first appears, you'll
definitely be frustrated to discover that the carriage reappears at the
end of the poem; and when it does, it's even more cryptic and filled
with strange implications than when it first showed up. As a reader, I
"got" Transtromer's metaphor of music as a house of glass right away,
but Ritsos's image is harder for me. I'm amazed that I went from the
lemon slice/carriage wheel to the whole carriage and then the possi-
bility that death is inside the carriage ("Is it possible, then, for death
to come in that kind of carriage?")—and then the carriage goes away
again, but not really, not really; it's waiting somewhere in a weird and
haunting way.

In this next poem, from Madagascar, the anonymous poet is
probably a farmer responding to an alarming aspect of his life: the
periodic appearance of locusts—a kind of relentless grasshopper that
descends in huge swarms to devour and desolate the farmer's fields.
Although the poet knows his locust well and can name every part
of its body and every action it engages in, Naming is not adequate
to the emotional experience that the locust brings to his world; only
metaphor and Imagining can give access to the mystery and misery
that it brings:

The Locust

What's a locust look like you ask?
Its head's a seed of corn;
Its neck is a jackknife hinge;
Antennae? Little bits of thread.
Chest? A shiny bronze breastplate.
It's whole body polished smooth
And solid as a knife handle.
Legs? a saw blade; spit
From its mouth? Ink.
Its underwings—thin cloth
You'd wrap a corpse in.

When it's on the ground,
It's constantly laying eggs.
When it's flying, it's like
The darkest cloud you ever saw
Gliding across the sky.
                    And when
It descends, it's noisy, glittering
Raindrops from a thick sunshower.
Whatever plant stalk it lands on—
Its scissors start cutting it up.
When it moves on the ground,
It's a crowd of razors
Shaving the earth bare.
When it crawls across your field,
Desolation crawls with it.

                    Anonymous, translated by Gregory Orr

■ ■ ■

The pleasure and dazzle of Imagining is experiential—you feel it almost immediately, or you don't feel it. Much can be said, perhaps— metaphors can be analyzed and explained to some extent, but finally their mystery and delight are beyond explaining or persuading.

■ ■ ■

In Aristotle's view, how far apart the two elements of comparison are is an important issue. We might say that the assertion of connection should be surprising and unusual, but also somehow credible and grat- ifying. We seem to value surprise, pleasure, and some intuited insight in such comparisons. Aristotle argues that if the claim or compari- son is too odd or the connection too distant, then the metaphor will fail to please. And of course a metaphor's two elements cannot be too *close*, either. You cannot compare a cookie to cake, for instance. To say "this cookie is a cake" will not help anyone's poem or arouse anyone's interest. Nor, I suspect would Aristotle have cared for a poem that claimed "this cookie is a turtle" or "this cookie is a mountain."

"This cookie is a mountain." Sounds a bit dubious, sounds like a surrealist image. I began this discussion of Imagining with an example from Guillaume Apollinaire's poem "Zone." Although not a surreal- ist himself, Apollinaire did invent the word. When the French poet André Breton went on to write the first *Surrealist Manifesto* (published as a booklet in 1924) and founded a movement that would profoundly influence Western art in the twentieth century, he defined surrealism as a reconciling of the "two realities" of human consciousness: *waking* reality and *dream* reality. According to Breton and the surrealists, these two distinct and seemingly contradictory forms of consciousness were to be reconciled into a "higher reality" or "sur-reality." Breton's mani- festo celebrated metaphors as the surest way for a poet to achieve "the marvelous"—a highest value in surrealism.

In poetry, surrealism called for metaphors and similes where the connections between two objects (what Aristotle called the "intu- itive perception of the similarity in dissimilars") were arbitrary or almost impossible to "understand" in Aristotle's sense. And yet surrealism has so permeated twentieth-century Western culture that even now, when we see a really weird or improbable event, we're likely to declare it "surreal" without even pausing to consider where the term came from.

Nevertheless, it's not surprising that a Saying poet like W. H. Auden would be skeptical of surrealist Imagining. In a letter from Auden to Frank O'Hara in which he rejected O'Hara's book for the Yale Younger Poets Award, which he has just given to John Ashbery, Auden comments skeptically about surrealist metaphors:

> I think you (and, John, too for that matter) must watch what is always the great danger with any "surrealistic" style, namely of confusing authentic nonlogical relations which arouse wonder with accidental ones which arouse mere surprise and in the end fatigue.

■ ■ ■

AN IMAGINING EXERCISE

Metaphor-making is a curious and exciting way of writing. There's a great sense of delight that comes from having brought together two dissimilar things and linking them powerfully. Still, it's hard to teach someone about metaphor-making. I think the best strategy is to introduce it as a kind of game in which the poet gives herself or himself permission to make outrageous metaphors just to see what happens. As I have noted, the French surrealists were deeply excited about metaphors and specialized in odd and sometimes outrageous comparisons.

To prepare for this exercise, you're about to read a long love poem by André Breton, the founder and leader of the surrealist movement, that is structured as a list of metaphors for parts of his beloved's body. Think of the structure of Breton's poem in terms of the interplay between disorder and order. You can visualize the poem as composed of two columns going down the page. The left-hand column is a list of human anatomy parts (in this case, the beloved's)—this list is more or less systematic and ordered (it goes from tip to toe, lingering at certain places and skipping around a bit). The right-hand column consists of the things that the poet associates with this or that body part—this list is highly disordered and unpredictable, even chaotic and/or outrageous at times. The two columns together enact a pair of lists that we can assume tries to get at the wonder and strangeness of passionate, romantic love. Of course, it's important to realize that the order (left-column body parts) and disorder (right-column strange comparisons) is held together tonally by a presiding and unifying emotion (celebration of the beloved). This disorder and order unfolding within a unifying emotion or tone or theme is, of course, the basic nature and true lure of lyric. But enough talking about the poem. Here it is, a surrealist love poem bristling with metaphors:

Free Union

My woman with her forest-fire hair
With her heat-lightning thoughts
With her hourglass waist
My woman with her otter waist in the tiger's mouth
My woman with her rosette mouth a bouquet of stars of the
*   brightest magnitude*
With her teeth of white mouse footprints on the white earth
With her tongue of polished amber and glass
My woman with her stabbed eucharist tongue
With her tongue of a doll that opens and closes its eyes
With her tongue of incredible stone
My woman with her eyelashes in a child's handwriting
With her eyebrows the edge of a swallow's nest
My woman with her temples of a greenhouse with a slate roof
And steam on the windowpanes
My woman with her shoulders of champagne
And a dolphin-headed fountain under ice

My woman with her matchstick wrists
My woman with her lucky fingers her ace of hearts fingers
With her fingers of new-mown hay
My woman with her armpits of marten and beechnuts
Of Midsummer Night
Of privet and angelfish nest
With her seafoam and floodgate arms
Arms that mingle the wheat and the mill
My woman with rocket legs
With her movements of clockwork and despair
My woman with her calves of elder tree pith
My woman with her feet of initials
With her feet of bunches of keys with her feet of weaverbirds
    taking a drink
My woman with her pearl barley neck
My woman with her Val d'or cleavage
Cleavage of a rendezvous in the very bed of the mountain stream
With her breasts of night
My woman with her undersea molehill breasts
My woman with her breasts of the crucible of rubies
With her breasts of the specter of the rose beneath the dew
My woman with her belly of the unfolding fan of days
With her giant claw belly
My woman with her back of a bird fleeing vertically
With her quicksilver back
With her back of light
With her nape of rolled stone and damp chalk
And a falling glass that's just been sipped
My woman with her hips like a canoe
With her hips of a chandelier and arrow feathers
And stems of white peacock plumes
Her hips an imperceptible pair of scales
My woman with her buttocks of sandstone and asbestos
My woman with the buttocks of a swan's back

My woman with her buttocks of springtime
With her gladiolus sex
My woman with her sex of placer and platypus
My woman with her sex of seaweed and old-fashioned candies
My woman with her mirror sex
My woman with her eyes full of tears
With her eyes of violet armor and a speedometer needle
My woman with her savannah eyes
My woman with her eyes of water to drink in prison
My woman with her eyes of forests forever beneath the axe
With her eyes of sea-level air-level earth and fire

André Breton (1923),
translated by Bill Zavatsky and Zack Rogow

You may or may not find this poem interesting. But chances are you "get it." That is, you understand how it was made, and you see that the poet gave himself permission to make up all sorts of outrageous comparisons. I suggest that in this exercise modeled on the Breton poem, you give yourself the same permission and also give yourself the same kind of steadying (ordering) structure that the anatomy parts gave Breton. So:

Choose an object that has a number of nameable parts (I'd say a minimum of at least six but more would be better) and use those parts to create a left-hand margin list. For example, a poem called "The Maple Tree" could have in its left margin the following list: *bark, leaves, branches, crown, trunk, roots*. You might use those terms to make something like this:

The Maple Tree

with its bark of week-old newspaper
with its leaves of lemon and artichoke
with its branches of God's candelabra
with its crown of sorrow and light

with its trunk of dreams
with its trunk of cathedral pillars
with its roots of tiny fingers sifting the earth,
with its roots of the buried mirror of branches

Or you could write a poem called "My Toyota":

with its tires of . . .
with its chassis of . . .
with its bumpers of . . .
with its engine of . . .
with its windshield of . . .
with its seats of . . .
with its steering wheel of . . .

After choosing an object (or person) to praise and listing the parts in the left-hand column, then go wild with associative metaphors in the right-hand side of the poem. Really let yourself go—there's no particular reason the metaphors have to make sense. (Although you're also welcome to make them as evocative, coherent, and emotionally cohesive as you wish.) Play is a form of freedom. Freedom to imagine is crucial; freedom to range freely in imagination is an essential form of permission that a poet gives herself or himself. The point is to experience the playful liveliness of Imagining and the fact that metaphoric imagination can make discoveries and create meanings in its own special way.

■ ■ ■

EXTENSIVE AND INTENSIVE METAPHORS

The great Chilean poet Pablo Neruda (1904–1973) wrote a group of poems he called "Elemental Odes." In this series, each poem begins by focusing on a simple (elemental) thing—artichokes, salt, a book, a medical technician—and generates a flurry of metaphors to show the poet's response to the object, a response that simply Naming or Saying wouldn't be adequate to accomplish. In this particular poem, there's even a minimal "story line" to structure the images: the poet gets the gift of the socks, considers his feet, puts on the socks, ends his poem. But what a set of images, what a dazzle of firework jewel images is strung on that thin story-line thread:

Ode to My Socks

Maru Mori brought me
a pair of socks
which she knitted herself
with her sheep-herder's hands,
two socks as soft
as rabbits.
I slipped my feet
into them
as though into
two
cases
knitted
with threads of
twilight
and goatskin.
Violent socks,
my feet were
two fish made
of wool,
two long sharks
seablue, shot
through
by one golden thread,
two immense blackbirds,
two cannons,

my feet
were honored
in this way
by
these
heavenly
socks.
They were
so handsome
for the first time
my feet seemed to me
unacceptable
like two decrepit
firemen, firemen
unworthy
of that woven
fire,
of those glowing
socks.

Nevertheless
I resisted
the sharp temptation
to save them somewhere
as schoolboys
keep
fireflies,
as learned men
collect
sacred texts,
I resisted
the mad impulse
to put them
in a golden

cage
and each day give them
birdseed
and pieces of pink melon.
Like explorers
in the jungle who hand
over the very rare
green deer
to the spit
and eat it
with remorse,
I stretched out
my feet
and pulled on
the magnificent
socks
and then my shoes.

The moral
of my ode is this:
beauty is twice
beauty
and what is good is doubly
good
when it is a matter of two socks
made of wool
in winter.

Pablo Neruda (1954–57), translated by Robert Bly

I most love the passage with the socks as birds in a golden cage, partly
because I say to myself, "yes, a sock does vaguely, crazily have the
shape of a bird," and that discovery fills me with silly joy. I also love
the humor of "twice" beautiful and "doubly" good because of *two*
socks—that absurd humor and its practical basis appeal to me (after

all, what good or beauty resides in one sock?). And finally, I love the secret politics of the poem—a politics that celebrates simple, reciprocal gift-exchange in human relations: Maru Mori gave me these socks; I give her this poem (and honor her by Naming her in it). I'd like a world where things were that simple and straightforward and generous.

■ ■ ■

One of Neruda's poetic heroes and forebears was Walt Whitman. I've already noted that Whitman is a great namer—that is one of his major strengths as a poet, which isn't surprising since he was a professional journalist and had to be accurate with his facts, his Namings. He loved the variety of the world and loved to catalogue that rich variety in the list poems he made.

But there were times when facts and accurate noticing and Naming weren't adequate to the mystery Whitman intuited. This was especially true in relation to the central symbol of his imagination: grass. Here's a section of his long lyric sequence, "Song of Myself," in which he denies his ability to name the mystery inherent in a handful of grass and then switches to a series of metaphors to evoke that mystery, a series of what he calls "guesses" but which are, of course, actually metaphors or Imaginings:

A child said, *What is the grass?* fetching it to me with full hands;
How could I answer the child? I do not know what it is any more
    than he.

I guess it must be the flag of my disposition, out of hopeful green
    stuff woven.

Or I guess it is the handkerchief of the Lord,
A scented gift and remembrancer designedly dropt,
Bearing the owner's name someway in the corners, that we may see
    and remark, and say *Whose?*

Or I guess the grass is itself a child, the produced babe of the
    vegetation.

Or I guess it is a uniform hieroglyphic,
And it means, Sprouting alike in broad zones and narrow zones,
Growing among black folks as among white,
Kanuck, Tuckahoe, Congressman, Cuff, I give them the same, I
    receive them the same.

And now it seems to me the beautiful uncut hair of graves.

Tenderly will I use you curling grass,
It may be you transpire from the breasts of young men,
It may be if I had known them I would have loved them;
It may be you are from old people and from women, and from
    offspring taken soon out of their mothers' laps,
And here you are the mothers' laps.

This grass is very dark to be from the white heads of old mothers,
Darker than the colorless beards of old men,
Dark to come from under the faint red roofs of mouths.

O I perceive after all so many uttering tongues!
And I perceive they do not come from the roofs of mouths for
    nothing.

I wish I could translate the hints about the dead young men
    and women,
And the hints about the old men and mothers, and the offspring
    taken soon out of their laps.

What do you think has become of the young men and old men?
And what do you think has become of the women and children?

> They are alive and well somewhere,
> The smallest sprout shows there is really no death,
> And if ever there were it led forward life, and does not wait at the end
>   to arrest it,
> And ceas'd the moment life appear'd.
>
> All goes onward and outward, nothing collapses,
> And to die is different from what any one supposed, and luckier.
>
> "Song of Myself," section 6 (1855)

Notice how the poem begins with the child's (difficult) question. It's as if the poet is in that notorious situation of a father being asked by his child one of those simple-sounding questions—"Why is the sky blue?" Not always easy to answer. And the scientific or fact-based answer doesn't really work either, because it doesn't address our human curiosity exactly or our longing for meanings. But Whitman has no sooner claimed his own ignorance about "What is the grass?" and declined to come up with a "fact" definition than he begins to provide *metaphoric* definitions: Grass is:

> *a flag and a handkerchief (both based on rectangular shape of a lawn*
>   *or field, perhaps) then a child*
> *then a hieroglyph*
> *then the beautiful uncut hair of graves*

In mid-poem, the anatomy images shift from hair to tongues (by way of the term *dark*), and then the poet offers to translate what the tongues are saying (earlier he translated the hieroglyph as a symbol of democratic equality). It turns out the tongues are saying something about death.

By my count, Whitman presents *six major metaphors* for grass, a number of which get explored and expanded upon. In the course of these metaphors, Whitman has brought in sex (flirting rituals involving the "designedly" intentional dropping of a scented handkerchief with initials in the corner) and death and resurrection. Plus youth and old age and a notion of political and cultural equality. All these *meanings* are the product of associative connections the poet or reader makes with the metaphors and the metaphorical transformation of the original object (the handful of grass). Something ordinary (grass) is shown to be extraordinary through the addition that Imagining has brought to it.

■ ■ ■

The introduction of a metaphor into a poem often affects the poem's momentum. This happens because it's in the nature of metaphor to "split" the poem into two levels. In the Whitman poem, the split narrative takes on momentum when it gets to *graves* because death is one of the main mysteries that Whitman's imagination (all human imaginations) must engage and transform. The two stories that his various metaphors implied were all over the map (seduction, birth, radical democracy) until he got to the central mystery: death. Death is one of Whitman's obsessions: his language and imagination spiral around this theme with one metaphor after another until he is finally ready, at section's end, to make a powerful pair of Sayings about it: "And to die is *different* from what any one supposed, and *luckier*" (emphasis mine).

■ ■ ■

The metaphors in Whitman's poem can be thought of as being *extensive*—that is, as the reader takes them in, they broaden or extend the poem's frame of reference; they widen and enliven the world of the poem (and of the reader, also, one hopes). Such a scattershot broadening is also the case with the metaphors in Neruda's "Ode to My Socks."

But metaphor can also function *intensively* in lyrics, as in this one by Emily Dickinson (1830–1886), in which the metaphors establish, intensify, and reinforce the poem's dominant emotion or tone:

Empty my Heart, of Thee—
Its single Artery—

Begin, and leave Thee out—
Simple Extinction's Date—

Much Billow hath the Sea—
One Baltic—They—
Subtract Thyself, in play,
And not enough of me
Is left—to put away—
"Myself" meant Thee—

Erase the Root—no Tree—
Thee—then—no me—
The Heavens stripped—
Eternity's vast pocket, picked—

Emily Dickinson, #587 (1862)

I'll attempt a paraphrase of Dickinson's poem in order to explain her metaphors and show how they feed toward the emotional and dramatic center of the poem, the theme of "how much I love you and need you." I attempt this clumsy paraphrase in order to clarify the metaphors. It's not much fun to do to a poem, any poem, but Dickinson is so compressed and intense in her writing that it isn't easy for many readers to follow her language and imagination as it unfolds. Here goes:

You are the single artery that feeds/goes from/is my heart (and love)—to eliminate you/forget you would be my death date. Stanza 2: There are many oceans/waves in the oceans, but only one Baltic ocean (a unique ocean). If you were taken away from me, there wouldn't be anything left—basically "you" are me in the sense that without you, I'm nothing. Stanza 3: Eliminate the roots and you have no tree; eliminate you and there's no me left—such a situation would be as if the sky were entirely empty of clouds (again deprivation) or as if something as vast as Eternity had had its pocket picked by a thief of something valuable (namely, "you").

As I say, paraphrases of poems are awkward and reductive, but I hope you can see my point: the theme of Dickinson's lyric is lost love or fear of loss of love (*you*) and how that deprivation would desolate the speaker. Although the metaphors are various (ocean and waves, tree, artery and heart, sky), they all feed into the poem's central theme: deprivation of the beloved, or the threat of such deprivation and how it would affect the speaker. The metaphors point toward the poem's center; that's what I mean by saying they can function intensively. This thematic center is reinforced by the poem's key verbs also: *empty . . . of, leave out, subtract, erase.*

■ ■ ■

MORE IMAGINING EXERCISES

Here's another variation on the Imagining exercise; this is a bit more complicated but could also prove interesting or fun. It has *three parts* (object, abstraction, comparison) rather than the *two parts* (part of body, comparison) of Breton's poem. Whether that will make it more interesting for you, I don't know.

Take an object that's natural and archetypal: taken from nature, the human body, or culture (door, window, house, soup, etc.). This will remain steady throughout your poem (order). Then link this object to an *abstraction* and finally to a *sensory image*. Combine these elements into lines and string them together; make up at least ten. Your tone can be solemn or funny or both. But let yourself go. I gave myself an object (rose) and a dramatic context ("I . . . stared at") and a set of abstractions (oblivion, death, hope, despair, rage). Then I tried to give those abstractions some sensory characteristics of roses (the presiding object) to see what would happen. Here's what I came up with in ten minutes—you're welcome to take longer, but not more than half an hour (to keep the pressure up). What I ended up with isn't a poem, but it was lots of fun:

When I first stared at
The rose of oblivion

With its bare-bones
And its petals of ice,
I saw it in no way resembled
The rose of death
With its velvet petals,
Or the rose of hope
With its thousand open mouths.

I saw that it had nothing
To do with the rose of despair
With its ragged leaves
And its bowed stalk;
Nor the rose of rage
That shivers in the wind
Despite its cloak of thorns.

I saw that it was cousin to . . .

My writing students frequently say to me that they "don't get met-aphor," by which they mean they don't know how to make them, or they're afraid to let themselves go with their imagination. There's something a bit daring and audacious about metaphor-making. When Frost remarked that once a person has made a metaphor it ruins him or her for honest work, I think he was slyly saying that the pleasures of metaphor-making are so intense and instantly gratifying that we are suspicious of them and of ourselves for making them.

■

Here's another imagining exercise that builds on the "I Remember" experience from Chapter 1. The premise is this: there is an Other (a person, a tree, a place even) that was once part of the speaker's life, the I's life, and so the I has a memory of that Other and of some specific aspects of that Other, as in "I remember your lips." The other dimension of this premise is that the speaker is *no longer near or within sensory contact* with the Other, so the speaker must *imagine* what the "lips" are now. The final premise is that time and separation and/or absence have *transformed* that aspect of the Other. My first example:

> I remember your lips.
> I imagine they have become a blimp
> made of pink neon now.

The structuring elements to be filled in by you and your imagination are these: "I remember your . . . I imagine they are/it is . . . now."

My second example:

> I remember your mouth.
> I imagine it is the open grave
> of another's dreams now.

The trick this time, if you wish it to sound like a poem, will be to try to keep all the Imaginings *tonally consistent* so as to unify the language and thereby make it into a poem, or as close to a real poem as a coerced assignment can be. My "blimp made of pink neon" is probably not tonally consistent with my "open grave of another's dreams," and it's unlikely they could inhabit the same poem. Although, who knows? It would depend on what other Imaginings I might array in the list I make.

Think of this exercise as a possible poem, or try to make it into a poem. Let yourself go, and don't worry much about the tone in the first ("permission") phase; but try to get a bunch of lines of Imaginings going, and then later you can rearrange them into an *effective dramatic structure*. As you consider that final step, ask yourself: Where would it be most effective to start? What Imagining would make a great ending?

■ ■ ■

Part Four

WHY POEMS?
WHY POETS?

CHAPTER TWELVE

Ecstasy and Engagement

There is no surer way to escape the world than through [poetry] art, and there is no surer way to tie oneself to it than through [poetry] art.

JOHANN WOLFGANG VON GOETHE

In the last section, we considered how poets Sing and Say and Name and Imagine with words and phrases. Such activities make language more lively, and poets are as fascinated by the possibilities of lively language as painters are by color. I hope the discussion of the four forces gave a sense of the energetic disordering and ordering that words and phrases can be made to enact. We've also seen how the liveliness of language gets shaped into two main forms of poetic coherence: story and lyric. In this final section, I want to shift from lively language and shaping forms to the psychology of the poet himself or herself. Specifically, I hope to explore some primary motives for writing poems and what they might tell us about the identity and purpose of the individual self as he or she embarks on the project of writing poems of self-expression.

The Goethe quote that begins this section seems to be a good place to start our consideration of primary motives for writing lyric poetry. I think he has it right: lyric poetry can free us from the world and can also, in a seeming contradiction, connect us powerfully to that same world. By way of parenthesis, I've altered Goethe's generalized term *art* to *poetry*. What I love about Goethe's remark is that it contains a deep insight into two things we want from poetry: to be freed or liberated from all confinements, and (almost its opposite) to be meaningfully connected to the world and the things and people in it. These two wishes (to be freed and to be meaningfully connected) not only are what we often seek in poetry, but they're also deep impulses that motivate us to write it. For our purposes, I'm going to give a name to Goethe's desire to "escape the world"—I'll call it the desire for ecstasy. And the wish for connection I'll call engagement.

Engagement and ecstasy: two of the most powerful impulses in the human spirit. Engagement is the impulse to engage things in the world—to do, to act, to encounter—to "tie oneself to it." Ecstasy is an impulse to "escape the world"—to rise up out of the body and out of time. If I were to glance back at the topics in the last chapter, I would note that the Singing aspect of language serves the ecstatic impulse well, just as Naming lends itself to the purposes of engagement.

But let's look closely at these two terms. The word *ecstasy* derives from the ancient Greek words *ek stasis* ("to be or stand outside oneself") and refers to "out of the body"—the experience of being released from the body as the center of experience, released from the body-self. For ecstasy to make any sense, the self needs to be experienced as consisting of two parts: say, a body and a soul. To the early Greeks, the dual nature of the self as body and soul made possible an understanding of the universal human phenomenon of dreaming. According to the Greeks (and a number of other cultures), when the body is asleep the soul goes off and has adventures in the world (or other worlds) in the form of dreams. When the soul returns to the body, the person awakes. The universal experience of dreams is not the only situation that has given rise to notions of ecstasy. Humans have always felt that being a body in time can become a burden or a bore and have always cultivated means of release. Ecstasy, of course, is one of the gifts of popular song. The chorus of the song "Drift Away," by Mentor Williams, captures this perfectly when it speaks plaintively of how the beat of rock and roll frees the soul, and how the longing is to "get lost" in it and "drift away." In this song and in many others, the assumption is that the soul is the part of our consciousness that wants to exist free of the body and its sufferings and troubles.

Perhaps the anthem of ecstatic experience could be Charles Baudelaire's prose poem "Get Drunk!" with its acute awareness that drunkenness is a metaphor for the self's desire for a purified intensity free of all constraints. Baudelaire (1821–1867), a French contemporary of Whitman, is quite certain that one of the main functions of lyric is to release the self, the soul, from its confinement in time and body:

Get Drunk!

Get drunk and stay drunk—that's the only thing worth doing. That way you won't be bent-back crushed by the sheer, hideous weight of time, won't be ground into the dirt—your only hope is perpetual drunkenness.

But drunk on what, you wonder? On wine, on poems, on your own self-righteousness—it doesn't matter what substance you use. Just so it gets you totally drunk.

And if it happens (and it will) that you wake up sprawled on the marble steps of some stranger's mansion or face down in a weedy ditch or alone in your grubby room and you feel your high fading or already gone, then all you have to do is ask the passing breeze or the sea wave, or a star, or a bird flying by, or even the clock—ask anything ephemeral and trapped, anything that knows it's tossed agonizingly about—go ahead, ask anything that can sing or speak "Hey, what time is it?" and it (whether it's star or wave or wind) will clue you in: "It's time to get drunk! If you don't want to be just one more martyred slave of time, you better get drunk and stay drunk—on wine, on poems, on your own righteousness—it doesn't matter what."

Charles Baudelaire (1869) translated by Gregory Orr

Time and the body and the mortality it implies—these are powerful motives for ecstasy. *Engagement* has equally powerful attractions for poets. Let's return to the notion of "connect us to the world." You may recall that in Part One I spoke of the poet's fundamental decision to "turn the world into words." Another way of saying that might be: "the poet makes a world out of words." Yes, but what world? What does it mean to make a world out of words? And why would anyone do it? Again, in Part One, I spoke of how almost all of our experience exists in our minds as memory: specific, concrete memories of the world—an iceberg tip we touched in the "I Remember" exercise. When a poet decides to write a poem, sometimes the motivation is a desire to *re-engage* events in her or his past—to focus on them and dramatize them as a poem, to dramatize a key moment in the life of the self. Thus, we have Theodore Roethke's "My Papa's Waltz" (see pg. 98) and Robert Hayden's "Those Winter Sundays" (see p. 95)—poems in which the poet has chosen a specific past situation (kitchen at night, cold house on a winter Sunday morning) and specific relationships (child/son to father in a family home context) to "bring back to life" with words.

A moment that (like all moments) has vanished as reality can be brought back by words and memory and be dramatized as lyric story in such a way as to express its meaning or meanings. We could say that Roethke's motive is to celebrate an intense (though unnerving) moment in his childhood; that Hayden's motive is to remember and honor and also apologize or express regret ("What did I know? What did I know . . ."). And both poets are reconnecting with their fathers in order to celebrate or explore a lost moment that continues to reso-nate in their present consciousness. The same could be said of Sylvia Plath's "Daddy"—poetry allows her to reconnect with her dead father and speak to him as if he were still alive so that she can dramatize her anguished relationship of love and hate and awe and despair.

In his Preface to *Lyrical Ballads* (1800), William Wordsworth famously defined poetry as "the spontaneous overflow of powerful feelings," a statement that clearly endorses the need poets feel for self-expression—we're feeling something so powerfully that we have to express it, and we do so in a poem. But a few pages later he defines poetry a second time and with a slight difference: poetry, he says, "takes its origin from emotion recollected in tranquility." Emotion is still at the center of the definition, but a new set of terms is also present. I'm going to update that second definition, rescue it from its old-fashioned phrasing, in order to highlight its deep insight into the poet's motives. Instead of *recollected*, substitute *remembered*. Instead of *tranquility*, let's say *from a place of safety*. Aren't some (many) lyric poems "emotion remembered from a place of safety"? Isn't that what poets often do when dramatizing a past moment, especially an intense or traumatic or overwhelming one—re-engage the world of their experience from the safe place of a later moment? "The whisky on your breath / Could make a small boy dizzy, / But I held on like death: / Such waltzing was not easy," says Roethke, and brings back out of oblivion a childhood memory that he turns into words *in order to dramatize it and engage the experience, and thereby reveal or discover some of its meanings.*

And on the subject of traumatic experiences recalled and dramatized in poems, let's note that traumatized people are, by definition, powerless against forces that harm them. But when poets go back by way of memory and imagination to past traumas to engage or re-engage them, then those poets are taking control—are shaping and ordering and asserting power over the hurtful events. In lyric poems, they're both telling the story from their point of view and also shaping the experience into an order (the poem) that shows they have power over what (in the past) overpowered them.

■ ■ ■

Not all engagement with our past is characterized by crisis. Wonder, love, loss—these mysteries are woven through the fabric of our daily lives. I love the way the English poet Thomas Hardy (1840–1928) expresses this sense of the wonder of the ordinary world that we sometimes miss when it's happening (as Hardy says below, "we were looking away") and only realize later, after it's gone. The good news about this loss of wonder is that writing lyric poetry is one way of trying to bring it back, to re-inhabit and praise what has vanished.

The Self-Unseeing

Here is the ancient floor,
Footworn and hollowed and thin,
Here was the former door
Where the dead feet walked in.

She sat here in her chair,
Smiling into the fire;
He who played stood there,
Bowing it higher and higher.

Childlike, I danced in a dream;
Blessings emblazoned that day;
Everything glowed with a gleam;
Yet we were looking away!

Thomas Hardy (1917)

Maybe it's a coincidence, but Hardy's poem is like Roethke's "My Papa's Waltz"—both of them feature a child (the speaker/poet) dancing in a past moment, under the eye of parental figures. Dancing is a form of animal exuberance (even ecstasy) and cultural ordering meeting in the same place: the individual, responsive human body. A French writer once said that prose is walking, poetry is dancing. That's a fine metaphor for the pleasurable intensification of emotion, language, and rhythm that is at the heart of poetry.

■ ■ ■

While I'm speculating about ecstasy and engagement, I might as well say that some poets are temperamentally inclined toward ecstasy (the lyric end of the lyric–narrative spectrum) and some are inclined more toward the pleasures and urgencies of engagement (the narrative end of the spectrum). As an example of the contrast of temperaments, we can consider Wallace Stevens and Robert Frost.

Wallace Stevens was drawn to the ecstatic lyric, and he made frequent use of Singing and Saying to lift his poems up out of the world of circumstance. He once defined poetry as "a momentary existence on an exquisite plane." Stevens's definition is clearly a reference to the ability of lyric itself (especially the lyric of Singing) to function as a brief ecstasy. It's also a sly repudiation and parody of another famous definition of poetry by his contemporary, Robert Frost, who said that poetry is "a momentary stay against confusion."

Frost was a great poet of Naming, and of Naming extended and organized into story. In other words, he was a poet of engagement of self in the world (or the second world of words). While Stevens's definition highlights the moment in which poetry itself bring us into a state of Singing bliss ("exquisite"), Frost's definition stresses the power of poetry to engage the confusing world and make it briefly coherent and stable.

It's fun to contrast Stevens's and Frost's definitions, because they highlight these two powerful but different motives that drive poets. In contrast, some poets are acutely aware of both impulses in themselves—for example, I think the tension between ecstasy and engagement is magnificently enacted in Keats's "Bright Star" sonnet, which we have already explored in terms of lyric with a ghost-narrative on page 104. In this poem, to "be" the star would mean to be timeless and ideal and unchanging—all of which have an appeal. But it would also mean being alone and isolated (the "lone splendor" of a hermit) in one's ecstasy. And one of Keats's chief longings was for the sensuous pleasure and intimacy that comes with engagement and embodiment—in this case, with his "fair love." Here's his poem again:

Bright Star

Bright star, would I were steadfast as thou art—
Not in lone splendor hung aloft the night,

And watching, with eternal lids apart,
Like Nature's patient, sleepless Eremite,
The moving waters at their priestlike task
Of pure ablution round earth's human shores,
Or gazing on the new soft-fallen mask
Of snow upon the mountains and the moors—

No—yet still steadfast, still unchangeable,
Pillowed upon my fair love's ripening breast,
To feel forever its soft fall and swell,
Awake forever in a sweet unrest,
Still, still to hear her tender-taken breath,
And so live ever—or else swoon in death.

John Keats (1819)

Keats wants both experiences: the unchanging stability of the star that ecstasy would grant, but also the sensuous intimacy that only time-bound engagement can allow.

BODILY BEING

Many poems that dramatize the tension between ecstasy and engagement involve a deep discomfort with bodily being. One of the best examples of this is T. S. Eliot's "The Love Song of J. Alfred Prufrock." To my mind, this poem is one the great dramatizations of a young person (male) trying to engage the attractions and anxieties of romantic, erotic desire. He is drawn toward the women he sees at the parties, but at the same time he is either alarmed or astonished by their physicality:

And I have known the arms already, known them all—
Arms that are braceleted and white and bare
(But in the lamplight, downed with light brown hair!)

Presuming that the sensory details of the women's arms as "braceleted and white and bare" are approving or celebratory, then it seems that Eliot's parenthetical "But" and further noticing of the "downed with light brown hair" represents a kind of anxiety about the physicality of the idealized beloved. In this passage and others in the poem, Eliot dramatizes his speaker's ambivalence—what William Blake in *The Marriage of Heaven and Hell* called the "Contraries" of "Attraction and Repulsion" that create tension in human lives. The speaker of Eliot's poem is not only hyper-aware of the female figures but also totally self-conscious about his own body. At one moment he's proud of how he has dressed up to create an attractive impression at social encounters:

> My morning coat, my collar mounting firmly to the chin,
> My necktie rich and modest, but asserted by a simple pin—

only to reveal in the next line that he is totally insecure in a bodily way:

> (They will say: 'But how his arms and legs are thin!')

Prufrock enacts the horrible, bodily self-consciousness of late adolescence (being a body as misery, not mystery). He dramatizes it, he enacts it; but his enactment doesn't lead to an engaged resolution of the poem in normal social terms—he will never speak to the woman, never feel comfortable with intimacy. By poem's end he is longing to be some other creature, a well-defended crab or lobster (crabby; safe in his shell), rather than a vulnerable human self:

> I should have been a pair of ragged claws
> Scuttling across the floors of silent seas.

Finally, his imagination at poem's end proposes a resolving scene of solitude and an image of mermaids that expresses his erotic longing and fuses it with his despair at ever achieving anything in the world of engaged intimacy:

I have heard the mermaids singing, each to each.
I do not think that they will sing to me.

I have seen them riding seaward on the waves
Combing the white hair of the waves blown back
When the wind blows the water white and black.

We have lingered in the chambers of the sea
By sea-girls wreathed with seaweed red and brown
Till human voices wake us, and we drown.

Those last lines about the "waves" and the "sea-girls" are a heightened musical rapture that lets us know that ecstasy has taken over—that Singing has released the speaker from his self-conscious and body-conscious anxiety in a final scene where living and dying, waking and drowning, are the same thing. It's a great poem of the mysteries of Eros and of being a body in time, written by a poet who cannot make peace with embodied desire. It will last as long as young men and women try to meet in a civilized context (e.g., at a party) to enact their mutual drama of attraction and fear, desire and paralyzing self-consciousness. "Prufrock" was written by a young man about his uneasy relations with women; but from my experience teaching the poem, I find that young women have no trouble responding to its central drama and recognizing it as something they've also felt.

■ ■ ■

The ecstatic impulse in young poets is not only tied to the story of being a body-self, it's also connected to youthful idealism and the desire to go directly to the essence of something. That's a young poet's temptation, for sure. It manifests often in the writing of poems that are made up entirely of abstractions and with little attention to the Naming of things, an orientation in a real world (who, what, where, when), the presentation of characters (especially an "I" and a "not-I" of some sort), or a consistent unfolding of action. The wish to reach essence directly, to simply say a concept and thereby conjure or grasp it; the loss of the wisdom of "show, don't tell"—how do these impulses happen in young poets?

When I say that young poets want to go directly to rapture and bypass engagement, I think of the two poems by Wilfred Owen on pages 174 and 175. In the first poem, he's creating a fantasy *ecstasy* world out of abstractions and flowing language. By the time he writes the second poem, though, Owen has been totally overwhelmed by his wartime experience in the horrors of trench warfare, and he's determined to use language to *engage* this experience as Naming and narrative. Young people are often inclined to idealism, but that can be a form of evasion of embodied experience. When Owen comes to write the poems "Dulce et Decorum Est" and "Mental Cases," he has learned to glance from heaven to earth, from earth to heaven; and if his poet's pain contains much of the earth-bound horror that he encountered, that makes sense and is appropriate and indelible.

CHAPTER THIRTEEN

A Second Self in a Second World

I n Part One of the book, we considered the nature of the world as we experience it: its randomness and disorder (both inner and outer) and our own need for order. I proposed that the initial act in the direction of poetry-writing is turning the world into words. Although I think that the simple urge to self-expression can explain a lot of the motivation to make a poem, I'll add another one here.

Sometimes a poet wants to make the world into words in order to *remake* the world. When you turn the world into words, you're not just translating the material world and the people and creatures in it into language; you're also arriving at a place where you can transform the world—or at least the version of it that you've chosen to encounter on the page or your laptop. The one you've chosen to shape with the poet's pen.

Such a remaking, a retelling of the story of yourself in the world, is often at work in poetry of engagement. Among other things, lyric gives us an opportunity to be a different self—the imagined self who could speak the words of our poem. A self that might be freer, bolder, more authentic and honest, more passionate, or more gentle.

It might imagine powerfully in the direction of its yearning (as Keats in "Bright Star" or Eliot in "Love Song of J. Alfred Prufrock"), or it might say (at last) what it really feels about something (maybe you *always* knew how you felt about it, or maybe the very act of writing revealed to you how you felt or feel). The point is this: we have a freedom to choose or create a new or a modified self when writing poems. It may be when we start writing a poem or start writing poetry in general that we don't even know "who" will be speaking them, but that's okay. What's most important at the outset is to understand the possibility that the self speaking your poems, the *I* of your poems, doesn't have to be defined or confined by your daily sense of who you are. It's something William Butler Yeats grasped and expressed in this epigram:

> The friends that have it I do wrong
> Whenever I remake a song
> Should know what issue is at stake,
> It is myself that I remake.

Yeats's friends (like our own) may have a need to see us in a certain way, as a certain kind of person with certain set characteristics; when we revise our poems or revise our own identities, they might find it upsetting. But for us, it's different; it's a chance to be or speak differently and freely. Much of who we are or long to be is suppressed in day-to-day social and economic interactions. When Emerson says: "The man is only half himself, the other half is his expression" (also read: "The woman is only half herself, the other half is her expression"), he's on to something essential about writing. But Emerson's phrase makes it seem like a deficit—as if we're less than complete without an expressive form. I prefer to think of it this way: that we are *more than* just who we are in the everyday world—and that "more" can come into being through acts of imagination such as writing and reading lyric poems.

WHITMAN AND THE SELF

In a wonderful poem entitled "There Was a Child Went Forth," Whitman offers a version of how one's sense of identity as a self might be formed beginning in childhood. According to Whitman's poem, the child-self is like a permeable membrane—the child doesn't have clear boundaries between its own being and what's outside it, between self and not-self (not-self being everything in the world that surrounds us: people and creatures and things). According to his poem, the self takes gradual form by interacting with what's outside it—the child "becomes" the thing and then absorbs the thing into himself (or herself), into a personal sense of identity. We recognize this "becoming" as another example of Whitman's radical "sympathy" or sympathetic identification/empathy:

> THERE was a child went forth every day;
> And the first object he look'd upon, that object he became,
> And that object became part of him for the day, or a certain part of
>   the day,
> Or for many years, or stretching cycles of years.
>
> The early lilacs became part of this child,
> And grass, and white and red morning-glories, and white and red
>   clover, and the song of the phoebe-bird . . .
> from "There Was a Child Went Forth" (1891–92)

Whitman's poem makes a simple and bold claim: we are the dynamic residue of our encounters. We *are* perception ("he looked upon") turning into memory: I am (Whitman's speaker is) the lilacs and the lambs and the fish of earliest childhood memories. I am the product of the self–parent relation, the son–father relationship in which the father is strong but also violent and abusive and manipulative:

The father, strong, self-sufficient, manly, mean, angered, unjust,
The blow, the quick loud word, the tight bargain, the crafty lure . . .

The son–mother relationship also:

The mother at home, quietly placing the dishes on the supper-table;
The mother with mild words, clean her cap and gown, a wholesome
   odor falling off her person and clothes as she walks by, . . .

These relations are a combination of sensations ("a wholesome odor")
and memories ("quietly placing the dishes").

I am (Whitman's speaker is) also the product of self–peer relation-
ships and self–social relationships:

And the old drunkard staggering home from the out-house of the
   tavern, whence he had lately risen,
And the school-mistress that pass'd on her way to the school,
And the friendly boys that pass'd—and the quarrelsome boys,
And the tidy and fresh-cheek'd girls—and the barefoot negro boy
   and girl,

I am also the product of my inner states and altered states of conscious-
ness, as when the self first wonders and doubts in the daytime and in
the dark: What is real?

—the sense of what is real—the thought if, after all, it should
   prove unreal,
The doubts of day-time and the doubts of night-time—the curious
   whether and how,
Whether that which appears so is so, or is it all flashes and specks?
Men and women crowding fast in the streets—if they are not flashes
   and specks, what are they?

Whitman's poem makes a certain kind of obvious sense: the things we encountered and saw as we grew up become part of our identity, our sense of who we are. Some experiences were pleasant, some not so; but we entered into them (e.g., "that object he became"), and then they entered us (e.g., "that object became part of him") as memories. Some stayed for a long time ("cycles of years") and formed our sense of who we are. But how does this relate to poetry? It's simple: these encounters and relationships didn't just form our identity; they're also a major source of our attitudes and values and sense of meaning. They are the raw material out of which we can (and do) make significant lyric poems.

SOME SELF–OTHER RELATIONSHIPS

I have no wish to present a psychology of identity formation here, any more than my forces of language and kinds of language use had anything to do with linguistics. What I'm after is an important source of poems—Whitman's poem suggests as sources the kinds of encounters (animal and plant nature) and categories of people with which the self, as it grows up, interacts. Such interactions can be dramatized into poems. Whitman is interested in a list that begins in childhood and moves toward adulthood—like much of his work, it tries to cover a lot of territory (a whole life!). I'd rather take a lesson from his ambitious poem—a lesson about where we as poets might look for subject matter for our poems. That is, we might think about these categories of people and things and ask: "Do I see or remember anything particular when I think about this category, and could I dramatize a self and not-self poem based on that experience?" For example, let's say there's a category called self–father relations. When you think about that category of relationship, does any scene come to mind? Any person other than your actual father? (After all, a step-father might fit in this category also.) A person and a scene or situation—something you might turn into words and dramatize. Isn't that what Roethke does in "My Papa's Waltz" and Robert Hayden in "Those Winter Sundays"—dramatize a personal experience of the self–father relationship? Doesn't Sylvia Plath do the same in "Daddy"?

Plath's "Daddy" allows us to highlight something important about human experience: if a figure (e.g., father) is important, then that person can be important even when absent. Plath's father in "Daddy" is no longer alive, but his *absence* is as significant and capable of generating meaning—generating a poem—as his presence might be. A figure's presence or absence can be deeply important in the life of an individual; either one can be dramatized into that form of meaning we call a lyric poem. This presence-absence paradox is something that any orphan or child of divorce, or divorced person, or survivor of a significant loss can testify to and that myriad poems have dramatized. It's a key fact of the second world of lyric poetry: poems create expressive meaning out of absences just as often as they do out of presences.

At what is probably a lesser level of intensity, we could extend this matter of presence and absence and poems: for a country person trapped in the city, the longing for the rural can be a meaningful absence; for a lonely person, the absence of a beloved is often an active presence in the imagination.

But I've gotten a bit ahead of my topic here. With Whitman's poem in the back of my mind, I'm going to offer a little list of possible categories of relations between a self (us) and a not-self. My list won't be exhaustive, but I'm making it in hopes that it will stimulate your own imagination and memory in such a way that you might discover a specific figure, scene, or creature that could be the basis for a poem dramatizing some aspect of that relationship that you find to be interesting or significant. (Or you might look at poems you like and ask: "What self/not-self relationship is being dramatized in this poem?")

Here's my list, sometimes broken up into subcategories:

Self–parents (self–father, self–mother, self–stepfather,
    self–stepmother)
Self–sibling or family member (sister, brother, cousin, uncle, aunt,
    grandmother, grandfather)

Self–creature (pets, wild animals, farm animals, neighborhood
creatures—a mouse or cockroach in a house . . . what is that
relationship?)

Self–nature or self–landscape (wild nature, backyard, park or garden,
woods, river or rivers, lake, wilderness, urban, suburban, rural)

Self–divine (could have to do with God or gods or with religious
rituals, ceremonies, experiences)

Self–beloved (love poems or poems of longing for love)

Self–hero (a hero or mentor figure, present in your life or in history)

Self–altered states of consciousness (drugs, madness, ecstasy, dream—
situations or experiences in which the self sometimes has a sense
of being divided or there/not-there)

Self–vegetative world (trees, flowers—recall Hopkins's "Spring and
Fall" from pg. 107)

Self–object world (some thing or object that fascinates or upsets you—
recall Neruda's "Ode to My Socks" from pg. 253–55)

Self–body (oddly enough, we often experience our bodies or parts of
our bodies as "separate" from us and have opinions about them:
e.g., "I love my feet" or "I hate my toes")

Self–past self (remembering yourself at a younger age or in a certain
situation long ago and addressing that self as if he or she were
another person)

Self–future self (another version of the previous relationship—why not
write a poem to yourself in the future? Who says we couldn't or
wouldn't want to dramatize such a relationship to see what emerges?)

Self–technological gadget (this must be a recent category of
relationship, but think about how intense and complicated it
sometimes is—your relationship to laptop, iPhone, iPod, apps,
virtual reality games and gadgets)

Self–art (there are poems addressed to or dramatizing an encounter
with paintings, pieces of music, etc. In a moment we'll look at one:
Rilke's "Archaic Torso of Apollo.")

This is just a partial list of relationships that could be considered as possible sources for your poems. Various poetry websites have huge repositories of contemporary poems organized by categories that they call themes or subjects, such as "brothers and sisters," but that might more usefully be thought of as relationships between a self and a not-self that poets have dramatized in one way or another in order to create or discover meaning.

Any of these relations can be experienced as either positive or negative. Walt Whitman and Frank O'Hara loved New York City, and their poems are full of the excitement of that relationship. In contrast, when the Spanish poet Federico García Lorca came to the same city in 1929 to study at Columbia University, he was traumatized by the experience; the anguish and despair of the relationship between himself and the huge, bewildering city fills his surrealist collection *Poet in New York*.

Another point: not all categories of self/not-self are meaningful to all of us. For someone growing up in the city, the rural landscape or wilderness might be an "empty" category of relationship. That is to say, the person would derive no meaning from that relationship and would probably have trouble writing poems about it, whereas the self–city relationship might be central to his or her being and the source of numerous poems.

■ ■ ■

Here's something obvious that I haven't mentioned: relationship is a two-way street. In each of the categories of self and not-self relationship, it isn't just the "I" that acts on the "not-I." This mutuality of interaction is expected when the not-self is a person or a creature, but it can extend past living beings to seemingly inanimate objects as well. For example, many readers feel that Rainer Maria Rilke's "Archaic Torso of Apollo" is one of the most effective enactments of the reciprocity of relation between a self and an art object:

Archaic Torso of Apollo

We can't see what's gone: his mythic
Head's vanished, the ripe fruit
Of his eyes unknowable now.
Yet what's left: his partial body
Glowing as if a lamp inside shone out—

Somehow what remains is suffused
With the all the intensity his gaze
Once had—otherwise, the shining
Curve of chest couldn't disturb so,
Nor your eyes detect a curving smile
Descending from either side toward
That dark and absent groin where
His force flared forth. Otherwise,

This stone body would seem marred,
But instead it descends as sparkling waterfall
From marble shoulders, it glistens
Like a wild beast's fur, it bursts out

Of its confinement with all the power
Of a star. Now, hiding's useless: it sees you
Completely. You must change your life.

     Rainer Maria Rilke (1908), translated by Gregory Orr

When the poem begins, the speaker ("you") is looking at the headless, limbless statue of the Greek god of beauty—looking at it intently, as we often do when we study something in a museum. But the power of the relationship shifts—it isn't just the "you" looking at the object; the statue itself quickly reveals that it is a source of light and energy ("glistens / like a wild beast's fur"), and by poem's end it has increased its energy level (it's now a star) and taken control of the relationship.

Now the statue is seeing the "you" with a power that culminates in a transformational demand: "Now, hiding's useless: it sees you / Completely. You must change your life."

■ ■ ■

We poets cannot dramatize all our relations. We're lucky if we can dramatize even the most important ones. It takes luck and skill. Lyric poetry doesn't aspire to a complete dramatization of self, which is impossible. But it makes sense to attempt dramatizing those relationships that are important to you. And yet we need to bring the relationship, any relationship, into dramatic focus. In trying to dramatize an important relationship (e.g., self and mother), we're often tempted to try to say *everything* about that relationship in a single poem—and that impulse can quickly create a muddled rather than a focused utterance (recall the discussion of lyric revision in Part Three).

■ ■ ■

EXERCISE FOR A POEM ADDRESSED TO YOUR YOUNGER OR YOUR FUTURE SELF

This exercise focuses on the self/earlier-self relationship. It asks that you first imagine (as we usually all do) that the person you were ten years ago isn't the same person you are now, so you can write a poem in which your present self speaks to this earlier self. Here are the suggested guidelines. Write a poem (at least twelve lines long) in which you speak as an "I" to an earlier you—to yourself at five years of age, or ten. Pick a time or a situation in which that earlier self is either in crisis or about to enter into a new experience. Experiment with your attitude toward that earlier self. It seems obvious that compassion and goodwill would be sensible, but maybe not; maybe you're angry or frustrated with that earlier version of yourself. Frustrated that he or she is, say, willfully blind to a particular situation or exhibits some personality traits or attitudes that you will later wish were not present or not

dominant. For example, I remember as a kid being paralyzed with shy-
ness and inhibition—almost afraid to speak. I could be compassionate
toward that affliction now, but I could also give my earlier self a dose of
hard advice and a warning about what was to come.

Alternatively, write a poem (again, at least twelve lines long) in which
you address a future you—a self ten years from now. What would you
say to this person? Are you proud of who he or she has become? Dis-
appointed? Frustrated? Do you feel a need to justify your present self
to this future person? Let your imagination and emotions lead you. If it
helps the language and imagination to flow, imagine that your poem is
in the form of a letter to your future self.

Whichever version of this exercise you choose, give yourself utmost
permission to put down whatever comes into your head. Find an open-
ing sentence that puts an attitude and an engagement in the fore-
ground, and then let it flow. (For example, I could write: "Look at you,
dawdling in the halls—by the time you get to the lunchroom, all the
food will be gone . . ." imagining myself reluctant to be in the school
lunchroom in third grade, where our teacher prowled up and down
and terrorized us into eating everything on our plates.) If the language
wants to go to a different place, let it—just follow along behind it and
write it down. Don't worry where it's headed or what it will discover. The
more vividly you imagine this past-self or future-self, the more some
event or attitude will emerge from the flow of the language.

You don't have to generate a completed poem in this first phase;
all you need to do is explore. It's easy to revise by trimming down
excess phrases and lines and leaving only the heart of the action and
the Saying. But that shaping by exclusion comes later in the process.
For now, just allow the flowing that discovers. It might also be helpful
to approach this exercise over a period of a few days, a few separate
efforts, in order to give your imagination time to consider different pos-
sible attitudes and situations.

EXERCISE FOR A POEM ABOUT SELF AND BODY

As we saw in the brief look at Eliot's "The Love Song of J. Alfred Pru-frock" and as we probably all know from our own experience, people have strong and complicated relationships with their own bodies or aspects of their bodily being. The poet Lucille Clifton has written a number of poems celebrating her bodily being ("homage to my hips" is a fine example). However, who hasn't heard someone say (or heard themselves say): "I hate my nose" or "I hate my curly hair"? Because we're rarely neutral and detached on the subject of our own bodies, that relationship can be a rich source for an emotionally charged poem.

Write a poem of at least twelve lines in which you dramatize a self–body relationship. Use your own body or a body part as the other character you're addressing: "Poem to My Feet," for example. The poem might begin by addressing them directly as if they were separate beings:

Where would I be without you?
How would I stay in touch with the ground?
Useful in the extreme, I find you are also
Beautiful, and it makes me sad
To cover you with socks each morning . . .

Or you could write the poem from a less intimate or personal perspective. Instead of addressing your own body or body part, you could dramatize from a more general place. For example, you could call it "Poem against Noses" and begin like this:

I have never liked noses—
Not small ones or large ones.
The small ones make me think
Of rabbits; the large ones
Are just embarrassments,

> *Always getting in the way,*
> *Always getting scalded*
> *By soup or coffee . . .*

Again, the trick might be to choose some aspect of your bodily self or of bodies in general and then give yourself permission to just start writing and see where it takes you. Later, if parts of it seem true or strong or strange and interesting to you, then those may be the lines that should survive the lyric "surgery" of revision; those may be the lines that create a unity of tone or attitude that reinforces the dramatic focus of the subject matter (be it noses, or knees, or hands, or feet).

■

EXERCISE FOR A POEM ABOUT A CREATURE

Write a poem of at least twelve lines about a particular animal. Use the "I" as a participant in the poem, almost like the "I Remember" exercise. It might begin something like this:

> *The first lemur I ever saw*
> *was in the Chicago Zoo . . .*

And then the poem could extend itself from there: What happened next? What did you notice or do? Such a poem, as it went on and extended itself, might be about lemurs. Or it could be about the Chicago Zoo as a place, or about Chicago itself, or about zoos in general (e.g., sad lemur = bad zoo). Write and write without trying to control it too much, and see where the language and your memory and imagination lead you. Maybe the topic *will be* lemurs, or maybe it will go elsewhere.

As a variant on this self–creature exercise, try this: leave out the "I" so that the focus is more on the creature, and the language will probably stress Naming and noticing (or Singing). For example:

Lemur with your eternally startled expression—
as if you were caught
picking someone's pocket . . .

Or else a poem about lemurs that doesn't mention the speaker as an "I" participant might begin like this:

It was hunched over the branch like an old man . . .

Before you begin this self–creature exercise, just sit quietly and let your mind (memory? imagination?) wander a bit in the animal world. See what creature comes to mind, and consider if you might enjoy writing about that one.

■ ■ ■

THE SHARED PASSIONS

When we consider writing poems that are self-expressive and that communicate to other people, we might want to think about the world we share with other people. As we've just seen, we all have in common a number of self/not-self relationships that have gone into making up our identity. There are also certain basic emotions that all humans have experienced at one time or another. Exactly which emotions are universally shared was demonstrated by an experiment devised by the social psychologist Paul Ekman. He showed photos of faces expressing a wide variety of intense emotions to people in a wide variety of cultures scattered around the world. He found that people in all cultures he approached recognized six of these emotions, even if they belonged to a culture that had no specific word for that emotion. Lacking that word, they would tell a story showing how that emotion could emerge from experience. For example, instead of saying "fear," they might say: "He's just turned a corner in the jungle path and finds himself facing a tiger." (It's interesting for us, as poets, to note that stories can convey emotions as effectively as Naming or labeling.)

Here are the six emotions or passions recognized by all humans:

happiness, sadness, fear, anger, disgust, surprise

Earlier, we considered categories of self–other relationship. We could think of these categories of self and other as two nouns: for example, the self–nature relationship of a poem about tulips. The emotions can define that relationship with a verb-as-emotion word that connects self and other:

I (hate, love, fear) tulips.

Does "fearing" tulips seem imaginatively implausible, even in a poem? Read Sylvia Plath's "Tulips." True, the tulips in her poem are transformed under the pressure of her emotion and her imagination—they become a dozen red lead sinkers wrapped around her neck; they become the open red mouths of jungle cats. The tulips, with the colorful vitality of their own being, threaten the speaker's desire to perish (she's ill in a white hospital room, wishing to have her being vanish into blank oblivion).

To dramatize meaning, all we need is our basic pronouns of self and not-self. Let's go with *I* and *you*, and then a basic emotion-verb inserted between them that establishes a relationship:

I love you
I hate you
I fear you
I sadden you
I disgust you
I surprise you.

Or vice versa:

You fear me.

You love me.

You sadden me.

Etc.

Here we are, firmly established in the territory of human nature (emotions) and human experience (self/not-self relationships) that is widely if not universally shared. Here we are in the world of relationships and emotions that lyric poetry has always dramatized in order to express what individuals feel and connect them to other individuals. It's a puzzle to me that some people can think poetry isn't important, when it so clearly is concerned with emotions and relationships that are central to being alive. And I haven't even mentioned those universally shared encounters or experiences we could call mysteries—the universal mysteries of birth, of love, of loss, of suffering, of wonder.

EMOTIONS, RELATIONS, AND MEANINGS

Every passion is capable of animating a lyric and thus becoming or enacting a meaning. For example, George Herbert's seventeenth-century poem "The Collar" begins with the speaker in an emotional state of egotistic rage and frustration: "I struck the board and cried, 'No more! / I will abroad!'" (Translations: "board" means "table-top"; "I will abroad!" means "I'm out of here!") The poem is the rant of a priest who wants to be free to enjoy the pleasures of the world (wine and food and adventure) rather than be restricted to his duties and religious renunciations. Here's the poem; it may seem old-fashioned (it's over three hundred years old), but its drama (sensuous desire versus restraint) is still current, as is the child–parent relationship (here the parent is God the Father) that so startlingly appears in the last two lines and completely changes the speaker's emotional state:

The Collar

I struck the board, and cried, "No more;
    I will abroad!
What? shall I ever sigh and pine?
My lines and life are free; free as the road,
Loose as the wind, as large as store.
    Shall I be still in suit?
Have I no harvest but a thorn
To let me blood, and not restore
What I have lost with cordial fruit?
    Sure there was wine
Before my sighs did dry it: there was corn
 Before my tears did drown it.
  Is the year only lost to me?
   Have I no bays to crown it?
No flowers, no garlands gay? All blasted?
    All wasted?
Not so, my heart: but there is fruit,
   And thou hast hands.
Recover all thy sigh-blown age
On double pleasures: leave thy cold dispute
Of what is fit, and not. Forsake thy cage,
   Thy rope of sands,
Which petty thoughts have made, and made to thee
Good cable, to enforce and draw,
   And be thy law,
While thou didst wink and wouldst not see.
   Away! take heed;
   I will abroad.
Call in thy death's head there: tie up thy fears.
   He that forbears
   To suit and serve his need,
    Deserves his load."

But as I raved and grew more fierce and wild
    At every word,
Methought I heard one calling, *Child!*
    And I replied *My Lord*.

                    George Herbert (1633)

The speaker-priest wears a clerical collar, but (this is a pun) he's also feeling "choler" (rhymes with collar)—which is an old word for rage and anger. He's sick of behaving in a way that's appropriate to his priestly identity; he sees that others are having fun, and he wants some, too: wants wine and some good food, and how about a flower-crown to show he's a good-time guy? He's not just frustrated; he's angry that he's been inhibited by his own timidity and by his obedience to rules that have restricted him ("Thy rope of sands"—they shouldn't have the power to confine him, but they did; they were strong ropes—"Good cable"—because of his cowardice). He goes so far as to claim that anyone who is too cowardly to break free deserves his confinement (but not him; he's out of here, right now!). He's cranked himself up with his rant until he's almost totally out of control ("I raved and grew more fierce and wild / At every word").

And then suddenly, in the last two lines of the poem, the speaker completely reverses course and changes his emotional state totally. Up until that moment, he has been like a roaring drunk in a barroom—talking aloud to himself, working himself into a frenzy. And then he hears a voice—the voice of an Other—and enters into and/or returns to the relationship of child–father. How the tone changes completely in that last line! When the voice calls "Child" (remember, it's the voice of God the Father), the speaker suddenly knows himself to be nothing but a spoiled child, and he collapses into acceptance as any child might when reprimanded by a loving parent after throwing a bratty tantrum.

CHAPTER FOURTEEN

Craft and Quest

To sum up: one main motive for writing lyric poetry is self-expression. The self we express is made up of experiences we've had, emotions we've felt and feel, thoughts we've had or have, and relationships between ourselves and the world around us (a world made up of people, places, creatures, things). We express this self largely by dramatizing relationships, experiences, and emotions in the heightened language of poetry (a language that mingles Naming, Singing, Saying, and Imagining). When we do this, we open ourselves to disorder and confusion and vital energy, but we also have the power to unify the material that we engage. We unify through lyric focus and also through story. Not to mention traditional ordering principles of poetry that our culture sometimes presents (and that I haven't emphasized much, because I've mostly been eager to talk about these other topics that seem more basic and urgent and accessible; less intimidating).

There's one more topic I'd like to discuss. How we grow as poets has a lot to do with reading poetry. When we start out as young poets, the notion of reading other poets doesn't necessarily seem important or interesting. We're eager (and afraid) to express what we feel and what we've experienced. We either don't care that much what other poets have experienced and written, or we don't think it's relevant to what we're up to ourselves. Or, and this is very common, we're afraid to be unduly influenced by other poets—we think that to become a poet we must express our own unique self in our own unique way.

All this is true enough, but the fact is that all serious poets grow through reading other poets and other poems.

CRAFT VERSUS QUEST

Let me step back again and approach this final topic from another direction. If you're lucky enough to be studying poetry-writing in a school, you're probably doing so in a workshop. In recent decades in America, we've institutionalized the teaching of poetry-writing in high schools, colleges, and universities. It's a project modeled on schools for visual artists and, further back, on the painting and sculpture work-shops of Renaissance Italy. In that system, young people learned techniques under a master craftsman and then went on to do their own work. The assumption is that a young aspirant might learn the craft from an older practitioner. We've modified this master–apprentice model further to include the merits of the peer workshop, in which fellow aspirants respond to one another's efforts with observations and encouragement.

Having worked within this workshop system as a teacher for over forty years, I've seen many young writers grow and flourish under it and I'm hesitant to repudiate it. That said, I've come more and more to feel that poetry-writing consists of two distinct things, which I choose to call Craft and Quest. It seems to me that issues of Quest are seldom addressed or even understood by teaching institutions. (In line with my sense of their importance, I'm going to dignify both terms with initial capitals for the purpose of discussing them.)

Craft consists of all the things one can do with words on a page— those linguistic skills you're naturally gifted with, and also those things you learn about poetry as you read it, study it, and write it yourself. When your chosen art is poetry, you're lucky—the road of craft goes on forever into new and unknowable countries. Chaucer seems to lament this fact when he says in the opening line of his fourteenth-century poem "The Parlement of Foules": "The lif so short, the craft so long to lerne." But I suspect he's really pretty happy with his fate. What if you (or Chaucer) had chosen to devote yourself passionately and wholly to the game of checkers instead of lyric poetry? With three years of serious study and play, you'd probably know everything there is to know about checkers. You would have mastered the game entirely, and then the rest of your life would be nothing but the boredom of triumph. But because you've chosen poetry, you're condemned to wonder at skills and felicities of language or imagination in the poems of others that you yourself may never achieve, no matter how hard you work toward them—things that will always be beyond your reach but also will always be luring you on. Not that I wish to sketch a hopeless situation—on the contrary, poetic craft in general is learnable, even though there's more to it than we can master in our lifetime. But if you're like me, you'll never know enough about it—always there is something for me to learn, some lovely trick I can't do (and that other poets seem to do effortlessly).

But I'm actually after another notion here—what I've called Quest. Quest has to do with the intersection of your own personal life and the art of poetry in your time and place. It has to do with what you want to do with poetry and what poetry wants to do with you. It has to do with coming to understand who you are and who you hope to be when you are reborn through language and imagination as a poet.

GAUGUIN'S QUESTIONS

Craft can be learned. We learn it by reading poems, by writing them, by listening to other practitioners of the art, by experimenting and imitating. Craft is learned in solitude, but it's also learned with and from others. Quest, in contrast, has to do with our personal sense of ambition, motive, or need in relation to the writing of poems. Quest is harder to talk about, and probably no one can identify its directions and nature except the individual poet herself or himself.

That said, I want to suggest some aspects of Quest. The late-nineteenth-century French painter Paul Gauguin (1848–1903) spent a significant part of his life far from Paris. He lived on the South Pacific island of Tahiti for many years. We needn't become overly concerned with the complexity of motives involved in his chosen exile, but we could note that he imagined that by living in a "traditional" world he was coming closer to basic existential questions about life. In line with this thinking, he gave a number of his paintings titles that indicated their metaphysical or mythic aspirations. Among them is a long horizontal painting of figures in a landscape—it's fairly easy to see that these figures and their actions are meant to symbolize three phases of life: childhood, adulthood, and old age. What isn't obvious in Internet reproductions is that Gauguin wrote three questions in white paint across the bottom of the painting. These brief questions essentially function as the painting's title. They are as follows:

Where did we come from? What are we? Where are we going?

The three questions correspond to the three scenes that structure his painting.

I propose that we can adopt and adapt Gauguin's questions for the purposes of understanding Quest in our lives as lyric poets:

Where did I come from? What am I? Where am I going?

And I'll add a fourth question as well:

What am I here for?

You'll notice that I've shifted from the plural pronoun *we* to the lyric pronoun *I*. If we choose to use the pronoun *we*, then the answers and thoughts we have will take on a mythic or collective tone. There's nothing inherently wrong with asking and answering big questions by framing them in social, universal pronouns. There's nothing wrong with it, except that that's not how lyric poetry works. Lyric places the *I* at the center, and it speaks with the voice of an individual. It's not self-centered in the simplistic, egotistical sense of the word, but it's centered in the self. (Where else can an individual center?)

"Who am I? Where did I come from? Where am I going? What am I here for?" These are significant questions for a person or a poet seeking to grow, *but* I don't think they can be answered directly.

In trying to understand Quest, you'll think about who you are, since part of it involves such givens as your inborn temperament or personality. You'll also delve into your personal childhood and adolescent experience, since Quest also involves awareness of your past and how it feeds or afflicts your work. But you'll also be exploring an impersonal past: you'll read everything you can find, especially poets from other times and places. Why? Not just to become familiar with what's been written before so that you can appreciate the range of possible craft strategies and tricks that poets have discovered, but also because reading other poets is an essential aspect of Quest. Yet for all the importance of the Quest questions, it's difficult to answer them directly. Sometimes we come at our truest selves best by indirection. As Emily Dickinson says: "Tell all the Truth but tell it slant— / Success in Circuit lies. . . ." Here are two "slant" approaches to these urgent and essential questions:

Reading for Kindred Spirits

I am assuming that in seeking to grow as a poet, you know that reading extensively in poetry is an essential part of your development. In the course of your reading, when you come across a poet for whom you love four or five or more of their works, it may be that you've found one of your "poetic kin." Just as we were born into a biological family and grew through our family relationships in various ways, so poets often feel as if they're reborn into a poetic family—that through reading they discover poet-fathers and poet-mothers, brothers, sisters, cousins, and so on. The wonderful thing this time around is that you get to choose, or "recognize," this kinship—you intuit your response, but you also become active and decisive in this choosing.

It's hard to exaggerate the necessity of finding "poetic parents" in order to be successfully reborn into poetry. Some poets, like Wordsworth and Keats, were actual orphans; but many poets have a vague sense of bereftness that is addressed by this Quest search. Here's the rapper Jay-Z on this phenomenon, from *Decoded*, his memoir:

> We were kids without fathers, so we found our fathers on wax and
> on the streets and in history, and in a way, that was a gift: We got
> to pick and choose the ancestors who would inspire the world we
> were going to make for ourselves. . . . Our fathers were gone, usu-
> ally because they just bounced, but we took their old records and
> used them to build something fresh. (pg. 255)

One of the wonderful things about thinking of your poetic lineage, your poetic family tree, is that the poetic figures you choose don't have to be compatible with one another, any more than your in-laws or aunts and uncles have to get along with one another. What's important is that something in them is sent down to you—some genetic theme or formal blood that flows in their veins is also flowing in yours.

Gathering Together the Poems You Love

When we seek our poetic kin, we are looking for poets whose work seems to share some overall quality or aspiration with our own. A sign of this kinship is that we respond to a group of poems by that poet, perhaps even a large body of his or her work. A different kind of experience happens when we have an intense response to an individual poem—when we are stunned by it. And yet, other poems by the same poet might leave us utterly unmoved or unexcited. What to make of this phenomenon? Why not make an anthology of those poems that stunned us or stirred us? Such an anthology will be deeply personal (and perhaps it should be kept private, who knows?). Personal, yet essential. These poems we love most will prove crucial to us in our quest for our own poetic identity.

■ ■ ■

TWO QUEST EXERCISES

A Poet's Family Tree

If you're a young poet, this exercise might be a bit premature for you. Quest in general is something that takes place over time (over our life-time, actually), and the poetic kin project definitely calls for patience. Still, you might give it a try.

Using a variation on the traditional form of a genealogical family tree, make your own family tree of poetic kin. Imagine that the trunk of the tree represents you, and the branches are your ancestor poets—those whose work you feel feeds your own poetic identity. Draw this tree on a page, and label its branches with the names of the poets (and writers or songwriters) you feel kinship with. When drawing the tree, think of poets (and writers and songwriters) with whom you feel a connection based on a number of their works and an intuited kinship with their ideas, feelings, attitudes, themes, and/or the style in which they express themselves. It should be a broader connection than simply loving a single poem. (I'm not saying that the passionate love for a single poem isn't important for your quest—it most definitely is central; but you'll get to address the experience of passionate attachment to a single work in the exercise that follows this one.)

Another advantage of drawing this scheme of poetic kinship as a tree is that eventually it can enable you to discover how some poets are connected back to other poets through time. For example, if Mary Oliver is a branch on your tree, you might see that two other branches coming together to help her form her work (two "kin," or influences on her) were poets from an earlier generation: James Wright and Theodore Roethke. Whether these poets, in turn, become part of your own "poetic-kin tree" is another question, but the thinking and the drawing constitute a good way of understanding the history of poetry as a series of passionate responses of later poets to earlier poets. It is this living history that can feed your own life and your own poetry.

Also, odd though it may sound, there's something about the physical act of working—in this case, drawing—with a pen ("the poet's pen") as a tool that makes things real for poets. And it's interesting to see in front of you the names of your kin and to marvel that such different figures and personalities could all feed into and nourish your own, personal poetic being.

A Poet's Personal (and Passionate) Anthology

If we are moved by a poem, it has meant something, perhaps something important, to us; if we are not moved, then it is, as poetry, meaningless.

T. S. Eliot, "The Music of Poetry"

As a young man and aspiring poet searching for his way in the world, Ralph Waldo Emerson felt he needed to take an active role in shaping his own direction in life. He was frustrated by the notion that he should passively accept received wisdom from the past—"Why should we grope among the dry bones of the past?" he asks in his essay "Nature." Instead, he wished to have "an original relation to the universe"—a sense that meaning would emerge from encounters between himself and what surrounded him, especially nature (he was a follower of Wordsworth, among other influences—Wordsworth was definitely part of his "poetic-kin tree"). To help orient himself in the world of reading, he urged himself to put together a collection of poems and literary and philosophical passages that meant the most to him. Here's how he put it in his journal:

Make your own Bible! Select & Collect all those words & sen-
tences that in all your reading have been to you like the blast of
triumph out of Shakespeare, Seneca, Moses, John, & Paul.

from *Journals* (July 1836)

Why not make such a document for yourself in relation to lyric poetry?
Why not sit down and think of all your favorite poems or parts of poems
(or brief excerpts from novels, philosophy, songs, or other texts, sacred or
secular) and make a list of them? The fifteen or twenty poems and songs
you love most. Absolutely love. Wouldn't want to live without. Would feel
less full and real if you didn't know them. Those that stunned you with
wonder or truth or beauty when you first read them or first "understood"
them. Once you've made that list, gather copies of those poems and pas-
sages together. Bring them together into your own personal anthology
that would merit the status of being "your bible."

When you do this (and I urge you to in the strongest terms), it's
a good idea to place a strict *limit* on the number of pieces in your
selection, so that you have to make difficult choices and weigh one
love against another. Start with twenty poems and songs and passages,
but then cut them back to only a dozen. Which ones will you keep?
Which ones will you reluctantly let go? This may seem like a cruel and
pointless part of an important project—this elimination of poems that
you've already decided you love. But by doing it, you can learn more
about what really matters to you—what themes stir you, what images or
rhythms lift your spirit or cast it down into a significant abyss. Pay atten-
tion to what passes through your mind as you pare down your list and
make these difficult choices, weighing one love against another. What
are your thoughts and feelings? What do your responses say about
yourself and your relation to poetry and to the world?

This project of "making your own bible" is, to me, one of the most
important ways of growing as a poet and of coming to know yourself as
a poet (and person). What you love most or deem most important will
reveal to you something about yourself. I don't mean that all of liter-

ature is about us, but I do mean that we read (especially lyric poetry) in order to know more about ourselves and our possibilities as selves. And when we respond strongly and passionately to a poem or a passage, it means that it's somehow a part of us or is revealing something significant about our experience and thus, indirectly, about who we are.

Elsewhere, Emerson counsels us to be "active souls," and that's the heart of this project—to be dynamic in our own behalf by recognizing what we love most. I'll go so far as to suggest that you type up your poetry bible's contents or even write out the poems and passages by hand, so that you can take the words into your own body, through your own body. And memorize them; make them a part of your being, phrases or poems or passages you can call up in time of need or when they seem most important and true.

Keep this small anthology in a folder somewhere. Take it out and look at it every once in a while; recite the poems you love aloud. When you encounter a poem that stuns you, consider adding it to this collection; consider giving it this status of importance in your life.

Will your poetic bible change as you change? My own experience is yes and no. For example, you might well place in it the first poem that ever moved you. And at some later date, you may ask yourself if you cherish that poem for nostalgic or sentimental reasons, or because (naïve though it might be) it represents the first time you discovered that the rhythmic language of poetry could be a door into your own self and into the world. New poems and songs and phrases will come along and demand to be admitted. Admit them, admit them. But consult the whole document periodically—read it aloud to yourself; edit it if you must, if you feel a poem's force fading in your life.

As a lyric poet, you could do worse than to consider the body of the world's poetry and other literature as the raw material from which you're free to cull great and sustaining sentences and poems. Cull them and place them together—create a passionate, personal document of writing that has changed you or charged you with a sense of the meaning of your existence.

■

Spread those poems, song lyrics, and quotes out in a circle on the floor around you. Not every day or month, but once a year, say. Do you see yourself and feel yourself in them? Do they, in a kind of rough composite way, reveal significant parts of your own being? Perhaps they suggest a theme or storyline (e.g., love, longing for intimacy, an abiding sense of loss, delight in the sensory world); perhaps they reveal some form of linguistic delight that you value—a certain kind of Singing that you respond to and also aspire to. Perhaps there are places that are blank in this mirror made of pages—blank spots waiting to be filled in by poems that you haven't discovered yet, or perhaps that you yourself will write.

■ ■ ■

Acknowledgments

This book came into being out of an encouraging conversation with Jill Bialosky, my editor, and her responses and guidance have helped hugely in bringing it to completion. Melissa Flamson at With Permission knows only too well my debt to her skills and patience. First, last, and always, my thanks go to Trisha Orr, whose faith in my notions sustained me and whose patience and good sense in responding to early drafts made this book possible.

Glossary

accent A greater stress given to one syllable than another in pronouncing English, or to some words more than others in a sentence of single-syllable words. When we accent the first syllable of content, we mean subject matter; when we accent the second syllable of content, we mean we're happy. English is a heavily stressed language, partly because a good part of its vocabulary derives from Anglo-Saxon, which derives from West Germanic dialects. Dictionaries provide a guide to relative stresses within multisyllabic words.

accentual meter An ordering principle by which the number of stresses, or accents, in each line makes a pattern for the poem; for example, a poem might have four stresses, or strong accents, in each line, or it might alternate lines of four stresses with lines of three stresses. Accentual meter doesn't necessarily keep track of unstressed syllables in a line.

accentual-syllabic meter An ordering principle for poems that counts both the number of stresses, or accents, in the line and the number of syllables in the line; for example, iambic pentameter consists of lines of ten syllables divided up into five (penta) iambic feet with a stress on every second syllable (iambic).

alliteration The repetition of an initial consonant sound of words in near proximity in a poem; for example, the bl sounds in "... all their sparkles bleared and black and blind" (Thomas Hardy, "The Convergence of the Twain").

anapest   See metrical foot/feet.

anaphora   A structuring technique that involves repetition of the initial word or phrase at the beginning of lines. It was much used by Walt Whitman to order his unrhymed poetry in *Leaves of Grass* (1855).

apostrophe   A direct address to someone or something as a way of creating relationship and engagement in a poem, even if the person or thing addressed is not alive. For example, in "Ode to a Grecian Urn" John Keats speaks to the urn, and in "Ode to a Nightingale" he addresses the bird as "you." Apostrophe in lyric can be addressed to a person, a thing, or even an idea.

assonance   A sonic effect achieved by the repetition of a vowel sound within words in near proximity to one another; for example, the long *a* sounds in this line from Robert Hayden's "Those Winter Sundays": "with cracked hands that ached / from labor in the weekday weather made / banked fires blaze." (See *consonance* for the equivalent sonic effect with consonant sounds.)

blank verse   Unrhymed lines of iambic pentameter.

closure   The sense that a poem has reached a climax or resolution of its themes or sonic patterns, or both, at its conclusion.

colloquial speech   Speech that is modeled on the ordinary way people speak (though in poetry it is a literary approximation of ordinary speech, which usually means it is more sonically dense than actual speech). When, in his *Preface to the Lyrical Ballads* (1799), the romantic poet William Wordsworth insisted that poetry should sound like "a man speaking to men," he revolutionized the notion of how poems could sound and pushed poetry in English farther toward a colloquial model.

connotation   The suggestive associations that a word can arouse in a reader, as contrasted with the word's *denotation*, or precise dictionary meanings. Connotations can be particular to a culture or an individual—thus, being based in the reader's reactions, they are not easy to control; but they enrich the meanings of words and poems.

consonance   A sonic effect that links consonant sounds within a poem; for example, the *r* sounds in the opening lines of Theodore Roethke's "Cuttings": "This <u>urge</u>, <u>wrestle</u>, <u>resurrection</u> of <u>dry</u> sticks, / Cut stems <u>struggling</u> to put down feet, . . ."

couplet   A two-line stanza in a poem.

dactyl   See *metrical foot/feet*.

denotation   The precise meaning of a word (as distinct from its *connotation*), best determined by consulting a dictionary.

diction   The kind of language used in a poem; having to do with word choice and vocabulary.

dramatic situation/context   The circumstances or setting of a poem, presented in relation to what is going on (who, what, where, when); comparable to the opening scenes of a play, in which someone is somewhere at a certain time doing or saying something.

duration   The length of time a syllable is held (or can be held) when it is pronounced aloud. Thus, the two single-syllable words *bit* and *doom* have different durations, *doom* taking longer to say aloud. Duration is an element of rhythm; it is usually a result of the vowel within a syllable, as in the two monosyllables above.

elegy   A type of poem concerned with death, grief, or loss.

ellipsis   The omission or suppression of a word or phrase as represented by a punctuation mark, usually three dots (. . .).

end rhyme   The matching of final sounds in words that occur at the ends of lines, as in these couplets that formt he opening of John Keats's *Endymion* (1818):

A thing of beauty is a joy forever:
Its loveliness increases; it will never
Pass into nothingness; but still will keep
A bower quiet for us, and a sleep
Full of sweet dreams, and health, and quiet breathing.

end-stopped line   A line of poetry that ends with a complete pause, which is often indicated by a punctuation mark. (See *enjambed line* for contrast.)

enjambed line   A phrase or sentence that continues beyond the line's end and reaches completion in the following line; for example:

Like to the lark at break of day arising
From sullen earth, . . .
　　from Shakespeare, Sonnet 29

Here the phrase "From sullen earth" completes the meaning of the preceding line. Also called a run-on line.

epigraph   A quotation that precedes a poem and either creates a context for the poem or subtly interacts with the poem itself; often set toward the right margin, after the poem's title.

figurative language   Language that serves to compare or transform rather than to name, denote, or speak literally; includes metaphor, simile, and personification.

free verse   Verse that is "free of" traditional metrical ordering principles; the poet determines the nature and length of each line and thus the overall arrangement of lines on the page. In English, free verse became popular early in the twentieth century, although certain poets such as Walt Whitman in his collection *Leaves of Grass* (1855) were clearly writing an early version of free verse. When, in 1918, Ezra Pound counseled young poets: "as regarding rhythm: to compose in the sequence of the musical phrase, not in sequence of a metronome," he was urging them to write free verse with a more varied rhythmic structure than the simple tick-tock of iambic meter or a metronome.

haiku   A Japanese poetic form consisting of three lines of five, seven, and five syllables, respectively. In addition to the syllable structure, a haiku must make use of sensory language and, usually, contain a word indicating the season in which the poem is set. Haiku focuses on a single scene or moment.

heroic couplet   A rhymed couplet in iambic pentameter.

iamb   See *metrical foot/feet*.

iambic pentameter   A line of accentual-syllabic verse consisting of ten syllables with stress on every second syllable.

image   A word or several words that convey sensory experience (sight, sound, smell, taste, touch). Unfortunately, in discussions of poetry the word *image* also often refers to figurative language (metaphors and similes). Thus, the potential confusion between sensory language and figurative language occasionally makes discussions of poems challenging.

imagery   The language used in a poem to evoke sensory experience.

incantation   The formulaic repetition of phrases or words for rhythmic effect. Incantation in a poem either intensifies a statement or alerts the reader to different possible meanings in the same phrase; for example:

> What did I know? What did I know
> Of love's austere and lonely offices?
> > from Robert Hayden,
> > "Those Winter Sundays"

internal rhyme   Rhyme that occurs within a line or adjacent lines of a poem rather than at the end of the lines; for example:

> The grave cave ate will be . . .
> > from Sylvia Plath,
> > "Lady Lazarus"

list poem   A structuring or ordering device in which a poem is modeled on a list of objects or events.

lyric   A poem based in an individual point of view, likely to stress that viewpoint or perspective; often presented as being spoken by an "I," but not always. By and large, the lyric attempts to dramatize an intense moment in the poet-speaker's emotional, experiential, or imaginative life (or a combination of them all). It is a form of poem present (as song or recitation or written piece) in all cultures and throughout all human history (so far as we know). The English term *lyric* comes from the Greek, which referred to a poem sung or chanted to the accompaniment of a lyre (a stringed instrument). This meaning persists in English when we refer to the words of a song as its lyrics. Popular song and lyric poetry exist on a continuum—they are variations on the same self-expressive impulse. By and large, lyrics tend to focus on a single dominant emotion that constellates the poem's language around a center.

lyric sequence   An extended poem made up of individual lyrics that follow a narrative arc, but each poem in the sequence constellates around its own imaginative and emotional center. The narrative or thematic connection between the individual lyric units is assumed rather than spelled out as in a narrative poem. One effect of lyric sequence is to achieve the intensity of lyric (individual poems in the sequence) as well as the scope and extension through time available to narrative poems.

metaphor   A basic form of figurative language in which one thing is said to *be* another thing ("A *is* not-A"—a logical impossibility); for example: "My heart is a fire engine."

meter   An ordering principle for the lines in some poems that provides an overall structure based on certain patterns. Meter is a regularizing of one aspect of a poem's words to create a recurring, stable pattern that, among other things, frequently determines the length or relative length of each line. In English, the most common forms of meter make use of a recurring pattern of syllable and accent count (accentual-syllabic meter), or accent alone (accentual meter), or syllable count alone (syllabic meter).

metrical foot/feet   In scansion or when composing in accentual-syllabic meter, the poetic line is imagined as a series of units called feet. A pattern of such feet constitutes an ordering principle in the poem. Thus, a line in a poem composed in iambic pentameter has five iambic feet. The most common metrical feet in English poetry are: iamb (an unaccented syllable followed by an accented one), trochee (an accented syllable followed by an unaccented one), anapest (two unaccented syllables followed by an accented syllable), dactyl (an accented syllable followed by two unaccented syllables), and spondee (two accented syllables).

mixed metaphor   In figurative language, the comparison of more than two things at the same time. In the statement "My heart is like a fire engine swimming toward its destiny," the heart is said to be a fire engine, but the verb *swimming* also indicates that the heart is a swimmer. Often, when more than two things are compared, the reader becomes confused or disoriented; thus, mixed metaphors are considered to be ineffective or even harmful to a poem. Of course, a series of metaphors (each of which is a one-to-one comparison) can be exhilarating (see Pablo Neruda's "Ode to My Socks," on pg. 253, or Walt Whitman's "Song of Myself," section 6, on pg. 258).

monologue   The thoughts of a single speaker presented as if spoken aloud.

narrative   A poem structured as a series of actions unfolding in time and related by sequence, cause and effect, or action and reaction.

narrator   The person who is telling a story or poem. A first-person narrator is usually expressed through the pronoun *I*, although it can also be *we*. A third-person narrator (*he* or *she*) tends to speak as if from outside the story as an observer but with the ability to communicate his or her own subjective responses.

near-rhyme   (See *off-rhyme*.)

ode   An extended lyric that praises a person, thing, event, or personified abstraction. Odes have been addressed to "Intellectual Beauty" (Percy Bysshe Shelley) and to "Artichokes" (Pablo Neruda).

off-rhyme   (also *near-rhyme* or *slant rhyme*) This occurs when two words have similar but not identical sounds, as in *store* and *stare* or *fame* and *flume*. People's ability to hear off-rhyme varies; it is generally most effective when placed at the ends of lines, where it's as likely to be recognized by eye as by ear.

parallelism   A construction of syntax that involves a paired repetition of words or phrases. It is used as an ordering element in many poetries, including Hebrew poetry of the Old Testament—as in this example from the "Song of Songs" (here rendered in English), which combines figurative language with syntactical parallelism:

I am the rose of Sharon,
and the lily of the valleys.
As the lily among thorns,
so is my love among the daughters.
As the apple tree among the trees of the wood,
so is my beloved among the sons.
  from "Song of Songs," King James Version

paraphrase A restatement of one's understanding, in one's own words, of the plot or unfolding theme of a poem from beginning to end.

pastoral A poem about nature or the rural life that tends to stress its joys or benefits.

persona poem A poem in which the poet speaks in the voice of another person, historical or fictional.

personification A figure of speech in which nonhuman objects or creatures are given human qualities such as emotions or agency.

pitch An element of rhythm. (See also *vowel pitch*.)

point of view The perspective from which a poem's events, characters, or details are presented.

prose poem A poem organized into sentences and paragraphs rather than individual lines. One could say it was invented by the French poet Charles Baudelaire in his 1869 collection *Paris Spleen*.

pun A play on words in which one word that sounds the same as another can mean two different things. Elizabethan love poetry relished puns relating to hunting deer, so that the beloved was *dear/deer* and *heart/hart* (a hart being an adult deer). If sustained, puns in poetry allow two levels of meaning to coexist at the same time.

quatrain A stanza of four lines.

repetition   See *incantation*.

rhyme   A sound effect that announces itself to the reader when two words have the same final, stressed vowel sound and/or the same final consonant sound following it; for example, *shame* and *fame* or *alarm* and *farm*. Rhyme can appear at the ends of lines to reinforce a sense of pattern, or it can appear within lines that are near each other (see *internal rhyme*). If too many syllables are identical, it can undercut the pleasure of rhyme, as when *following* is rhymed with *hollowing*. (See also *off-rhyme*.)

rhyme scheme   In a poem making use of end rhyme, the repeating pattern of the rhymes in each stanza or over the course of the entire poem.

rhythm   A sense of pattern or recurrence; in poetry, an inclusive term for the complex sound patterns made by phrases and sentences. Meter, if present in a poem, is part of the far more complex phenomenon of rhythm, which also involves a great number of different elements of language, including among other things: duration, (vowel) pitch; such sound effects as assonance, consonance, alliteration; phrasing and pauses, syntax, punctuation, rhetorical devices and incantation. These elements operate not in isolation, but in relation to each other, creating the overall oral or sonic performance of the poem, that "sense of musical delight" Coleridge insisted was essential to poetry.

scansion   A process by which a poem's lines are analyzed in terms of a scheme consisting of metrical feet arranged in a pattern of accented and unaccented (stressed and unstressed) syllables.

sectioned poem   A poem divided up into several sections in order to cover a theme or subject across a longer time period or from different points of view. The sections of such a poem can be imagined as brief lyric poems or partial poems that become units in a larger or more extensive poem whose unifying principles are looser than those of a conventional lyric (see further discussion, pgs. 110–13).

sestet   The last six lines of a sonnet (which contains fourteen lines).

simile   A form of figurative language in which two things being compared are linked by *like* or *as*; for example, "My love is like a red, red rose."

slant rhyme   See *off-rhyme*.

sonnet   A traditional form of poetry consisting of fourteen lines, usually of rhymed iambic pentameter; brought from Italy into Elizabethan English society. The Shakespearean or English sonnet consists of three rhymed quatrains and a final rhymed couplet. The Italian or Petrarchan sonnet consists of a grouping of eight lines (octave) followed by six lines (the sestet).

speaker   The voice or person imagined to be speaking the poem. It may or may not be the poet in an autobiographical sense, but the identity of the poem's speaker is central to its meaning(s).

spondee   See *metrical foot/feet*.

stanza   Derived from the Italian word for "room," a stanza is a grouping of lines together into a unit.

stress   See *accent*.

surrealism   A literary and artistic movement founded in 1924 by the French poet André Breton; it sought to combine the nonrational elements of dream reality with the waking reality of daily life so as to create a "higher" reality, a "sur-reality." Originally an avant-garde movement, it was so widely influential that the term *surreal* has become part of the everyday vocabulary of people who are not even familiar with its origins. Surrealism celebrates imagination and "the marvelous": "The image is always marvelous" (André Breton, first *Surrealist Manifesto*).

syllabic meter   A (rare) metrical principle by which a poem is ordered through a pattern of line length established by counting the syllables in each line. If a poet writing in syllabics desires an eight-syllable line pattern, then whenever the line length gets to eight syllables, the poet breaks the line and puts the next words on the following line.

symbol   A symbol is present in a poem when a named object suggests meanings beyond its own. W. H. Auden said this about symbols: "A symbol is felt to be such before any possible meaning is consciously recognized; i.e., an object or event which is felt to be more import-ant than the reason can immediately explain is symbolic. Secondly, a symbolic correspondence is never one to one but always multiple, and different persons perceive different meanings" (*The Enchafed Flood*, pg. 62).

syntax The arrangement of word order in a sentence to create meaning. Syntax can be varied—the sequence of words can be rearranged, but only within a certain range in English. For exam-ple, "The man bit the dog" is simple English syntax (sentence subject, predicate/verb, object of verb). It can be varied to mean something almost the same: "The dog was bitten by the man." But it can't be varied too much: "The bit man dog the" contains the same words as our original sentence, but does not have meaning in English.

tercet A group of three lines.

tone The overall emotional weight or slant of the voice of the sup-posed speaker of a poem or of the poem itself as intuited by the reader; similar to a person's tone of voice. Poems tend to display a consistent tone (e.g., cheerful, melancholy, angry) as a means of creating unity of effect, intimacy with the reader or listener, or emotional impact.

trochee See *metrical foot/feet*.

unity Relates to a reader's expectation (and a poet's aspiration) that the language and imagined events in a given poem will cohere and be related in some obvious or subtle way. The degree of unity varies from poem to poem (and the need for it from reader to reader), but it seems to be a presiding human longing in relation to poetry (which is the most unified and patterned language use we know, with the exception of the "language" of mathematics).

villanelle A fixed form of poetry consisting of five rhymed, three-line stanzas followed by a four-line stanza. The first and third lines of the first stanza recur throughout the poem as the end line of succeeding stanzas. Such famous villanelles as "One Art" by Eliz-abeth Bishop and "Do Not Go Gentle into That Good Night" by

Dylan Thomas indicate the form's power to dramatize an obsessive theme until it achieves resolution or revelation.

voice   A quality of language that gives the reader the sense that a consistent and coherent personality is presenting or speaking the words of the poem. Voice goes a long way toward making the poem feel cohesive and unified. It is often related to an emotional tone that unifies the words and images (e.g., sad, joyful, anxious), but it can also dramatize the speaker's attitude (e.g., ironic, boastful, satiric).

vowel pitch   The "highness" or "lowness" of vowel sounds as formed by forcing air up through an open throat; such sounds roughly correspond to higher and lower notes on a musical scale. The patterning and variation in vowel pitch constitute one element of a poem's overall rhythmic effect.

Credits